The Form of News

The Guilford Communication Series

THE FORM OF NEWS

A HISTORY

Kevin G. Barnhurst
John Nerone

THE GUILFORD PRESS
New York   London

© 2001 The Guilford Press
A Division of Guilford Publications, Inc.
72 Spring Street, New York, NY 10012
www.guilford.com

Printed in the United States of America

This book is printed on acid-free paper.

Last digit is print number: 9   8   7   6   5   4   3   2

LIBRARY OF CONGRESS CATALOGING-IN-PUBLICATION DATA

Barnhurst, Kevin G., 1951–
    The form of news : a history / Kevin G. Barnhurst, John
Nerone.
        p.   cm.—(The Guilford communication series)
    Includes bibliographical references and index.
    ISBN 1-57230-637-8 (cloth)   ISBN 1-57320-791-9 (pbk.)
    1. Newspapers — Social aspects. 2. American newspapers —
History. 3. Newspaper layout and typography — United States.
3. Electronic newspapers.   I. Nerone, John C.   II. Title.
III. Series.
PN4749 .B29   2001
302.23'22–dc21   2001023038

PREFACE

We began this book in the late 1980s, when we were young and single assistant professors in the College of Communications at the University of Illinois. Barnhurst had just begun sowing his wild oats as a promiscuous coauthor (he eventually did at least one article with almost everyone in the office) and wanted to investigate the then-fashionable notion of a design revolution in the 1970s and 1980s, but Nerone proposed to go back a bit further, "Oh, say, a hundred years." And that set the direction. Neither of us foresaw spending so many years in collaboration, but one thing led to another.

In the process, our initial notion of what we were studying mutated. At first we thought to study only the layout and typography of newspaper front pages. That research put us squarely in territory that was then the traditional identity of journalism departments, but their identity was changing through a growing dialogue with other traditions of design and criticism. So our work redefined itself within the greener pastures of visual culture and communication. In the process, we crossed boundaries, expanding into any other area we could find that would involve design conceived broadly. We began looking at illustrations and photography, and also interrogating textual forms: the ways reporters discussed visual things or made things visible in text. Gradually we discovered that what held our investigations together was an interest in the entire experience with newspapers, what we now call the form of news. Hence our title.

At that point we also began thinking of our work together as a book rather than as a series of articles, and we began discussing the project with Peter Wissoker of The Guilford Press, whose encouragement we came to rely on. We would present bits of the research at scholarly meetings, and he would meet us at some nearby venue, dog-tired after a day of conferencing, invite us for a drink, and ask probing questions, the sort that made his intellectual interest clear and made us think again. His patient generosity nurtured the project till now.

We intend the book to be an accessible treatment of a particular dimension of the newspaper's history in the United States. Although some of the detail included will engage only specialists (in journalism, in history, in design), we wrote the book so that a general reader can use it. We consistently found that, no matter how detailed or focused our discussion was when it commenced, it always ended up looking outward to the broadest social, cultural, and political concerns.

Our ultimate topic, then, is civic culture. We think of our work as part of the growing body of academic thinking that dwells on the decline of citizenship. Because we are professors who also teach young adults, we are always mindful of the frontiers of our political culture. We know that our students, even the journalism majors, don't read newspapers and don't think much about public life, although they are voracious consumers of other kinds of media. We would like our students to love the newspaper form as much as we do, and we would like the newspapers of our day to deserve that love, because we think it would be good for the republic. In that we are as pretentious as all our colleagues who preach similar sermons, and, preaching only to the converted, satisfy themselves that they're being heard.

We brought to the book distinct but complementary bundles of expertise. Barnhurst once worked in commercial design and teaches courses on visual representation and media studies; any passage that uses the words "expressionism" or "Bodoni" originated with him. Nerone is trained as a historian and teaches courses in the history of communications; any passage beginning "Historians disagree on . . ." originated with him.

But we think of this work as a true collaboration. Every passage has been rewritten by both authors, often to the point where we ourselves can no longer tell who first drafted what. Most chapters began with a conversation, usually in an unlikely setting: at a bowling alley in Champaign, Illinois, or Albany, New York; sitting on a park bench in Syracuse, New York; or in Chicago, on a bridge over the Chicago River or during memorable evenings over coffee at the Java Cat, beer at Big Chicks, and/or jazz at the Green Mill. With most chapters, that initial conversation produced a strategy for collecting samples. Then, after we'd gathered a pile of stuff, another conversation produced some initial take on it. Then one of us would draft preliminary findings, generating a text that would zip electronically back and forth between us, gradually evolving into penultimate form, then going off to publication or presentation elsewhere.

Chapter 1 was presented in slightly different form as "A Critique of News Form: Newspaper Production and Social Meaning in U.S. History, 1750–2000," to the International Communication Association (ICA), June 2000, in Acapulco, Mexico.

Chapters 2 and 3 grew out of a National Endowment for the Humanities fellowship at the American Antiquarian Society. We are also indebted to the staff of the Society for their assistance in researching the images used to introduce each section of the book. Research assistance in gathering photocopies of newspapers came from Paula Saukko. Richard R. John and Jeff Pasley generously read and critiqued these chapters, catching some errors and therefore procuring a share of the responsibility for whatever inaccuracies remain.

For an earlier version of Chapter 4, see John Nerone and Kevin G. Barnhurst, "Civic Picturing vs. Realist Photojournalism: The Regime of Illustrated News, 1856–1901," in *Design Issues 16* (1) (Spring 2000): 59–79. It received the Catherine Covert Award from the History Division of the Association for Education in Journalism and Mass Communication (AEJMC), as the best mass communication history article published that year. We appreciate the assistance of Craig Robertson, who selected the issues of the newspapers analyzed. The research was supported, in part, by the National Endowment for the Humanities fellowship program at the American Antiquarian Society. The work was presented as "The Regime of Illustrated News, 1856–1901," at the ICA convention, San Francisco, May 1999.

A longer version of Chapter 5 is available. See Kevin G. Barnhurst and John Nerone, "The President Is Dead: American News Photography and the New Long Journalism," in *Picturing in the Public Sphere*, Bonnie Brennen and Hanno Hardt, eds. (Urbana: University of Illinois Press, 1999), pp. 60–92. The research was first presented at the ICA annual convention, Montreal, May 1997.

Chapter 6 grew out of a much shorter quantitative study, Kevin G. Barnhurst and John Nerone, "Design Trends in U.S. Front Pages, 1885–1995," *Journalism Quarterly 68* (Winter 1991): 796–804. We thank the UIUC College of Communications for financial assistance, Ellen Wartella and D. Charles Whitney for technical assistance and criticism, and Holly Kruse, Gilbert Rodman, Rob Goldsmith, and Jochin Reicher for coding assistance on the study.

Chapter 7 first appeared as John Nerone and Kevin G. Barnhurst, "Visual Mapping and Cultural Authority: Design Changes in U.S. Newspapers,

1920–1940," *Journal of Communication* 45(2) (Spring 1995): 9–43, and was supported by a grant from the Research Board, University of Illinois at Urbana–Champaign, and by additional funding from Syracuse University. Jack Bratich shared insights and assisted on the chapter. An earlier draft was presented by Matt Ehrlich at the ICA convention, Sydney, Australia, July 1994.

From Chapter 8, the analysis of newspapers on the Web was published as John Nerone and Kevin G. Barnhurst, "Beyond Modernism: Digital Design, Americanization & the Future of Newspaper Form," *New Media & Society* 3(4) (December 2001): 467–82. The exhibition of international newspaper design was supported through a grant from the National Endowment for the Arts design program and appeared at the Lubalin Center, Cooper Union, New York City, April 12 through May 15, 1995. A catalog of the survey was published (see Barnhurst, 1995) and was also presented as a multimedia display, "Global Twentieth-Century Newspaper Design," created with technical assistance from Stephen Masiclat of Syracuse University, at the annual AEJMC convention in Washington, D.C., August 1995. The survey of Spanish newspaper design was supported by a sabbatical grant from Syracuse University and a visiting professorship at the University of La Laguna, Tenerife, Spain. The exhibit traveled from there to Barcelona, Bilbao, and Madrid, December 1996 through June 1997. The catalog appeared on-line (see Barnhurst et al., 1999). José Manuel de Pablos co-curated the exhibit; Francisco Javier Fernández Obregón edited the catalog; Itanel Bastos de Quadros, Jr., Claudia Irene de Quadros, and Eva Bocco assisted and translated; and Araceli Álvarez and Javier Rodríguez also assisted with the exhibit.

Like all large projects, this one left a trail of indebtedness, most notably to our immediate families — Ivy Glennon and Miranda Glennon-Nerone, Richard Doherty and Joel, Andrew, and Matthew Barnhurst — and to our colleagues at Syracuse University and at the Chicago and Urbana–Champaign campuses of the University of Illinois. Paul and Barbara Nerone have always been supportive, and John always has them in mind as the first readers of anything he writes. We hope we did not try the patience of those near us too much, but we did have fun along the way, including many long laughing fits by phone and some harried all-nighters carried out trans-Atlantic-ly.

KEVIN G. BARNHURST   JOHN NERONE
Stoddard, New Hampshire   *Urbana, Illinois*

CONTENTS

Contents

CHAPTER 1

THE FORM OF NEWS

Style, Production, and Social Meaning, 1750–2000

The newspaper has always been a privileged form of communication in the United States. Law accords it a seriousness often denied other media, and popular culture endorses its power to expose and enlighten. Although the content of the newspaper is often criticized for bias or sensationalism or silliness, the form of the newspaper is almost sanctified. One might say that the form supplies the standard against which the content is measured.

The newspaper form derives its sanctity from its relationship to civic culture. Thinkers endowed the newspaper with a special role in supporting the public conversation of the U.S. republic at a very early point in the nation's history — at a point when newspapers were really incapable of playing that role. Norms arose from this expectation, however, and inflected the design and development of the newspaper, giving it an iconic status it still enjoys, even though it has long since discarded many of its civic responsibilities. Very little in a modern newspaper enacts or even recounts political debate, but Americans still like to think that democracy is rooted in deliberation (Is it any longer? Was it ever?) and that the newspaper helps make deliberation possible.

This book explores the connections between the newspaper form and democratic civic culture. It does so by examining the history of newspaper form over the long course of its development in the United States from the colonial era to the present. It takes seriously the sanctity that the newspaper has commanded as an instrument of democracy, and asks how and when it has lived up to its mission; how and whether it has reconciled its sacred political work with its profane commercial operation; and how it might be reworked in a changing media environment. Throughout we presume that deliberation is the soul of democracy.

There are many ways of thinking about deliberation (as there are many ways of thinking about democracy), and some suit the newspaper (real or imagined) better than others. One prevailing sense, especially among communication scholars, is that newspapers support deliberation by transmitting information to people, who in turn feed back preferences in various ways — by their votes, of course, but also through letters to elected officials, poll results, or other political expressions. In this model, good newspapers provide adequate, reliable information in a clear and transparent fashion; good readers receive the information and process it rationally; and then the readers become good voters who express preferences informed by the news and responsive to justifiable values. This particular version of the so-called transmission model makes sense as well to many in the media, and to a certain extent it makes sense to us.

There is much, however, that the transmission model fails to capture. As James Carey (1988) has pointed out, it fails to capture the ritual functions of the media: the way news helps communities form and sustain themselves. It also fails to capture the dense overlapping network of relationships that any medium exists to sustain.

Any medium constitutes a complicated network of relationships. A *medium* is, after all, something "in between," something that mediates among and connects other things. A newspaper connects sources of news with readers; it brings them into or facilitates particular relationships. A simple transmission model of news imagines a unidirectional circuit: the world makes news, the newspaper reports it, the public consumes it. But each way station along the route stands for something much more complicated. The world that makes the news is actually a disparate collection of institutional and noninstitutional sources: governments and their agencies, the police, stock markets, sports associations, entertainment industries, polling organizations, the wire services, and so forth. The newspaper too is a collection of disparate actors: reporters and editors and all sorts of production personnel, from printers to paperboys, of course, but also lawyers and accountants and marketing experts. The public has always been segmented by age, gender, race, class, income, religion, and the like (although newspapers have only recently become more inclined to think of their audience as a group of disparate markets). So, just thinking within a transmission model, a newspaper sets up a very complicated, multidimensional set of relationships. The *Boston Globe* simultaneously maintains relationships between the Red Sox and their fans, between the high-tech industries along Route 128 and their investors, between City Hall and the voters, and between Shaw's supermarkets and shoppers. In a *material* sense, the newspaper itself is the combination of all these relationships (see Nerone, 1994). But news is not just about material relationships.

There is another order of relationships constituting a newspaper, one that we call *represented* relationships. These are the ways that the newspaper imagines and proposes that it mediates in the world. Often these are expressed in truisms: The press is the eyes and ears of the people, or The press is the restless adversary of corruption, or The press is the palladium of liberty. In formulations like these, the press proposes that it relates to the citizenry as their champion, and to powerful public and private institutions as their watchdog. Obviously, this represented order of relationships works to explain and justify the material relationships that also constitute the newspaper.

Such representations crystallize in the form of the newspaper. By *form* we mean the persisting visible structure of the newspaper, the things that make the *New York Times,* for example, recognizable as the same newspaper day after day although its content changes. Form includes the things that are traditionally labeled layout and design and typography; but it also includes habits of illustration, genres of reportage, and schemes of departmentalization. *Form* is everything a newspaper does to present the look of the news.

Any media form includes a proposed or normative model of the medium itself. Put another way, the form includes the way the medium imagines itself to be and to act. In its physical arrangement, structure, and format, a newspaper reiterates an ideal for itself.

This ideal is not a description of the material work of the newspaper. The form proposes ideal relationships between the world and the public, for instance, that will not correspond exactly to the material relationships it actually sets up. The newspaper will figure its reader as citizen on one level and as consumer on another, as self-controlled rational investor on one level and as emotion-driven buyer or fan on another, and so on. The relationship between material and represented relationships in any medium tells a lot about the work that the form does in the world. It is not accidental that we phrase this relationship in a way that echoes Althusser's famous definition of ideology as representing "the imagined relationship of individuals to their real conditions of existence" (1971, p. 162). Our analysis of form will often read like an ideological critique. One premise of our critique is that form embodies the imagined relationship of a medium to its society and polity.

We hope that approaching the newspaper through its formal dimension will offer a new perspective on a familiar subject. The newspaper is perhaps the oldest and best understood mass medium, and has been the subject of many histories and scholarly treatments. *Content analyses* have looked at all sorts of news matter, examining images as well as words. *Audience studies* have not only measured trends and demographics but have also explored the act of reading — for example, by tracking eye movements of readers, analyzing depictions of readers in the fine and graphic arts, and doing ethnographies of practices among actual and historical readers. *Structural research* on the newspaper industry has revealed changing patterns of ownership and competition and probed shifting professional standards. All of these research traditions share a concern with the political consequences of news. The rapidly growing field of political communication draws on all of them to explore the relationship between news and the agendas of public institutions.

The many studies out there that illuminate one or more aspects of the newspaper don't necessarily combine to reveal the larger whole. They tend to understand the newspaper as a fairly simple transmission channel, bracketing many of the material relationships the newspaper constitutes, and slighting the order of represented relationships. We think that formal analysis offers a promising framework for considering the whole newspaper. The form of the newspaper, encompassing words as well as images, gives a physical existence to the full range of imagined relations that scholars have described piecemeal.

Newspaper forms have a complicated history. In the United States alone, tens of thousands of newspapers have been published. Obviously we could not give an account that includes all the varieties of newspaper form. Instead, we have hewed to the mainstream, looking for the most typical or hegemonic way of putting together a general interest newspaper at any given time. Surprisingly, this story has not previously been told — sadly, too, because we would be happier critiquing a mainstream narrative for what it excludes. Our revisionist instincts frustrated, we have aimed for simplicity and elegance, trying to balance faithfulness to detail (all the "noise" of real history) with the clarity about the form of news as a whole that our account requires.

With those caveats, we have constructed a narrative based on a series of different newspaper *formations*: printerly, partisan, Victorian, and modern. Each formation combined a *look* with a system of newspaper production (or *type*) and a broader cultural configuration. The *printerly newspaper* combined a bookish appearance with craft production and the republican values of the

American Revolution, including a fantasy about the public sphere. The *partisan newspaper* used a larger format and a more elaborate division of labor, with editors as chief operating officers, and was integrated into the rise of mass politics and the market economy. The crowded potpourri of *Victorian newspapers* emerged as publishers directed a news industry generating printed products for a newly imperial nation. And the *streamlined, modern newspaper* combined bureaucratic production with expert explanation in an era of monopoly capitalism.

CONTENT, READERS, POLITICS, FORM

Most newspapers end up in the trash, and the consumer may easily associate their value with their fate as physical objects. Here we espouse the opposite view. Cultures leave behind a record of their lives, concerns, and power arrangements not only in self-conscious, lofty venues — chronicles and books, works of art, and monuments — but also in their litter. The detritus of daily life contains another record of public spaces, practices, and politics, one that describes the environment where people confronted and shaped those loftier ideals. Ordinary folk throw away the paper once they've read it because they think of news as information, and they assume (separating the two) that content matters, not form.

Common sense proposes a relationship between content and readers, imagines a politics coming out of this relationship, and in the process leaves form invisible. In common sense, an ideally transparent newspaper carries content to ideally sovereign readers, who sift through the content, extracting the usable matter by applying self-conscious intelligent values. Everything about this relationship is pragmatic. Editors and reporters, the content providers, hardheadedly refine the grand mess that is the world into reliable dispassionate stuff, and newspaper readers, the most worldly and discerning of all media audiences, look hardheaded right back. The politics that comes out of such a relationship pushes citizen involvement and empowerment. The newspaper tells you the truth, and the truth sets you free; the newspaper gives you knowledge, and knowledge is power. Not that anyone really believes all this. Hardheaded people know that reporters can't escape bias, that everyone has a hidden agenda, and that ordinary people are fallible, even stupid. They expect the relationship to fail. But it remains the yardstick with which they measure the performance of the media.

Scholars to some degree have shared these commonsense notions.

Those who assumed that the content has effects in the world set out to content-analyze reporting, to measure scientifically its real (as opposed to its apparent or impressionistic) content. Their initial attempts ignored important qualities of news, such as the role it plays in perpetuating and transforming culture and ideology. Historians now pay attention to those qualities, although their accounts deal with aspects of form only haphazardly, if at all (Schudson, 1978; Leonard, 1986; Emery, Emery, & Roberts, 1996; Sloan & Startt, 1996; Folkerts & Teeter, 1998).

Our approach to form builds on this cultural and ideological perspective and takes it a little further. This requires us to adopt a critical understanding of the relationship between content and readers and of the politics that emerges from their interaction. No piece of this big equation can be understood without considering form.

News comprises more than the sum of its informational content, which arrives embedded in what we call form. Another premise of our critique is that the form of news creates an *environment*: it invites readers into a world molded and variegated to fit not only the conscious designs of journalists and the habits of readers, but also the reigning values in political and economic life. The newspaper provides a three-dimensional experience, with particular sights, sounds, and smells that become reassuring through repeated exposure. At any moment in its history, news form seems natural and pretends to be transparent — an order of words, images, and colors within pages and sections, reflecting and containing events that remain distant and yet distinctly present. Form structures and expresses that environment, a space that comfortably pretends to represent something larger: the world-at-large, its economics, politics, sociality, and emotion. Not that form is autonomous: the forces operating in daily life themselves mold the space we call the newspaper along with everything else, leaving obvious scars and embellishments. The form of news works to hide these scars; it works to present itself as a picture of the changing world, an unchanging witness to change. But the form has changed profoundly. At each phase of U.S. history, newspapers have matched that history not with a picture of the world or a particularly reliable witness of events but with an environment: a paper armchair, a newsprint backdrop, a surround that itself proposes a way to see.

In so doing it inscribes its own *readers*. Just as it hides its own form, the newspaper proclaims its readers to be sovereign individuals, self-conscious users of transmitted information about the world. Critical scholars object to this account, arguing that information is presented in ideologically fraught forms, but they imagine that ideological effects occur because readers read ideologically constructed stories and pictures. This account also misses the mark. Readers do not read bits of text and pictures. What they read is *the paper,* the tangible object as a whole. They enter the news environment and interact with its surface textures and deeper shapes. Readers don't read the news; they swim in it.

Research has tended to examine readers as receivers, detached from the things they read. First, media professionals developed an arsenal of techniques to describe and predict the impact of messages on audiences. These social science techniques treated the media as the source of meanings. Then, using reader-response theory as a rallying cry (Tompkins, 1980; Radway, 1984; Iser, 1989), critical scholars insisted that the act of *reading* (instead of the act of publishing) is the pivotal moment in the circulation of meaning. Historians in turn set to work recovering the experiences of historical readers (Brown, 1989; Leonard, 1995; Zboray & Saracino Zboray, 1996a, 1996b). Studies of past and present reading practices have provided a welcome corrective to the crude notions of an all-powerful culture industry that are often attributed to Frankfurt School theorists (such as Horkheimer & Adorno, 1944/1991). But we think they have overemphasized the sovereignty of the reader.

Readers may make meaning, but not under conditions of their own choosing. In the case of newspapers, the form constrains meaning making. Once readers enter the newspaper, they continue to make choices, but the form imposes tacit rules that allow for certain reading practices and work against others. Even when readers resist, they do so within an existing environment. Their practices, along with media industry practices, and for that matter a host of other cultural practices, become implanted in media forms. The resulting environment can survive for decades (and some aspects become fossilized for centuries). We therefore question the notion of individual sovereign readers. Instead, our critique follows the premise that the form of news constructs the audience's field of vision.

Another way to describe our approach is to say that we're more interested in *the public* than in *the people.* Although the populist strain in studies of reading practices appeals to us, it implies that the public *is* the people. The people comprise all sorts of individuals and groups with idiosyncratic habits and with heads full of all manner of unexpected intellectual anarchy. But the public is not simply the sum of the people, because the public does not exist except as represented. The people may be active and imaginative, but unless that activity is communicated to the polity in some form, it is not really public. So the public will always be a representation of the people, but will never be the people, until an age arrives when people can represent themselves publicly without mediation. In the meantime, news form intervenes, affecting the public in spite of the fact that individual people might not be moved by news messages or may use them in oppositional ways.

Our notion of news form suggests a powerful causality, but we want to be careful to distinguish it from the kinds of claims that some media scholars have made for forms of communication. The most familiar is Marshall McLuhan, whose work has influenced a broad array of thinkers. (McLuhan, 1964; Ong, 1982; Postman, 1985). Causality in this body of thinking comes from the phenomenology of communication – the way specific technologies interact with the sensorium, the collection of senses. Visual forms, which enter the brain through the eye, differ from oral/aural forms, which enter through the ear, and result in different mental capacities and operations. Likewise, different technologies have different temporal registers. Some, like the spoken word or the broadcast image, operate in real time and are evanescent; others, like the printed text, make time stand still, and allow messages to stand still and be dissected by the mind. Such thinking sees a strong causal link between printed forms and individualized, rational, critical discourse, and contrasts that with the visceral, instinctive, emotional, and collective behaviors of precivilized adolescence. Modern intelligence, modern subjectivities, and modern democracy come from printing, then, because of its formal characteristics. People easily divorce text from its rhetorical intentions, but submit themselves to imagery, which confounds their cognitive filtering systems. Newspapers make us smart; comic books make us stupid.

We depart from this tradition in several crucial ways. First, we reject the elements of technological determinism that it contains, and see technologies as only one element in a dialectical process that includes many others: economies, cultural values, political movements, the distribution of social power, and so on. Second, we question the dichotomies between rational and emotional, visual and textual, temporal and spatial. Every form of communication mixes these profusely. Third, we reject the model of causality that focuses on the individual mind being acted upon through the sensorium, arguing for a line of separation between the individual and the social, and for the social construction of the social.

For us, the power of form is not a matter of the abstract qualities of communication. Instead, in our view, it comes from the relationship of the form to a medium's material relationships. The form of the newspaper distributes power because of the complicated way it executes a range of material relationships while it proposes (somewhat different) political relationships.

Is there an essential politics to the newspaper form? Not in the sense that form can be read in vacuo, isolated from everything else about a newspaper. Today every newspaper makes some claim to being an instrument of democracy. Even under dictators, the press pretends to speak to the people as if they matter politically, as if public opinion guides the state. If fascists print newspapers, the newspaper form isn't essentially democratic. So is the specific form of any newspaper really related to the political work it does? Or is form simply the clothes that a newspaper wears, dress to deceive the naïve eye, making this look smaller and that look larger, giving a healthy appearance to fat, flabby, and flaccid public discourse?

We think form historically has run clear to the bone. The truism that one cannot judge a book by its cover (shifting the metaphor) — that the outward or visible form cannot indicate inward or essential character and meaning — goes too far. In fact, the form of news is never innocent or neutral (even deceptive book covers reveal the values driving the complex of actors and readers involved). Just as the content of news cannot present a simple window on events unclouded by the medium itself, neither is the form of the news transparent. The form reenacts and reinforces patterns of deference, just as do other formal aspects of culture, such as manners and dress or *Robert's Rules of Order*. Another premise of our critique is that the form of a medium encodes a system of authority. Some forms always allow for more democracy than others. We have found that newspaper form does political work even when ignoring politics itself.

By *political work*, we mean something other than the usual sense contained in the phrase "the power of the press." News, at least in the United States, has always been thought to play a political role, disseminating (and influencing) arguments and movements for everything from the amending of constitutional government to the waging of war. Research in political communication usually conceives of the work of the news, however, in terms of content (Iyengar, 1991; Cook, 1998). That concept has generated questions such as "What knowledge was available to citizens about such and such?" or "How did the press cover so and so?" Questions about content do matter. The power of the press to include or to exclude specific facts or opinions is *real* power; arguments over it are *real* arguments, but they often ignore any power of the *form* of news.

News form has an impact by establishing the environment of power. Our claim here goes beyond that usually made by critical scholars: they challenge mainstream research by arguing that the power of news operates not through its manifest content but through its subtext or as superstructure. Scholars interested in the power of news texts to encode biases, representations, and ideologies focus on the meaning lurking beneath the surface, the latent as opposed to the manifest content. Scholars who document the power of media businesses and institutions see content as alternately expressing or mystifying these underlying structures (Schiller, 1989; McChesney, 1999). The form of news acts as the canvas of institutions and ideology alike, a physical and cultural backdrop, an environment that itself feeds back into practice. To take the analogy further, we consider ourselves *media environmentalists*. The form of news records the imagined terrain of the social and political world and prescribes the maps and binoculars needed for navigation. We aim to describe the topography as something given a shape that has changed in the past and that might be nudged into change again, this time for the better.

The environment of power has a greater impact because the form of news plays out right under the reader's nose, when it is clearly visible and yet somehow beneath attention. The citizen-reader has a crude but usable vocabulary for distinguishing the flora and fauna in this environment, similar to but less sophisticated than the vocabulary of news professionals. But these taxonomies conceal the grand form even while they isolate and reveal the various species of little forms. Making distinctions that seem the most obvious — separating images from text, or splitting images into classes such as photographs, illustrations, charts, and the like — can go only so far toward building an understanding of the overall form (Barnhurst, 1994).

Histories that grow out of such distinctions can work against understanding when applied to news. Take the commonsense distinction between *word* and *image*. Ordinary people readily distinguish between neighboring texts and images as they skim the whole paper; some readers program themselves to not even see the pictures, assuming that all meaningful discursive content will be most usefully presented in text. But the distinction between word and image is far from natural. Making words and making pictures both originated from drawing, but no one confuses the two, at least partly because the distinction has been institutionalized. Schools train students to write in one class and to make pictures in another. Newspapers clearly organize photographers to work apart from writers, despite efforts to encourage teamwork. Researchers do the same. The theories and methods at hand, as well as the scholarly societies and journals, reflect the industrial divide between word and image work. The resulting studies of journalism pay scant attention to visual devices, and visual communication usually brackets the text.

Form understood as news environment bridges this divide. Newspaper content has run predominantly as text through much of history, but the words always contained visual descriptions and came arranged in physical space. In pursuit of form, our analysis crosses over into text, blurring the line between visual and textual communication. In this we avoid playing words against images and declaring a front-runner (e.g., Stephens, 1998).

When pressed, people will also subdivide images in commonsense ways. Scholars do the same, studying photographs apart from information graphics, for instance, or excluding comic strips from research on feature illustrations. The strategy seems obvious but risks reducing form to a list of different ingredients for content, which then invite comparisons: Does photography reflect events accurately? Do graphics convey information more efficiently than text? Even ethical questions may boil down to similar choices: Do pictures, headlines, or graphics treat minorities fairly? These questions fall into the *mimetic fallacy*, the assumption that images can and should reflect the external world. Recently a movement has grown up to decry conscious manipulation and expose the cultural power of imagery (Berger, 1972; Ewen, 1988; Messaris, 1993; Burnett, 1995; Hall, 1997). Political analyses of visual culture rightly debunk the naïve equation of pictures with reality, while working within a standard recipe. Cultural studies of journalism, for example, primarily examine television (despite exceptions, such as Ericson, Baranek, & Chan, 1987). Attending to one ingredient risks ignoring the flavor of the whole. When analyzing content here, we try to focus on the ingredients that get the least attention elsewhere, such as sketches and drawings or the bylines, logotypes, and so-called *sigs* that mark columns and sections. These items interest us for the ways they mix with others in systems of production and in the general social, cultural, and political setting. Each visible morsel holds our interest because it comes steeped in the big pot of gumbo we call form.

Focusing on particular visual elements produces a chronicle, listing innovations and crediting innovators, that wants to become art history. Older visual histories taught an appreciation first of the great artists and then of the social processes defining and manufacturing great art. The recent visual culture movement has redefined art as a social text, examining how images represent power relations and what political consequences result (e.g., Taylor, 1994; Jenks, 1994; Bryson, 1994). News, however, rarely aspires to art, and the narrative strategies of art history rarely fit newspapers. Scholars of images seek out the first, the most distinctive, or the most unexpected images, divining from them the broader shifts in art history. Critical histories reject the ideologies but retain the emplotments of their predecessors. Treatments of the history of photography moved from technique, to aesthetics, to social description and critique without shedding the shock of novelty as the central plot device (see Newhall, 1938/1982; cf. Green, 1984).

Not surprisingly, the emphasis on innovation yields a history of revolutions, many of them accumulating at the end of the twentieth century. Such narratives hold great allure for scholars of communication. The field is young and enamored of change; it understands itself as studying the communications revolution and understands the revolution as ongoing in its own time. The past usually appears as an earlier version of today's revolution (Beniger, 1986). History comes as an afterthought, as something to understand by using the template of present convulsions. McLuhan (1962), characteristically, argued that it was only because he understood how television (the contemporary communications revolution) rocked his world that he could explain how the printing press had earlier revolutionized human consciousness. The belief that one's lifetime contains the most significant portion of History has a strong affinity with the happy practice of using the present as a key to unlock the past.

Most design histories (Meggs, 1998), as well as the few studies of newspaper design, such as Allen Hutt's *The Changing Newspaper* (1973), which updated and extended Stanley Morison's *The English Newspaper* (1932), follow the model of art history. Besides building connoisseurship among viewers, they aim to improve practices among professionals, without paying much attention to social and cultural history. Such works implicitly assert the autonomy of professional design, a notion firmly rooted in the twentieth century. Design autonomy not only divorces visual devices from other kinds of content but also suggests that earlier newspapers were primitive, mere anticipations of modern designs.

Our inclination here is different. We look for elements in the past that are incompatible with present understandings, and we look for rhythms of change paced differently from revolutions. Because the form of news trumps all the particular elements within it, we do not limit ourselves to pictures but also study other aspects of news, including the words in type, the stories in layout, and the surrounding sections in format. We attend to visual details, but not to foster art appreciation or description for its own sake (Barnhurst, 1991). Although professionals may assert their autonomous domain, aesthetic principles and practices are socially constructed. The form of news emerged from one such construction site, from the physical conditions of work carried out under the pressures of social change. We have attempted here to identify the complex of forces, events, and processes inside the media and outside in society that crystallized in particular visual forms. John Hartley's *The Politics of Pictures* (1993), by examining how the British press visualized a public before the American Revolution, furnishes a prologue. A final premise of our critique is that the form of a medium comes rooted in the historical moment. We have found in the form of newspapers a history of everything we could think of.

DEVELOPMENT OF NEWS FORM

The complicated history of news form requires simplification. Not only have the thousands of published newspapers followed diverse paths of development, some genres have been self-consciously countercultural. We feel drawn to publications outside the mainstream and have elsewhere argued for paying more attention to these in journalism history (Nerone, 1990, 1993a, 1993b). In the case of newspaper form, however, we found that the history of the mainstream had not yet been written. By providing a first draft of that history, we aim to describe the series of hegemonic formations that the counterculture genres then countered. In the process, we have necessarily streamlined the process of change. Because there have been so many regional and generic variations, constructing a linear narrative of change requires doing some violence to the historical record. Similarly, because older styles and practices do not immediately and neatly cease when newer ones appear, we have had to cheat to achieve a clean division of events into periods, particularly before the twentieth century. Since the 1920s, the emergence of a self-conscious design practice has eased this problem.

To develop an outline of the different historical periods in the visual presentation of news, we first looked at a lot of newspapers. Based on their appearance, we made an initial distinction between modern and Victorian newspapers, and after pursuing our research further we added the prior category of printerly newspapers. Again, we based these distinctions initially on the appearance of newspapers. *Printerly newspapers* look bookish and home-made; *Victorian papers* seem crowded and busy; *modern newspapers* appear more purposeful and organized. The form of the modern newspaper clearly shows the hand of the design specialist, whereas earlier forms did not, although some notion of design is still evident. Both printerly and Victorian newspapers used a design sense that we call *vernacular*, emphasizing apparent balance and filling space with an increasingly varied but ad hoc typography. Vernacular design underplayed hierarchy or categorization; the news was largely unsegmented, presenting an impression of an unmapped and perhaps unmappable world. At first, even the boundary between advertising and editorial content was not clearly demarcated.

After further study, we concluded that appearance did not evolve independently, but instead emerged partly from what we call newspaper *type*. By this we mean the constellation of tasks and occupations involved in making newspapers. The syncretic presentation of content in printerly and Victorian newspapers expressed in visual form the habits of news work. Vernacular newspapers fit the routines and practices of journalism; certainly it was not an autonomous occupation, as design often is today. Although news appearance did follow stylistic movements experienced in the culture more generally, newspaper design grew principally out of journalism, as an extrusion of standard modes of news gathering or as an expression of systems of producing the newspaper. Form followed practice as well as other kinds of form.

From our initial broad categories — the vernacular designs of the printerly and Victorian eras and the self-conscious designs of the modern era — we constructed a chronology that traces the newspaper from its roots in the British American colonies to the present period of digital news. To cover so long a narrative, we developed a schematic view of different styles, types, metaphors, and formations of newspapers. The full meaning of these terms will become clear through the elaboration that follows. A synopsis of the overall course of development — from the printerly, through the Victorian, to the modern — will clarify these terms and frame our arguments about the details and mechanisms of change over time.

Before Modernism

First we examine the forms of news before modernism, covering the design of American newspapers from the eighteenth through the nineteenth century (Part I). We begin with a discussion of the newspapers of the colonial and revolutionary periods, then turn to the transformation of the newspaper that resulted from the growth of the market in the nineteenth century and the initial industrialization of print.

Schematically, our account moves on three levels (Table 1.1). The first, *style*, deals with the most immediate visual appearance of newspapers. We have identified several periods in the stylistic evolution of the press after the colonial era: Federal, Transitional, Partisan, Imperial, and Victorian. The changing *styles* overlaid three successive *types* (our second level) of newspaper, which we named according to the dominant position in its production. The printer's newspaper appeared during the colonial and Federal periods; the editor's newspaper emerged during the Transitional and typified the Partisan period; and the publisher's newspaper began in the Imperial and reached its height during the Victorian period. A master metaphor (our third level) explained and animated each type of newspaper-producing sys-

TABLE 1.1. EARLY NEWSPAPER FORMATIONS

A timeline of the principal formations, and the style periods, newspaper types of production, and controlling ideals that comprise them.

FORMATION	PRINTERLY				PARTISAN				VICTORIAN		
YEAR	1780	1790	1800	1810	1820	1830	1840	1850	1860	1870	1880
STYLE	Federal		Transitional		Partisan		Imperial		Victorian		
TYPE	Printer's paper				Editor's paper				Publisher's paper		
IDEAL	Town meeting				Courtroom				Marketplace		

tem. The printer's newspaper operated under a town-meeting metaphor, the editor's under a courtroom metaphor, and the publisher's under a marketplace metaphor. These master metaphors combined descriptive and normative dimensions, explaining both how the newspaper *did* function and how the newspaper *was supposed* to function. At specific moments, style, type, and metaphor crystallized to constitute a newspaper *formation*. Part I deals with three formations: the printerly, the partisan, and the Victorian.

The first newspapers in America were the creatures of colonial printing trades, and we begin with a cultural analysis of newspaper design in the age of artisan production (Chapter 2). From the earliest newspapers in anglophone North America until the mid-nineteenth century, the basic system of production was craft-oriented. The key figure was the printer, who operated a small shop with a couple (and in even the most elaborate cases fewer than a dozen) employees. The printer was the master of this establishment. His (and rarely her) bundle of tasks included what would today be the roles of the publisher, the editor, the copy editor, the reporter (occasionally), and the design specialist.

One element of practice in printerly newspapers was passive newsgathering. Colonial printers received correspondence and culled other sources, print or oral, to fill their pages; they did not actively report the news, and they rarely inserted their own voices in the newspaper. In the early nineteenth century, editors began to impose their voices on passively gathered material, but reporting was slow to develop. The bookish and austere printerly style was well suited to production routines in the printer's paper.

Thus the craft setting produced the forms and grammars of printerly design. Production routines called for austerity and simplicity, a style usually considered the poor stepsister of books. These newspapers, however, were quite sophisticated in articulating with social and cultural formations. Although considered visually primitive by today's aesthetic standards, such newspapers developed conventions that served to convey a particular kind of cultural authority, one suited to an austere and deferential society. The work of the newspaper, its reason for being, was politics and commerce. In the colonial era, newspapers tried to represent this realm as calm and gentlemanly.

The Revolution disrupted this terrain. Revolutionary leaders required newspapers to serve the movement, subsidizing and contributing pointed content to supportive newspapers while silencing others. The turbulent public arena changed the work of the newspaper, even though printers retained the forms of calm and passive management. The end of the Revolution did not return printers to their colonial situation. Instead, after the Revolution, the newspaper was expected to take part in the process of continually generating legitimate authority and to help sustain a sphere of rational public deliberation. The public sphere was ideally nonpartisan, but partisanism emerged nonetheless and with it an urge toward mass politics.

The age of mass politics marked the end of the printerly formation and the appearance of the partisan formation. Partisan activists augmented the printerly production of the newspaper by installing the editor, an autonomous agent of political organization not necessarily socialized into the printer's craft and values, as the chief functionary. The editor's newspaper remained a printer's paper in one sense, but prefigured a more elaborate division of labor.

The printer's paper yielded to the publisher's paper in the Victorian period. We next track the development of form as the newspaper shifted away from party news organ toward mass-market commercial product and relocated from print shops to mechanized factories (Chapter 3). In the early to mid-nineteenth century, a series of social, cultural, and political transformations reconfigured the public sphere and reconstructed the uses of the newspaper. The rise of mass politics had coopted the printer's newspaper, and party organizations installed editors whose job was to compose the content of the paper. The rise of a national market society and with it the commercialization of the press integrated newspapers more and more into business arrangements, producing the type we call the publisher's newspaper and the formation we call the Victorian.

The printer's newspaper had been a gentlemen's conversation about the colonial world and then a citizens' town meeting. The editor's newspaper was a partisan advocate in the courtroom of political opinion. The publisher's newspaper was a commercial tool and a marketed good. In combination, the twin moments of political and commercial transformation produced a newspaper that was expansive in appeal to the public. The political parties and the advertisers, which both subsidized editing and publishing, wanted to reach as many readers as possible. At the same time, these newspapers were expansive in their representation of the world. More and more kinds of material found their way into the paper, which grew in size and density as a result.

As the newspaper changed its social function and internal structure, its form also changed. News, redefined as an almost limitless compendium of the social world, came to resemble the burgeoning marketplaces of an industrializing society. Newspapers placed this undigested, complex barrage on the page in the same bewildering abundance that characterized so much else of the culture of the marketplace in the nineteenth century (Lears, 1994).

In Victorian papers, newsgathering became an occupation in its own right. Two types of reporting personnel emerged, recognized, in fact if not in name, as the correspondent and the scavenger. The *correspondent* was a manly observer of events and personages in distant and (usually) powerful places; he (rarely she) was a persona, although usually pseudonymous, who conveyed subjective impressions with an air of authority and confidentiality, like the colonial letter writer. The *scavenger* was not a persona but a completely anonymous newshound, combing first the exchange papers, then the police courts, the theaters, and the taverns for bits of information that might be conveyed in a sentence or a paragraph or that might be turned into a story of a column or so. The correspondent was a gentleman, the scavenger a piece worker, often paid by the line or the column inch. Their asymmetrical contributions were neighbors in the paper, making the overall content active and miscellaneous, qualities its presentation matched.

Typography was the dominant face of news. As the industrial organization of newspapers became more articulated in the nineteenth century, the task of setting news into type fell to the emerging printing trades. One feature of the shift from printer's to publisher's newspapers was the appearance of a divide between editorial work and production work. Typesetters, proofreaders, and press operators worked for the business side of the press, insulated from editorial newsworkers and under the supervision of publishers. It was the publishers who decided the visual vocabulary of their newspapers. They based typographic decisions on custom and convention and on financial considerations. Editorial statements in Victorian newspapers make clear that publishers attended to visual issues, and their choices accumulated into a recognizable style.

By the 1880s the eclecticism of Victorian design proved unstable. Its (not inaccurate) representation of the abundance of the new age clashed with the rationalizing spirit of the era of natural science and industrialization. Eventually, this spirit would produce modernist newspaper forms.

Pictures in Transit to Modernism

A key element in the move toward modernism in U.S. culture was the development of illustration (Part II). We next examine how illustration broke the monopoly of typography after mid-century and what role pictures played in making news an expression of the larger transformations occurring in U.S. culture. Scholars usually see illustration, especially photography, as naturally modern and as one of the key forces producing the modern. The technology, the very tools of illustration, supposedly drive its cultural impact. As the consummate modern device, the camera couldn't help but turn anyone using it into a modern as well. Such an account, however, elides a half-century of practice, a very nonmodern interregnum running from the point when illustrations entered news (around 1850) to the point when photographic reproduction dominated news illustration (around 1900).

To understand the older regime of illustrated news we looked at the two leading newsweeklies, *Frank Leslie's Illustrated Newspaper* and *Harper's Weekly* (Chapter 4). Initially, news illustration adopted the conventions of portraiture and storytelling, meant to reinforce then-traditional notions of civic culture. Far from transcending the order of words, these civic pictures remained integrated into it. Publishers found pictures useful as curiosities, to attract readers as much as to inform them. Pictures at first provided the background scenery upon which reporters' stories would unfold. The imagery pointed back into the text, still the primary mode of news. In design terms, images provided respite from the flow of text but were always interlopers. Custom came to require a clear separation between images and text, most often accomplished by framing illustrations with frilly bric-a-brac that, more than mere decoration, indicated a conceptual boundary. In sum, the strategies of representing the real during the second half of the nineteenth century followed a distinct visual regime: illustrated journalism underscored the author, dedicated itself to storytelling and observation, promised vicarious experience to its readers, and embraced a republican ethos of citizenship.

The regime continued until the late nineteenth century but was already entering decline by the time half-tone reproduction became common (around 1900). A new regime of modern photojournalism replaced illustrated news just as modern forms of cultural authority replaced the republican ideal. The advent of photorealism robbed illustrated journalism of its claim to authenticity and deprived pictorial reporting of much of its storytelling arsenal. The demise of civic picturing had a larger consequence: the loss of the republican mission of news. Operating by different rules from its predecessor, the photojournalism that dominated the twentieth century replaced any civic responsibilities for imagery with a commitment to populism and realism.

Replacing the older with the modern regime involved a complex interaction between text and pictures. We trace the triumph of daily photojournalism by examining how the *New York Times* and the *Chicago Daily News* covered the deaths of sitting presidents (Chapter 5). These events allow us to monitor techniques for covering a core aspect of news — the unexpected — at roughly twenty-year intervals from 1881 to 1963.

Text and picture changed in a dialectical fashion. We found an initial repertoire of verbal techniques for presenting visual information, including dramaturgy, depictions of demeanor, and the presentation of visual detail using the technique we call walking description. These fell largely into disuse as photographic depictions arose. Instead, news analysis came to dominate the verbal report, as many of the tasks of reporting shifted to pictures and as photojournalism replaced the older regime of illustrated news. Pictures acquired immediacy, conflict, prominence, and other news values, heightening the emotional register of news while replacing simple picture narratives with complex episodic arrays of multiple images.

Changes in the practice of news gathering and styles of news presentation marked the transition to modernism. Modern newspapers presumed a more autonomous reporting function, encouraging a stance of objectivity and expertise. Modern reporters, who as professionals are neither gentlemen nor waged workers, took on the task of authoritatively classifying and prioritizing events. Modern photojournalism, in a departure from the conventions of Victorian illustration, complemented that primary task of professional reporting, providing a sense of visual immediacy to go with the formally structured text. In both text and image, the emergent modern newspaper required the effacing of the persona of the journalist, who might have a name (registered in a byline), but who did not have a point of view, a set of values, or (usually) a style of writing. The modern journalist and photojournalist became experts, not authors. The photojournalist is sometimes still a scavenger — a throwback to the Victorian newspaper — although the reporter is not.

Modernism Arrives

Pictures reveal only one dimension of the rise of modernism, and the form of news includes a great deal more: typography and text, other imagery and graphic design, systems of departmentalization and hierarchy, and production processes. We next turn to these dimensions as accretions of broader cultural movements during the twentieth century, when newspapers adopted the visual vocabulary of modernism (Part III).

Schematically, we identify three types of newspaper, according to productive processes, since the 1880s: the *industrial* (which overlaps and continues our earlier designation, the publisher's newspaper), the *professional*, and the *corporate* (Table 1.2). We chose these terms partly to connote the larger cultural moment in which each type participated. The industrial newspaper extended until the First World War; the professional newspaper reached its height in the 1970s; and the corporate newspaper is still ongoing. The first two of these types corresponded to specific design phases that we call Proto-Modern, Classicist Modern, High Modern, and Late Modern. The corporate newspaper mixes period references in a self-consciously instrumental fashion, creating a regime with design ideas relatively autonomous from other productive processes. A master metaphor hailed readers into each type of newspaper: a department store for the industrial, a social map for the modern, and an index for the corporate newspaper.

Our examination begins with an overview of the rise of modern newspaper design. A longitudinal study of newspaper design elements from 1885 to 1985 (Chapter 6) answers the question, Did a visual revolution in newspapers occur after the founding of *USA Today*? One explanation usually advanced for such a visual revolution is that rapidly changing technology enabled newspapers to implement design innovations. This argument belit-

TABLE 1.2. MODERN NEWSPAPER EVOLUTION

A timeline of the stylistic phases, types of production, and ruling ideals for transitions in the modern newspaper formation

FORMATION	VICTORIAN					MODERN					
YEAR	1890	1900	1910	1920	1930	1940	1950	1960	1970	1980	1990
PHASE		Traditional		Proto		Classicist		High		Late	
TYPE		Industrial				Professional			Corporate		
IDEAL		Department store				Social map			Index		

tles the cultural significance of news forms, which are seen as merely the accidental result of new technical capacities. In fact, the capacity to change news designs had been available for quite some time, but journalists considered the existing form of news fully functional, which we interpret as suitable to the social and cultural uses of news at the time.

Another explanation advanced for a design revolution is a perceived need to compete with newer media, particularly television. This argument, like the previous one, attributes design innovation to technological exigency and belittles its cultural significance. We find it equally unconvincing, at least in its conventional form. Television was hardly the first new medium to challenge the newspaper's economic health, nor was it the first to make the appearance of the newspaper seem staid and uninteresting. Movies and radio, not to mention illustrated magazines, had already produced panics in newspaperland. The design response to these earlier challenges was to streamline the newspaper, to rationalize its appearance — in a word, to modernize.

We conclude that the question of a visual revolution must be answered with a qualified negative. The 1970s saw an acceleration of trends already in place since the 1920s, when modernism established itself in what we call the professional newspaper. Further analysis shows successive design *phases* within modernism over the course of the century, culminating in the current Late Modern phase, which likely marks the exhaustion of modernism just as design itself achieved its greatest prestige.

The rise of the modern newspaper encouraged conceiving of newspaper design as an autonomous arena. The modern newspaper accommodated artists, from the designers of information charts and graphs and the layout artists for each section to the managing editors and their assistant managing editors, who came to supervise layout, design, graphics, and photography. Organized as professionals, with a system of societies and awards, and often housed in the business offices of newspapers, these commercial artists worked anonymously, as experts, accumulating power through the several phases of the modern era.

The key moment for the rise of modernism came not in the 1970s or the early 1980s but much earlier, during the period between the world wars. We next explore that period in depth, examining the record of five newspapers during the key decades of change (Chapter 7). From 1920 to 1940, modernism became the established vocabulary of newspaper authority. A streamlined and rationalized front page with hierarchical story placement told the reader what mattered most in the world of the news. As newspapers grew longer, they divided internally into sections that further compartmentalized and labeled the news — as frivolous (sports, women's concerns) or serious (the front page, the editorial page, the business section). Design features developed to signify these valuations.

The innovations demonstrate how professional newspapers assumed the crucial modern role of mapping the social world for readers. The newspaper claimed a new level of ostensibly independent cultural authority, an elevation corresponding to other familiar developments in modern journalism, such as the creation of an ethos of objectivity and professionalism among journalists. Newspapers also reflected the two faces of modernism in the fine arts. At one end of a continuum, the reserved broadsheet adopted the abstractionism of modern art movements, and at the other end the emphatic tabloid adopted modern expressionism.

The timing of the overall cultural shift suggests that its genesis was partly economic. The mantle of professional authority worn by reporters depended on the economic power that accompanied the transformation of newspapers into industrial enterprises and the achievement of local monopolies within newspaper markets. Only when newspapers could believably claim to present *the* news rather than to represent *one view* of the news (as was the case in partisan and competitive markets) did the need and the opportunity to assume professional responsibility come into existence. Likewise, only then could the newspaper meaningfully claim to map the social world for its readers. The line from that set of changes to *USA Today* was a relatively direct one — no further revolution need apply. Visual mapping thus tied modern design to a new agency of cultural authority, modern journalism.

After Modernism

Finally, we trace the decline of the high modern moment of U.S. journalism during the closing decades of the twentieth century (Part IV), the age of the corporate newspaper. What scholars find true textually and ideologically (Hallin, 1994) also holds for form. Newspapers at the end of the century saw another period of visual experimentation that may mark the decline of the modernist style. In the end game of modernism, the collection of styles that we call corporate expanded beyond U.S. borders to confront a borderless world.

To understand the form of news in the final decades of the century, we examine the spread of U.S. newspaper form internationally, including a selection of the prestige press and large-circulation newspapers from every continent (Chapter 8). There is much at stake as the forms developed in the

United States are adopted, in turn, by newspapers throughout the world. U.S. news justifies its invasion of other countries by pretending to professional neutrality, but news design gives to political thought a form so latent that we compare it at one point to the Trojan horse. The form imposes a particular view of the commercial value of news, the authority of journalists, and the power of imagery, among other assumptions. U.S. design models, adopted without any cognizance of their ideological contents, have consequences in the larger understanding of events.

The wholesale redesigns of the late twentieth century have elevated newspapers into high culture, divorcing them from ordinary and everyday events and surrounding them with nostalgia heightened by a series of crises and preservation efforts. In an excursus on the Spanish press, where broadsheets have disappeared entirely, we found that, much like the interlude between the world wars, the current period has seen the breaking down of boundaries. Long-standing distinctions between the visual vocabularies of the modern broadsheet and the tabloid have now begun to dissolve.

The melange of styles and practices in printed and now Web-based newspapers, although postmodern in terms of scholarly and design thinking, might more meaningfully be understood as neo-Victorian. The new styles, embodied most famously in *USA Today* and its clones, mark a return to the mystifying abundance of facts and stories that newspapers of the Industrial Revolution made visually present to readers. They also imply the abandonment of the high authority of modern journalism, presenting the possibility of recovering some aspects of the old civic culture of news. At the same time they accelerate rather than reverse the marketing and industrial logic of the corporate newspaper. Although in some aspects the form of Internet news calls individuals back to citizenship, in other aspects the form pushes individuals away from the public sphere back into civil society.

As news begins to move onto computer networks, its form again enters a state of flux that invites speculation. We are uncomfortable making oracular pronouncements about the future impact of new media on the form of news, but the present moment of change presses such questions upon us. If our historical analyses point to ways that the form of news imagines, constitutes, and reinforces political systems, then how will the design possibilities of the Internet allow reformations (or deformations) of news? The fact that the same producers (such as the New York Times Co.) may operate in the new information environment should not obscure the changing politics of news form. As a network of material relationships, the Internet version of the *New York Times* might be the same as the print version, but the form of the Internet version differs markedly. It allows a greater disarticulation of discrete relationships and invites an unveiling of its sources of content supply. As a result, it makes it harder to believe in the *New York Times* itself as a kind of national town meeting, as the print version would sometimes seem to propose.

We conclude by summarizing how a different form for news can hail readers into various relationships with the events and personages of the day (Chapter 9), returning to our initial themes. The relationships empower readers and news differentially. The modernist newspaper, and much of the twentieth-century culture of the press, is based on a Baconian understanding of the maxim that knowledge is power: the function of democratic media is to present knowledge to a rational citizenry. This model presumes that the citizenry is in consensus on the larger features of an overall mapping of society — the personal, for instance, should be readily separable from the political. In this understanding, empowerment means acquiring information. Journalism should supply this information, preferably mapped according to the gross features that, common sense tells everyone, correspond to the essential structure of society. In this fashion, the modernist newspaper proclaimed its mission to give a complete and accurate account of the day's news in a context that gives it meaning.

The Baconian model is no longer believable. All the newspaper formations we discuss — printerly, Victorian, modern, and postmodern — are deeply implicated in legitimating existing concentrations of power by making them seem simply obvious. The modernist newspaper, the most implicated here, has combined the inescapable function of visual reputation with a journalistic claim to map the social fully and neutrally and with the economic power to make that claim believable. Put tersely, the project of mapping the social has always entailed more power for the mapper than for the citizen. The challenge remains to invent forms of news for a reinvigorated civic culture.

A FINAL NOTE

We write as members of a particular generation. We both came upon the newspaper in our youth as a familiar form but suddenly also as something wonderful. Once we grasped the *idea* of the newspaper, it seemed so curious and so real: the infinitely public news of the day, packaged and delivered to an alert populace in the face of all the corruptions of power. In our different ways, we made the newspaper an object of study too. What we loved in the idea of newspapers, the actual newspaper itself often betrayed. Newspapers break their vows, whether as social, cultural, and political institutions or as artifacts. These shortcomings have only strengthened the allure of the idea of the newspaper, an allure that we feel for no other medium. Certainly, television has been the great rising communication star of our lifetimes, just as the Internet seems to be for our children. Television doesn't much interest us, and we guess it is because no one ever pretended that television has a necessary relationship to self-government. Quite the contrary. As our friend Dave has always said, if people didn't buy TV sets, the government would give them away for free.

Perhaps the tension between our attraction to the idea of the newspaper and our criticism of actually existing newspapers pushed our interest in past newspaper forms. We have resisted the common idealist temptation toward nostalgia, although a critical reader might disagree. We do reject a happy progressive narrative of newspaper development and try to honor the virtues of past newspaper forms. Some things newspapers simply used to do better. They engaged readers better. They invited people (albeit especially white men) into politics better. They presented multiple voices better. They encouraged argument better. They told stories better. Many of these virtues have since been sacrificed to higher ends: clarity, precision, expertise, prediction, realistic photographic illustration. We wonder whether, in the long run, this has hurt self-government.

It is hard to believe in self-government now. After watching the presidential impeachment follies, who wants the political process involved in, say, setting interest rates? Surely we want to protect Social Security from politics. In this age, we approach the idea of self-government with the same adolescent yearning we feel for the idea of the newspaper. This might seem like nostalgia again. But it has always been the possibilities, not the actualities, that we love.

PART I

BEFORE MODERNISM

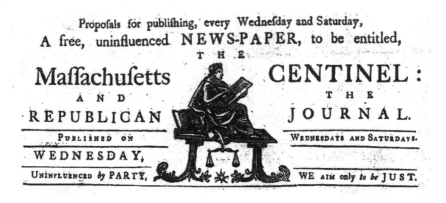

Proposals for publishing, every Wednesday and Saturday,
A free, uninfluenced NEWS-PAPER, to be entitled,
THE

Massachusetts   CENTINEL:
AND   THE
REPUBLICAN   JOURNAL.

PUBLISHED ON   WEDNESDAYS AND SATURDAYS.
WEDNESDAY,
UNINFLUENCED by PARTY,   WE AIM only to be JUST.

Warden and Russell, "Proposal for publishing . . ." nameplate with relief cut (American Antiquarian Society, Broadsheets, 41 × 22 cm), Boston, March 11, 1784.

Symbols of Citizens

Newspaper form not only carries content but presents it in ways designed to reach an imagined reader. Printers during the colonial era and the early republic, however, equated newspapers with the public itself, and perhaps this is why their iconography did not depict readers. Being integral to the audience, newspapers experienced no urgency to represent an external, hypothetical reader. In our perusal of the earliest phases of U.S. newspaper history, we found no illustrations of the audience. In fact, images of newspaper reading did not emerge generally in U.S. painting and graphic arts until the second decade of the nineteenth century (Leonard, 1993). Before then the press had a limited capacity to publish illustrations. One exception, where illustrations did appear, was newspaper nameplates.

Newspapers typically promoted their inauguration by printing a broadside prospectus. In its announcement, the *Massachusetts Centinel* presented itself in typography as a guardian for the commonwealth in imagery that represented it not as military but as civilian and not as masculine but as feminine. The seated figure faces right, in the direction of advancement, and holds a large tablet. She is not primarily a reader but a scribe in the act of writing, her page only partially filled. She represents an ideal surrounded by symbols of virtue: scales for Justice and a book for Knowledge, on a platform rooted in Nature. This depiction is allegorical, not ethnographic. The body (this goddess-like extension of the public) is pure and possessed of republican virtues. Its task is first to write, and in doing so it actually makes itself, both as a public and as a guardian of the public. The newspaper is thus an appendage self-made by the body politic. Its relationship to the public is immediate and unproblematic.

Later imagery would separate out the newspaper, as something for the citizen to challenge. For example, a book illustration after the turn of the century shows a gentleman leaping from the barber's chair, gesturing at the newspaper in his hand. Objects of ordinary life fill the scene — a wig hanging on its rack, fish hanging from the ceiling —

and two men look on. "D--n, D--n, The Author & Publisher I Say!" reads the inscription (Huggins, 1808). The newspaper stands rigidly away from its reader, the one quotidian prop to give offense. As an external object the newspaper is keyed to power, and that led to its use by the mid-nineteenth century as a symbol of male authority.

CHAPTER 2

THE FOUNDING FORMS

Politics and the Work of Newspapers, 1750–1850

The U.S. newspaper first acquired a distinctive form in the wake of the American Revolution. That form had many sources: the English tradition of provincial newspapering, the specific uses of the newspaper in the British American colonies, the ideological impulses of the Revolution, the formation of a national public sphere with particular norms and practices, the material development of print work and technology, and a variety of stylistic influences. This chapter begins by describing the development of this printerly formation. We base our analysis in this chapter on a combination of browsing newspapers from the years under study and a more systematic survey.[1]

The post-Revolutionary newspaper eventually became the Victorian newspaper. The Victorian formation, which prevailed by the end of the nineteenth century, evolved in response to, again, a whole array of influences: social, political, economic, stylistic, technological. This chapter outlines the moments of the evolution of the Victorian newspaper, and then begins to analyze the process of evolution by describing the political factors involved. Our premise is that politicization, or the integration of the news-

---

[1]For the survey, we first examined issues of the *Courant,* published at Hartford under several names, at roughly ten-year intervals from 1767 to 1789, to capture a close-up image of the colonial era and the Revolutionary period, followed by quadrennial issues in presidential election years from 1796 to 1884, covering the era from the early republic through the Industrial Revolution. The *Courant* provided one case of a continually published newspaper. We supplemented that long-term case study with other examples, selected at ten-year intervals from 1757 to 1867, including roughly a dozen separate titles as disparate as we could locate from the archives for each decade.

paper into an emerging system of mass politics, constituted an initial moment of the transformation of the newspaper. We begin with the colonial newspaper.

NEWSPAPERS AS "PUBLIC PRINTS"

Colonial newspapers perplex modern readers. Compared with contemporary news media, colonial papers were short, stale, dull, unintelligible, and unprofitable. Almost always four-pages long, they contained news so old we would hardly call it news and presented it in a form sure to deprive it of whatever intrinsic interest it might have. Even for the schooled reader of colonial newspapers, moreover, much of the content is obscure. Finally, we know that printers constantly ran short of cash. At first sight the newspaper culture flourishing in the British North American colonies by the mid-eighteenth century presents a mystery.

What were the uses of the newspaper in the colonies? The answer is summed up in the phrase common to those newspapers, and which is also the title of the best scholarly book on them, *The Public Prints* (Clark, 1994). The colonial newspaper understood itself as a public institution. As an accompaniment to government, frequently supported by patronage, it often declared itself "printed by authority."

The public prints were public in one sense of the word: they dealt with public affairs, which means affairs affecting everyone. They were not public in another sense of the word: they did not discuss affairs in a fashion that would be accessible to everyone. Instead, their content was coded and elliptical, indicating their printers' awareness that, although a newspaper might appear before anyone, even the most vulgar reader, the public prints should be intelligible only to truly public men, gentlemen, and sometimes their women.

One reason that so much of the content of these newspapers was unintelligible to ordinary readers is that it consisted of artifacts without an interpreter. Take, for example, "The Speech of his Excellency Jonathan Belcher," the governor, to the General Assembly of New Jersey, delivered on December 17, 1756, and printed in the *Pennsylvania Journal* on January 20, 1757 (Figure 2.1). The paper gives its readers simply a transcript of an official address, without commentary. The address runs a full column, and refers here and there to facts, events, and issues: a previous session of the legislature that failed in some way to achieve consensus on unnamed issues, a communication with Lord Loudon a few days earlier, a request for the rais-

The Speech of his Excellency JONATHAN BELCHER, Esq; Captain General, and Governor in Chief of the Province of New-Jersey, to the Council and General Assembly of the said Province, met at Elizabeth-Town, on Friday December 17, 1756.

Gentlemen of the Council, and of the General Assembly,

AT our Meeting in October last, I laid before you in the most particular Manner I cou'd, the State of our publick Affairs in that Time ; and in your Resolution thereupon, you said, several of the Matters were of extraordinary Moment, but desired a Recess for further Consideration therein; and I now hope you will have Recourse to my Speech then made to you, and duly delibrate, and do in the several Articles what may be necessary for the Honour and Interest of his Majesty, and the Safety and Welfare of the Province.

That there might be no Reason of Delay, in doing what may be necessary on our Part, for promoting his Majesty's Service I wrote to the Right Honourable my Lord Loudoun, the 14th Current, informing his Lordship that the Assembly would sit at this Time: and his Lordship's Answer to the said Letter I herewith deliver you, which I think full of Justice, and of a kind Regard to this Province; the best Return whereunto will be your doing all you can (in Conjunction with the other Colonies) in raising a good Number of Men for the common Cause, in, Defence of his Majesty's just Rights and Interests, as well as for your own Safety; and that you now come into such seasonable Resolutions; as may facilitate our acting up to our Duty, and which will also in the best Manner express your Gratitude to the Right Honourable the Earl of Loudoun, for all his Goodness to, and generous Treatment of this Province.

Gentlemen of the General Assembly,

I believe you will think it absolutely necessary to look into the State of your publick Funds, in which I understand by the Officers of the Treasury, there are Deficiencies, especially in the Want of Money to pay the Quarters of the Troops stationed in this Province; as also for the Payment of the Men lately under the Command of Col. Schuyler, but now devolved on Capt. John Parker, whose Letter of the 19th of November, I herewith deliver you; and upon the Receipt whereof I sent to the two Treasurers for the Money, whose Answers were, they had no Money for the Occasion; so I was obliged to send away the Messengers without any : I believe you will therefore think it best, in Justice to the People, and for preventing great Desertion, to send away the Money without Delay.

Gentlemen of the Council, and of the General Assembly,

I hope you will give every Thing laid before you in my Speech of the 13th of October past, as also what I have now said to you, their due Weight and Consideration, with good Dispatch; and thereby demonstrate your Duty and Loyalty to the best of Kings, who is always approving himself a nursing Father to his People.

Elizabeth Town, Council Chamber,
December 23, 1756,
J. BELCHER.

FIGURE 2.1. Governor Belcher's speech is shown in detail from the *Pennsylvania Journal,* January 20, 1757, p. 1.

ing of troops, some budget problems, and so forth. The governor concludes thus:

> I hope you will give every Thing laid before you in my Speech of the 13th of October past, as also what I have now said to you, their due Weight and Consideration, with good Dispatch; and thereby demonstrate your Duty

and Loyalty to the best of Kings, who is always approving himself a nursing Father to his People.

An ordinary reader would obviously know some of the background here: the back-country warfare with the French and their Native American allies that occasioned the call for troops, as well as the swirling geopolitical controversies associated with the superpower conflict between Britain and France. These larger narratives also framed other items in that issue of the newspaper: a five-column digest, apparently copied from an English newspaper, of events in Europe; a letter from a man who'd been captured by Indians on an unnamed North Atlantic island (Nova Scotia, probably); and reports of naval encounters, where French ships captured British privateers and vice versa. A goodly part of the context of the governor's remarks belonged to common knowledge, but not so a larger part. The casual reader might know who Lord Loudon was, but would not be able to interpret the significance of Belcher's communication with him. Nor could the casual reader summon up the content of Belcher's previous speech to the assembly. Consequently, no casual reader could readily understand the nature of this speech as a political act. The news remained inaccessible and opaque to anyone lacking the prior knowledge and the ability to decode the artifacts presented.

The same obscurity also clouded pieces intended to be controversial. Although political contentiousness was not routine in the colonies, sometimes factional strife broke out into public debate. The most famous example for historians of the press, the struggle in the province of New York in the mid-1730s, led to John Peter Zenger's acquittal for seditious libel in 1735. Even in that case, modern readers can puzzle out the dispute only partially from the controversial publications in Zenger's own *New York Journal*. The reason? Most of the matter appeared in the form of pseudonymous contributions and reprinted essays, all missing the background information essential to a full interpretation.

The language itself in political controversies tended to exclude those not liberally educated. Political arguments indulged in the long sentences and florid language of Ciceronian oratory, reveled in references and allusions to classical literature, and relished the dialectic give-and-take of lawyerly dispute. Most contributors adopted a fictional persona, like Cato or Candor or A Farmer. A dedicated reader could follow a long string of contributions and rejoinders week after week, but the high cost for admission to this reading club excluded all but the well-to-do with ample leisure time. Even more telling, mere dedicated readership wouldn't reveal Candor's identity. Some people would know him not by virtue of readership but because they moved in the appropriate circles. For them, reading Candor's argument had different meanings. Because a privileged circle of readers existed, one can surmise, Candor's political act presupposed their attention. They formed an interpretive community that was primary in the minds of authors. (At a later point in history, the rhetorical uses of the pseudonym became more apparent. In revolutionary Philadelphia, for instance, every reader knew that Common Sense was really Tom Paine.)

The forms of political controversy suggest that typically disputes took place between different members of what is called the political class. By *political class* we mean those who actively and continually followed political affairs and had a reasonable expectation to act in them. This level of activity went well beyond voting. Although political participation varied regionally, in most places only a small group of men (and sometimes women) actively followed politics. Unlike the class of all voters, the political class was quite small, restricted to gentlefolk (meaning folk who didn't work with their hands), along with some farmers and craftsmen. The public prints considered this political class their primary audience.

A large part of the political class and of the initial newspaper market consisted of officialdom. In fact many colonial newspapers, including all those south of Philadelphia, were founded by printers whose main income came from government printing (Steele, 1986, pp. 153–4, 164). In the seventeenth century, colonial administrators had considered printing a nuisance. By the early eighteenth century official attitudes had changed, however, and governments began luring printers to colonial capitals. Printers were hired to publish the laws enacted by colonial legislatures, along with other official documents, so that the far-flung justices of the peace and other officers of the law could work from identical authoritative texts (Rawson, 1998). Officials also encouraged state printers to publish newspapers, which carried the phrase "Printed by Authority" prominently in their nameplates. They were expected to provide a common diet of news and sentiment to the best men in the colony, and thereby to facilitate the work of governing.

Newspapers began, then, as extensions of privileged communication. One might think of them as an extended legislature, with all the privileges of legislative discussion, including one of the traditional perquisites of parliamentary debate: protection from broader scrutiny. For this reason (among others), colonial newspapers had the habit of referring to people and officials with elided letters, that is, not to Governor Hutchinson but G------r H--------n. To name the personage would violate the etiquette reserved for conversations that tradition held as privileged. Of course, the governor's name was widely known, as were the identities of many but not all of the coded personages mentioned in the newspapers. The form itself recorded an instinct to think of political communication as appropriately limited to the political class.

News of commerce followed the same pattern. Colonial newspapers dedicated a large portion of every issue to shipping and commercial news. Successful newspapers devoted another substantial share of space to advertising. Like the political content, the commercial content was aimed at a privileged stratum of society and acted as an extension of a non-print communicative arena: the conversations of merchants in coffeehouses and taverns. Such colonial gathering places boasted of the wide range of newspapers available for their customers, and patrons of any particular public house had a collective identity and constituted an interpretive community.

In its form and content, in fact, the colonial newspaper acted as a virtual tavern. It reprinted excerpts, making available the contents of a range of newspapers, just as the tavern promised. Its publication of controversy reproduced the conversation of the patrons of a tavern. Newspapers, however, differed in important ways. They lacked the strong identities of a tavern or coffeehouse, as well as the physical locale. There were fewer newspapers, and they couldn't really succeed without appealing to politically disparate readers (Conroy, 1995).

PRINTERS AS MERE MECHANICS

Until well into the nineteenth century, newspapers in America were produced by printers, who simultaneously handled the physical production of the newspaper, its business operations, and its editorial tasks. Of these three aspects of newspaper production, the editorial side received the least competent attention.

Business necessity obliged the colonial printer to adopt a humble and submissive attitude, as Stephen Botein (1975) has strongly argued. The printer, as a craftsperson, was conscious of working with his (sometimes her) hands. Only the fame of one colonial printer could have so obscured the humility of the rest. Benjamin Franklin, perhaps the first true international celebrity born in the colonies, became a political chieftain in his home province of Pennsylvania. Such a climb up the social ladder occurred only rarely. As soon as he had achieved substantial material comfort, Franklin took off his leather apron; now a gentleman, he found his craft background irrelevant at best, and embarrassing at worst. The typical printer struck a figure far less grand.

The hand of the printer, as a dutiful servant, everywhere marked the newspaper. Take for example an issue of the *Hartford Connecticut Courant,* on March 9, 1767 (Figure 2.2). The foot of the nameplate announces the printer's name and place of business: "Printed by THOMAS GREEN, at the PRINTING-OFFICE, opposite the STATE-HOUSE, in HARTFORD." Every item that followed began with "Mr. Green." In setting his own name in type, Green demonstrated his skill as a tradesman. The *Courant,* typical of colonial newspapers, used type in only one face on its pages. Within this limited palette, Green clearly preferred to display a mastery of his craft. Capital letters or lowercase, small capitals, letter-spaced or not, italics or regular — every combination appeared. This emphasis on variety he applied especially to the individual greeting, which appeared within one page in all capitals, in small capitals, and in widely letter-spaced large and small capitals combined. The issue contained an unusual number of contributions from readers, each of whom greeted Mr. Green in a different typographic tone.

Printers depended on the patronage of gentlemen. They dealt in, essentially, a species of luxury goods (books and newspapers were expensive). Their customers outranked them socially and disposed of greater and more stable economic resources. For these wealthy gentlemen, printers provided a range of commercial services by printing handbills and broadsides, legal forms, and the like.

In contrast to their patrons, print shops survived as precarious enterprises. The colonies chronically ran short of currency, and printers had continually to order supplies from England. Colonial industry produced none of the materials — type, ink, and, for a time, even paper — required to manufacture printed products. As a result, the defection of any significant portion of a printer's clientele would prove catastrophic.

When they composed the newspaper, printers (however conscious of the need for compelling content to attract and hold readers) always had to remain inoffensive. A reprinted speech by the governor or a long excerpt from another newspaper would be ideal. A controversial item from a reader could be profitable — contributors themselves customarily paid for publication — but also dangerous. Suppose some readers found it offensive? To avoid this danger, the printer reserved the right to reject anything deemed inappropriate and promised to keep the pages open for rejoinders. Around these practical considerations, printers built a positive ideology of the open press.

MONDAY, March 2, 1767.

Numb. 114.

THE

Connecticut

AND

WEEKLY

COURANT

THE

ADVERTISER.

Printed by THOMAS GREEN, at the Printing-Office, opposite the State-House, in HARTFORD.

Mr. GREEN,
SIR.

The following is from One who is willing to throw in a Caveat against whatever is inconsistent with Liberty, or that may prejudice it, even in the most distant Manner; and as the Press is open, he hopes that if the Observations are not just, they may be publickly confuted.

Fas est ab Hoste doceri.

THERE is a Law in France, which forbids Father and Son to be at the same Time Members of the King's Council, or of Parliament. This is said to be a very ancient Statute, and how far regarded by the late Monarchs, or ... Tyranny of that Kingdom, am unable to say; but thus much we may infer, that the French, now despised by us as Slaves, were once a free People, and entertained so high a Sense of Liberty, as to be peculiarly cautious of admitting any Custom or Usage which might in the least prejudice the perpetuating so invaluable a Blessing.——

The good Policy of this Law is very evident in thus wisely guarding against an undue influence in public Councils, which is in its self destructive of Liberty, and strikes at the very Root of communicative Justice. The Authority and Influence of a Father over a Son, the natural Dependance, and Duty of the latter to, and on the former, together with their Family Connections, which are to be strengthened, their Interest to be promoted, and private Views served, make it highly dangerous to the Public, that they should sit in the same Council, as the Voice of one will too naturally be the Voice of both; it is in Effect giving one Man two Voices in a Debate, and thereby enabling him by Degrees to gain such an Ascendant in Council, as may be extremely dangerous, if not fatal to public Liberty. This Danger increases, in Proportion as the Number of Councillors in any State are but few. And

I can assure the Public from very good Authority, that at the Time of enacting this wholesome Law in France, the Number of Councillors exceeded Fourteen several Times over.

And further our own History informs us that until the inglorious and unhappy Reign of CHARLES the First, it was unprecedented in England, for the King to call any Man into the House of Lords, during the Life, and Sitting there of his Father.

FREEMAN.

———————

February 17th, 1767.
Mr. GREEN,
SIR,

As you have extolled in your Paper, a scurrilous Piece, signed Plaind Facts, calculated, and no Doubt intended to stir up Strife and Animosity in the Government; and to disturb the late happy Establishment; (unless you will shew your self a Friend to a small discontented Party) must insist on your giving the following Remarks a Place in your Next:.

Your's, &c. A. Z.

WHEN the late detested STAMP-ACT was repeal'd, and the Government so happily put into the hands of wise and faithful men, I was ready to hope, that every one would be easy, and we should have no further strife & animosity among us; but was surpris'd (on reading in one of your late papers, a piece sign'd Plaind Facts) to find we had still some who were desirous of disturbing our present happy establishment, and raising up a party, against those worthy Gentlemen who so deservedly fill the chief seats in the Government. However, as I considered it might be the sudden start of some low born genius, who wanted to shew his wit and talent at satire; I determined to treat it with that contempt and neglect it disserved, but on reading your last week's paper, I find we are to be favoured with more of the same kind. Therefore beg leave to observe, that the ob-

vious design of this seditious writer, is to stir up a spirit of strife, among the people in the western parts of the colony, against those in the eastern, because the greater number of the principal authority hapen to reside there, as tho' the Governor and Counsellors were to be chosen by acres of land, or according to the amount of pounds, shillings and pence in the public list. And to inflame the people still more, he reckons the towns of Windsor, Hartford and Middletown, as tho' they were on the west; whereas a considerable part of those towns lie on the east side of Connecticut River; he does indeed remind us, that Windsor hath two, Hartford one, and Middletown two parishes on the east side of the river; had the author meant to tell us facts truly, he would have informed, that Windsor and Middletown have each of them three parishes east of said river. This I mention only as an instance of his unfair and deceitful conduct.——But to be serious, can this Gentleman believe that the present authorities living in the eastern counties can be any just objection against them? I admit, that in a popular government, 'tis best, generally speaking, that the rulers be equally dispersed all over the community, as near as may be; but yet the best men are to be chosen, let them live where they will; and the freemen are under a solemn oath to vote for such. If therefore Providence hath placed the best men in the eastern parts, (and the late united votes of the freemen evidences this) let us without favor or affection vote for such, as we are in duty bound to do. If the scale should hereafter turn, and more suitable or better men can be found to the westward, we in this part of the colony shall be content that they be called to the government, but till such an event take place, we think that every one should be easy with their present rulers.

Time has been, when the go-

FIGURE 2.2. On the front page of the *Hartford Connecticut Courant,* March 9, 1767, note the different ways of presenting "Mr. Green." Other variations appeared inside.

An open press, or a "free and open press" in the common phrase, differed markedly from the modern notion of the free press. Today's free press supposedly acts as an agent in news and politics: a watchdog for corruption, an adversary of special interests, and an advocate for the common good. The colonial open press, on the contrary, provided a passive instrument for the political class. Its virtue consisted in its evenhanded availability to those who deserved access. This bred an impartiality quite easily mistaken today as a precursor of twentieth-century objectivity.

The newspaper's appearance reflected its impartiality as public print and open press. Its columns were broad, calm, and orderly; its text typography undifferentiated; its items unheadlined. Everything about its appearance announced that it was the reader's job, not the newspaper's, to make sense of the world. Its pages, flat and plain, set a stage for others to act upon.

The look of the newspaper also cued its readers as gentlemen. Printers congratulated each other on the neatness of their productions. They gravitated toward typefaces that looked bookish, and they put together newspapers meant to be read like books. The book-like typography gave a consistency to the whole colonial period. The *Courant,* for example, used an old-style type throughout its pages, in text sizes resembling those used in books and pamphlets, set with the same cast-iron letters the printer employed for other commercial jobs. The paper produced variation by using different fonts of the same typeface, which bear a family resemblance built from the same basic forms.[2] In colonial newspapers, the single typeface provided a visual unity that gave a warm, cozy impression: all fonts on the page living in harmony with the others.

Although designed to look like books, colonial newspapers might not have encouraged reading to flow from beginning to end. The latest and most interesting news, often the last thing to go into type, would not sit at the front of the paper on top but usually toward the inside margin of an inner page. It became customary in the eighteenth century (and remained so through most of the nineteenth) to print first the outside of a newspaper sheet, pages 1 and 4, and the inside last. That order left the ink on the outside, on surfaces exposed to handling, drier and less prone to smudging. If colonial readers were like readers today, they probably would have skipped directly to the latest news and then worked their way back. But perhaps not.

---

[2]Computer programs have confused the term *font* with *typeface.* Typographers define a font as one set of the complete alphabet, such as the regular font, italic font, boldface font, or the like — what computers call styles. In various sizes, all matching fonts together comprise a typeface — what computer programs erroneously call fonts. See Barnhurst (1994) for the history, classifications, and meanings of typography.

The printer did intend each reader to read every item in the newspaper, with the possible exception of some ads. The expense of printed goods and the scarcity of appropriate information to fill the pages called for close attention by readers rather than a throwaway mentality. Ironically, this meant that little care need be exercised in composing the newspaper. The ordering of items mattered less for a reader who would read them all. Individually, each item moved in commonsense fashion from beginning to end (inside-out by today's style of journalism, which likes to lead with the end of the story, then move back to the beginning and run on through the middle). The overall content, moving from stories older and farther away to newer and nearer to home, also suggested a literary form, in which chronology tended to control and led the rising action to a satisfying climax. Because of the long time frame of the newspaper, with nearby news available right away and distant news arriving months after occurrences, the oldest items of any issue were older than the newest items of the previous issue, while its newest items were newer than the oldest items of the next issue. The content interlocked from issue to issue, encouraging readers to archive their subscriptions.

The pages reinforced a consensual map of the world, dictated as well by the exigencies of producing a newspaper, with contents arranged hierarchically in three tiers. The most important news came from England and Europe, and was gleaned from London newspapers that ships delivered to the major northeastern ports, Boston and later Philadelphia especially. Although it had its practical usefulness, such news played another role — perhaps the oldest for American newspapers — as a way for those distanced from the centers of power and culture to participate vicariously and to confirm their identity as civilized gentlemen (Sampedro, 1998; Clark, 1994).

Next came news from the Americas, including the British Caribbean. The distinction between European and American news was, however, permeable. Caribbean newspapers regularly printed important news from Europe, and even local reports from places like Barbados and Jamaica also doubled as indices of European events. A naval encounter off Kingston, for example, might signal hostile French policies. News from the Americas thus supplied items for gentlemen to scan in what amounted to peripheral vision for those whose gaze fixed on Europe.

Finally, the newspaper turned its attention to news from the colonies, mostly clippings (unattributed) from its sister newspapers arranged in chronological order. Rather than classifying things by topic or significance, colonial printers accumulated items, seemingly (though not really) passively. They in fact followed clear social and mechanical procedures.

The habit of clipping news from each other's pages underscored the way that printers worked in concert. Together they formed a de facto news service. Each individual printer's relatively minor input into the system might consist of just one or two local briefs. Take for example these items from the *Connecticut Courant* of 1767:

> Hartford, March 9.
> A few Days ago, the Wife of one Flint of Windham, was delivered of four living Female Children, at one Birth, but they all expired within Twenty-Four Hours.
> A few Days ago, a Dwelling-House, belonging to one Waterous of Marlboro' was consumed by Fire, together with a great Part of the Furniture.

Quadruplets and a fire — the sorts of things printers included in their papers did not appear just for the interest of local readers, who would have heard about them otherwise anyway, but for possible reuse. Other printers used them to fill another role newspapers played: to allude to the transcendent in the human condition. A distant printer who found some local item compelling to that end would label it "melancholy" or "tragic" or "marvelous." Such items operated as portents, their meaning not tied to specificities of time, place, and person. For that reason, "A few Days ago" sufficed as a date (Nord, 1990).

THE NEWSPAPER
AND SOCIAL PREDICATION

In the previous example, note the "wife of one Flint" as the protagonist. As a woman, she didn't get her own name, nor did Flint himself deserve a first name. Neither of them merited a title. Their presentation in the news indicated their social position. A later, superficially egalitarian practice pretended to disguise class distinctions by employing the same basic format for everyone — full name, domicile, and occupation — whether in a crime report, a news report, an obituary, or a letter to the editor (as if one's line of work, neighborhood, and family name conveyed no information about class). Colonial practice indicated otherwise; it tacitly acknowledged society's division into classes by supplying all a reader needed to know about some people: only gender, or race, or ethnicity, or occupation. News stories about "a farmer's wife" or "a laborer" or "a Negro servant," so common in the colonial press, designated the sorts of people who didn't really matter as individuals; they figured only as exemplars of particular social categories.

In contrast, certain other people in the newspaper not only appeared by name and title but engaged in action. Newspapers usually presented men who fully participated in politics as having full names, presuming on the wide recognition of such men as gentlemen, and so could abbreviate where appropriate. The form marked the distinction, not with an elided name or title but with hyphens drawing attention to the missing letters, in what amounted to a typographic wink. For less illustrious persons, no newspaper would report on "one Fl--t," to adapt the earlier example.

Underpinning the many classes of people it presented, the newspaper made a grand division into two gross classes, the historical and the everyday. Consider a bit from a report on bad weather in an issue of the *Pennsylvania Journal* of October 29, 1767:

> Monday last arrived the ship Ann and Dorothy, Capt. Greenway, who informs us, that in the above gale of wind of the 15th, he shifted his cargo and was laid on his beam ends for 12 hours, that one of his people was washed overboard and drowned, and himself narrowly escaped, as he was over, but happily caught hold of one of the staunchions by which he saved himself.

Being named indicates that Greenway was a man of substance, a ship captain, and therefore a privileged player in the transmission of information, who even gets a voice in the paper. The common sailor washed overboard and drowned, however, appears in the same register as the shifted cargo. His fate is melancholy and anonymous — simply another casualty of nasty weather. The captain is a member of the class of men allowed to participate actively in history; the sailor is one of the everyday.

The historical class occupied the world of decisive action, the everyday class the world of work and labor. Ordinary people toiled in a mundane world imbued with a timeless quality. Their activities followed the unending cycle that reproduced life and material arrangements, but lacked any role in steering the development of the polity. Men of action performed that role. They deliberated and made decisions in a sublime world invested with a protean character. These gentlemen, immune from the necessity to work at physical labor, had freedom to act in the direction of affairs (Arendt, 1958).

The grand division of the social world into gentle- and ordinary folk was so universally understood as to never require direct expression. Neither did it require elaborate forms or gestures of disguise. As one of the deep assumptions underlying colonial life, the duality of social class extruded into newspapers tacitly and without effort, taking visible forms that matched its visibility in social arrangements where it also remained unremarked. As a result, when situations arose that challenged its usefulness, the social division could rely upon no articulate justification. It fell as a casualty of the American Revolution (Wood, 1992).

REVOLUTION AND THE WORK OF NEWS

By the time the Revolution ended, newspapers could hold much more news. The visible change in sheer typographic capacity expressed the growth in the work of the newspaper. Rather than serving principally as a tool of gentlemen, allowing them to monitor international affairs and ritually identify with their London counterparts, it became a propaganda instrument. Its controversial function eclipsed its older informational and commercial functions without removing them. The process of change took visible form only gradually. Practical considerations and the traditional attitudes of printers combined to retard the changes in form. In the end, however, the Revolution changed the newspaper's work, overriding along the way its commitment to the ideology of openness.

Generations of historians have argued over the Revolution: its causes and effects, its central character, and its inevitability (see Nerone, 1994, ch. 2). Without going into these debates in any detail, we can say simply that the immediate controversies leading to the Revolution — arguments over taxation — held particular interest primarily to gentlefolk, and yet the justifications cited for resisting Britain involved everyone. Merchants and lawyers, for instance, would oppose import taxes on paper and tea for obvious reasons, but what could explain the allegiances of the laborers and farmers called upon to act? Somehow the gentlefolk persuaded the everyday folk that elite grievances meant something to everyone — that is, the colonial elites made their interests universal. They did so in the face of the British administration's effort to universalize its interests. The Revolution thus featured an ideological battle between a revolutionary leadership and the British administration.

Historians also argue about the ideological presuppositions of the revolutionaries. Again without going into detail, we can say that the revolutionaries, whatever the prevailing system of political thought or language, found it necessary to represent public opinion as unanimous in opposition to the

British administration (Figure 2.3). By *representing* public opinion, we mean not just persuading the public but also presenting a picture of the public, both to Americans themselves and to the polity overseas, including the British administration and Parliament. The need for unanimity came from the assertion that the Revolution represented the formative moment for a new political community. Such an event, in theory, required the actual consent of all members, not just the tacit consent of a majority.

Newspapers became central to the project of representing public opinion for two principal reasons. As public prints, the press could extend, at least in theory, to the entire populace. Meanwhile, as indices of current events, newspapers routinely made their way back to Britain, both in regular ships' packets and in the reports colonial officials sent their superiors. In other words, newspapers worked top-down to convey the leadership's messages to the population and bottom-up to convey a picture of the people's sense of things to the administration.

Those two tasks defined the revolutionary newspaper's work, at least in concept. In practice, this was too much work for the press. Circulations remained small throughout the period, reaching only a portion of the public. Content remained occasional and elliptical, drawing at best an incomplete picture of the public, and not allowing the public to represent itself. Ordinary people had grievances of their own, often against colonial elites, not the British administration. Throughout the colonies, everyday people became restive, even while being asked to support unprecedented political action and to make unaccustomed material sacrifices.

Thus the ideological battle of the Revolution took place on two fronts, as revolutionary leaders worked on the British public and government, on the one hand, and on the ordinary people of the colonies, on the other, even

FIGURE 2.3. In this detail from the *Pennsylvania Journal,* October 18, 1775, the well-known woodcut illustrates both the strategic importance of unanimity and the expanded repertoire of revolutionary printers.

while the British government targeted colonials with its own propaganda. This complicated political landscape drove the new sense of mission for newspapers. The revolutionary movement needed a media system that could present the appearance of the people in deliberation. Ordinary people would never go for revolution unless it seemed a spontaneous movement of the People. To newspapers fell the tasks of presenting the arguments and representing the public as universal and unanimous. Those tasks superseded the ideal of an open press. The polite diffidence with which printers had earlier accepted contributions from other ideological camps could not survive under conditions of revolution.

To take on the additional task of shepherding controversy, newspapers had to grow in capacity. They did not simply discard their existing functions in commerce and culture. They found a new format more appropriate to their enlarged role. They outgrew their bookish appearance and adopted a larger format, closer to that of magazines today. For example, the *Pennsylvania Journal* between 1757 and 1767 jumped to longer lines (from 10 to 11 words per line) and longer pages (from 97 to 132 lines per page). The increase of 50 percent in the capacity to carry words on the page showed dramatically and accompanied the rise of the controversial politics of empire. The change presaged a series of shifts that would progressively take the realm of news further away from the bookish domain of literature and science.

INVENTING THE PUBLIC SPHERE

The Revolution transformed the political role of the press from the fitful public arguments and occasional controversial expressions of the colonial era into something new: a full theater of deliberation. The transformation entailed nothing less than the invention of a national public sphere. The physical design of newspapers accommodated the shift. Calm typography, open circulation, and universal forms of address provided an ideal conduit for rational discourse, the central component of the public sphere.

In his influential book, *The Structural Transformation of the Public Sphere,* Jürgen Habermas (1963/1989) argues that the modern notion of the public sphere originated in the eighteenth century, after civil society and the state split into antagonistic spheres. Under feudalism, society and the state thoroughly intertwined, but in early modern Europe, with the emergence of the new capitalist economy and the new intimacy of life in bourgeois families, an autonomous social realm appeared. The upper strata of this new civil society, jealous of their freedom, set about limiting state intervention in the social realm by developing a discourse of individual rights.

The public sphere occupied the space between civil society and the state. It acted, on the one hand, as a buffer zone, protecting the realm of individual rights from state interference. On the other hand, it supposedly served as a steering mechanism for the polity as a whole. Public deliberation conducted in the public sphere would set the agenda for the state.

As a steering mechanism, the public sphere provided a deliberative space with very specific rules. There private citizens could discuss public affairs free of coercion from the state and free of undue influence from civil society. The public sphere could be a realm of equality, unlike civil society where inequality obviously reigned. The vagaries of economic affairs and the privacy of bourgeois family life guaranteed that men would experience wide variations in their fortunes. Although as individuals all of us might differ, the theory went, the public sphere guaranteed our equality as citizens.

Not that political equality was equally available to everyone. The very notion of a free society in the eighteenth century incorporated the then-common sense of non-freedom for women, children, non-whites, and wage laborers (as well as slaves and indentured servants). Civil society assigned all of *them* a set of rights, duties, and obligations fundamentally different from that assigned to the propertied white men upon whom they all depended materially. Although the equality of the public sphere putatively balanced and canceled the inequality of social arrangements, only the privileged could gain entrance there. The interests and concerns of all other classes were subaltern and invisible.

Equality within the public sphere required the negation of individual social interests and passions. For the public sphere to serve as a buffer zone, steering mechanism, and guarantor of political equality, it necessarily could not operate like the feudal model of representative publicness, the king's court, where public figures known to represent established social interests or estates met face to face. The new bourgeois public sphere presupposed a citizenry of abstract equals, not tied to social estates but simply independent, interested simply in the common good. The new public man was nobody in particular, an anybody. He was not a singular someone, such as a merchant or banker whose political actions expressed his own interests.

If the public sphere required citizens to negate their social selves, it also enjoined them to think of the public as very public indeed. Public expression occurred under the presumption of what Michael Warner (1990), in *The Letters of the Republic,* calls universal supervision. That is, anyone who spoke in public had to assume that everyone could hear. Public speakers must frame their arguments in terms that would appeal to all citizens *qua* citizens, not to specific interest groups in society. The new model of public man spoke as though he directed himself to everybody.

Habermas defines this kind of discourse — an anybody talking to everybody — as rational. This definition of what it means to speak rationally is a pragmatic one. If the public realm negates the particular interests of both speakers and listeners, in effect, only disinterested appeals remain. All participants must construct a universal subjectivity (in place of the interested one they usually inhabit). Rational discourse speaks only from that subject position.

Habermas has described an ideal type of public discourse, one that certainly never existed in its perfect form. The ideal did, however, inhabit the minds and works of the revolutionary generation. The norm of public discourse exerted a gravitational force, pulling actually existing politics toward forms of presentation that claimed rationality. The unobtrusive typography of the colonial newspapers, as well as their supposed reach to the citizenry, provided a transparent, universal vessel for rational discourse. Much of the controversial content of the period gives the impression of authors arguing to a phantom public mind, a supremely intelligent, observant, and candid rationality. The best revolutionary propaganda invoked a kind of populist Leviathan.

The high point for the norm of public discourse came after the Revolution, during the dispute over ratifying the Constitution. A long series of essays that entered the canon of political theory as the Federalist Papers provides a prime exemplar of the public communication Habermas outlined. Actually the product of three well-known leaders, James Madison, Alexander Hamilton, and John Jay, the essays first appeared in newspapers, all printed over the name Publius. The pseudonym, referring to a figure from Roman history but instantly translatable as *public man* or *citizen,* reinforced the negation of personal interests, just as the norms of public communication required.

In their form, that is, their appearance in newspapers, the essays met the norm of speaking to everybody (within the limits already described). Their content met another norm, the requisite voice of an anybody. They pitched the Constitution in pragmatic terms, to be sure, but in terms that were clearly meant to transcend faction and appeal to the candid minds of citizens, not to the material interests of, for instance, merchants or farmers. In that sense, the essays counted on universal supervision. Content as well as form projected the same audience: the everybody that publicness dictated.

THE NEWSPAPER OF THE NEW NATION

In the period following the Revolution, newspaper form sought to match the norms of the public sphere (Nerone, 1989). Although frequently partisan, printers always acknowledged the requirement of negation, and proclaimed the openness of their presses. Many newspapers, even obviously partisan ones, adopted the motto "Open to all parties but influenced by none." Printers thought of their newspapers as the infrastructure to the public sphere and presented them as common carriers for the information and deliberations of a rational citizenry. In part, this seemed like a return to the colonial ideal of the open press, but the new public prints differed in two ways. First, printers had acquired a repertoire of advocacy techniques during the Revolution that gave them an elevated sense of their own powers and responsibilities (Botein, 1981). Second, the ideal of the public sphere, coupled with political exigencies (the need to win popular support for novel governmental institutions and programs) exerted a constant pressure toward fuller penetration into the citizenry.

Because the new nation placed such heavy emphasis on generating its own legitimacy, it quickly adopted policies that encouraged newspaper growth. Early postal policies, for instance, provided de facto distribution and content subsidies to printers in the form of reduced postal rates for periodicals and free carriage of exchange papers between newspaper offices (John, 1995). Governments on all levels — local, state, and national — required themselves to publish official business in newspapers at advertising rates (Smith, 1977). The policy allowed the press to expand into smaller and more remote towns far more quickly than market conditions otherwise would have permitted.

Newspapers in the new nation were printerly in formation. The workplace routines, division of labor, entrepreneurial demands, and craft culture of printers all supported the notions of publicness that the new sense of the public sphere entailed. Printers represented themselves as public-spirited and nonpartisan at core, as earnest in the knowledge of their public responsibilities, as rational, and as servants of the activities of citizens. If they did consider themselves authors or political operators, they knew that they were supposed to conceal such pretensions behind traditional self-effacements. In form, the newspaper presented itself as unauthored. Printers did not hide their identities; they published their names prominently on their newspapers, sometimes including their surnames in the nameplate. But they did not present their proprietorship as authorship. Instead, they used forms designed to assign the authorship of everything in the newspaper to some other agency. Printers typically copied news from other newspapers or from official sources, much as they had done in the colonial era. Even the controversial material spoke from the position of an anybody. Although obviously the work of political activists, and sometimes of the printer him- or herself or of a crypto-editor, such material usually masqueraded as the ruminations of Publius or someone like him. Spectacular exceptions like Benjamin Franklin Bache and William Cobbett aroused such heated condemnation precisely because they violated sacred norms; other printers may have desired such influence or prominence, but practical and normative constraints discouraged them from acting.

Early newspapers embraced principles they called impartiality and impersonality. *Impartiality* meant assuming a neutral stance toward partisan competition, allowing either side to use the columns of a newspaper, and leaving to readers the task of making sense out of controversial arguments. *Impersonality* meant treating matters of public concern without reference to persons: discussing "measures, not men," in their phrase, and refusing to print *personalities,* a term they used to mean personal attacks. Printers developed formal conventions and a visual appearance for contents that matched these principles: the pseudonymous letter, digests of clipped news, reprints of apparently unedited government reports and official speeches, and rare and terse original local news. Even highly partisan newspapers, which were especially common around the turn of the century, adopted these forms.

Newspapers of the early republic operated under the master metaphor of the town meeting. Each newspaper supposedly provided a neutral, limpid mechanism for transmitting the information and opinions that its readers would use to govern themselves. The normative power of the town-meeting metaphor didn't, however, cleanse the press of other motives and practices. Practical politics drove in another direction.

Despite the conventional hostility to party, early national politics was in fact highly factional. Scholars continue to debate whether the divisions during the Washington, Adams, and Jefferson administrations constituted a real party system, but no one denies the vigorous and occasionally overheated factional disputes occurring in those years. Scholars tend to approach the newspapers of the period with an eye toward decoding their partisan agendas, in effect considering partisan activity the essential nature of the newspaper. Such an approach reduces the forms of impartiality that newspapers adopted to empty gestures, simply disingenuous and therefore meaningless.

On the contrary, newspapers did seem to take seriously the notion of rational public deliberation. Even the partisan newspapers assumed that their readers paid careful attention to the arguments of opposing politicos. When, for instance, Benjamin Russell's *Columbian Centinel* of Boston printed pro-Administration essays about the Jay Treaty — a flash point of partisan struggle — it did not itself print the rebuttals to those essays, leaving that task to the opposition *Independent Chronicle*. It did, however, assume that its readers also read the *Chronicle*, or were familiar with the arguments in it. The rejoinders in the *Centinel*'s columns paid minute attention to confuting those counterarguments. Such instances show that these partisan papers assumed the existence of a sphere of public deliberation and took responsibility for providing rational arguments to that sphere.

Most newspapers in the early years avoided open partisanship. The same array of concerns that had led colonial printers to avoid controversy now discouraged partisanship: most papers remained local monopolies, most print shops remained marginally solvent, and most printers remained wary of offending any patrons. Local conditions, however, often allowed a kind of nonpartisan partisanship. In many New England towns, for instance, the relevant local population — propertied men — were monolithically Federalist; thus the local paper could be Federalist and noncontroversial at the same time. If one ignores this context of local conditions, the early national press may appear rabidly partisan (a widely held but lopsided image; see, e.g., Fischer, 1965; Stewart, 1969).

The antipartisan strain of press culture drove news form through the first generation of the new nation's history. Its power persisted in spite of repeated violations and constant political innovation. Anyone looking for evidence of partisan activity in the press of the early republic will find ample evidence that newspapers allied themselves with activists and factions in all sorts of mostly covert ways, but almost always with a guilty conscience, or protestations of innocence, or an altogether virginal appearance. Only around 1820 did we find newspapers routinely appearing openly as partisan instruments without any sense that such behavior raised normative questions. We leave it to political historians to debate whether true partisan politics had appeared earlier; here we argue only that the form and norms of newspapering did not condone earlier partisanism. Clearly, by around 1820, partisanism became an accepted norm for newspapers. At that point, a tradition of advocacy that printers had embraced during the Revolution fully reasserted itself.

The history of political development inflected the form of the newspaper in fundamental ways that we can delineate after laying out a rough chronology of how the visual form of newspapers evolved.

PERIODS OF NEWSPAPER STYLE

The visual style of the U.S. press evolved in five stages from the printerly newspaper of the early Republic to the industrial newspaper of the Victorian era. Here we begin to describe the chief indicators of design change, period by period, based on our survey of newspapers. We especially rely on an intensive look at the *Connecticut* (later *Hartford*) *Courant,* a paper that published without a break throughout the long period and that consistently floated in the mainstream of the nation's newspapers.

The *styles* of news correspond roughly to three *types* of newspaper defined more or less by mode of production. The first type, the printer's newspaper, continued the tradition of the colonial press. The second, the editor's newspaper, resulted from an augmentation of the printer's paper that occurred when political parties coopted newspapers. An editor, a professional at composing the news and editorial content of the newspaper, took over these functions from the printer. The third type, the publisher's paper, involved another reorganization, when proprietors as publishers assumed the business control of the newspaper and consequently assumed power over both editors and printers. Our five periods of news style include three that correspond directly to the modes of production plus two other more-or-less transitional forms (see Chapter 1, Table 1.1).

In what follows, we will alternate between descriptions of styles and discussions of the emergence of new types of the newspaper. We have already discussed the development of the printer's newspaper. We will move next to a description of the styles associated with it: the Federal and the Transitional. Then we will discuss the development of the editor's newspaper, and describe the Partisan style. These pieces of the story were all driven by the great political developments of the years between the Revolution and the Civil War: the invention of a national public sphere and the rise of mass electoral politics. We will take up later the rise of the publisher's newspaper and its styles, the Imperial and the Victorian, which were driven by the other grand process of the first century of the republic: the market revolution (Chapter 3).

The form of news began as a visual whole and slowly articulated into interrelated segments reflecting the new work of the newspaper. The social tasks of journalism gradually gave shape to the stuff of news. The process began with grand distinctions and went on to fine ones. First came the separation of other matter of the newspaper from advertising (a subject we will consider in detail in Chapter 3). Three further separations followed: editorial opinion from news events, history from the everyday, and telegraphic news from postal or clipped news. Formal elements embodied each of these distinctions.

The final product, a newspaper structure based on industrial processes, did not pretend to give a coherent account of the world. Victorian design seems utterly chaotic by modern notions, but its readers as well as its composers took it wholly for granted. It figured the newspaper as a multiform series of conduits for intelligence, each operating by transparent procedures, and none involving the expert description of the world. That newspaper structure was a long step away from the colonial press, when the printer (albeit unobtrusively) composed — for readers taking the proper point of view — a coherent account of the way the world went. We return later to what happened to that function of the newspaper.

Federal Period, 1780s–1810s

Design throughout the seventeenth century remained relatively quiet, without innovation in typography or layout (Meggs, 1998). The early republic, although politically distinct from the colonial era, did not break abruptly with existing social arrangements. The evidence of newspaper form suggests the degree of continuity. During the period many classic qualities of newspaper appearance carried over, especially in the typography. Newspapers reflected the neoclassicism of other practical arts. The type remained generally uniform, using font variations for emphasis, just as did books. Few decorative touches appeared. Ruled lines ran only as horizontals, discretely separating, for example, one ad from another. Reflecting the return to social routines, the news in some ways lost the adventuresome spirit of the Revolution.

The *Courant* saw two principal differences emerge (Figure 2.4). A new, refined blackletter nameplate harmonized with the old-style text and display typography. The blackletter (sometimes called Gothic or Old English) provided a Germanic visual cue, referring to the Teutonic origins of the English people and their ancient order. The backward-looking reference missed a core quality of news — novelty — and contradicted the updating that newspapers otherwise manifested to their readers. Instead it offered a connotation in the opposite direction, one usually hidden in the values of news: traditional authority. At a time of political novelty, when federal forms of government began their period of testing, newspapers acquired in their blackletter nameplates an important sign of gravity and stability.

The other change occurred in the scale of the page. The format moved from the three columns characteristic of the colonial and revolutionary era,

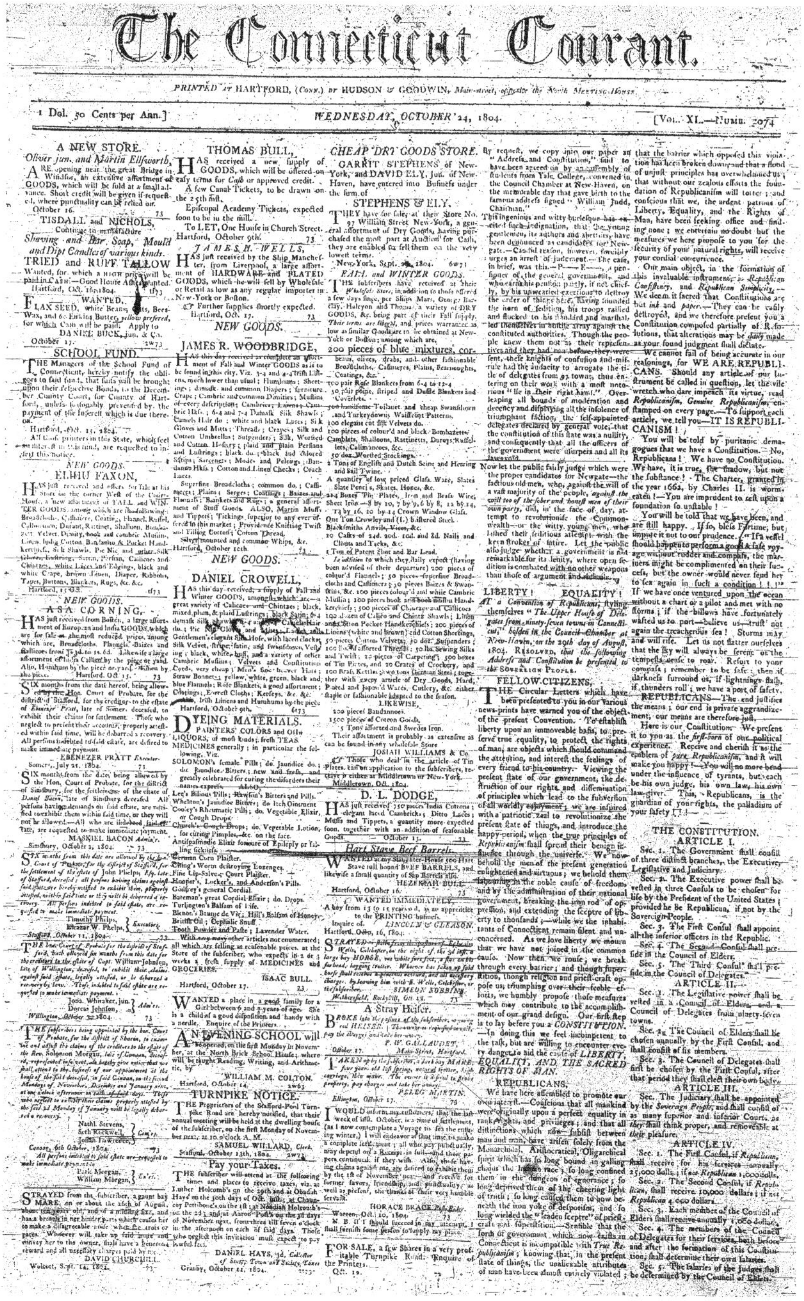

The Connecticut Courant.

PRINTED AT HARTFORD, (CONN.) BY HUDSON & GOODWIN, Main-street, opposite the North Meeting-House.

1 Dol. 50 Cents per Ann.] WEDNESDAY, OCTOBER 24, 1804. [VOL. XL.—NUMB. 2074.

A NEW STORE.

THOMAS BULL,

CHEAP DRY GOODS STORE.

TISDALL and NICHOLS.

JAMES H. WELLS,

NEW GOODS.

SCHOOL FUND.

JAMES R. WOODBRIDGE,

NEW GOODS.

ELIHU FAXON,

NEW GOODS.

DANIEL CROWELL,

ASA CORNING,

DYEING MATERIALS.

LIBERTY! EQUALITY!

FELLOW-CITIZENS,

D. L. DODGE,

Hart Stave Beef Barrels.

WANTED IMMEDIATELY,

A Stray Heifer.

AN EVENING SCHOOL

TURNPIKE NOTICE.

REPUBLICANS,

Pay your Taxes.

THE CONSTITUTION.

ARTICLE I.

ARTICLE II.

ARTICLE III.

ARTICLE IV.

FIGURE 2.4. A *Courant* front page, for October 24, 1804, shows the style of the Federal period.

growing first to four and finally to five columns. As that happened, of course, the page enlarged to accommodate the growth. Although the nameplate stayed relatively constant in its weight for the page size, the text and display type became smaller relative to the full page. The change lent a sense of fullness and final authority to the visual form. Nameplates dominated and provided an establishment flavor suitable for a settled political climate, indicating the aim (if not the reality) of achieving that stability.

These two major differences also affected other newspapers and set what became the fundamental visual vocabulary of newspaper authority. Some newspapers shifted to blackletter nameplates without any real change in the body of the pages. Two in Massachusetts, the *Political Gazette* of Newburyport and the *Salem Gazette,* both made such a change in 1796. The blackletter nameplate has continued until today as a sign of established importance in the U.S. press. So too has the large format. The *Scioto Gazette* moved from three columns in 1794 to four by 1807, and the *National Intelligencer and Washington Advertiser* moved to five columns. The changes, harking back to the large volumes used in university settings since the advent of books, today remain the authoritative form for newspapers in this country (but not in many non-Anglophone countries).

Other than these two foundational changes, newspapers of the period clearly had no rigid uniformity of visual design. Even within nameplate designs they followed changes in fashion. The general movement went from old-style roman nameplates, through blackletter, and eventually to fat face (an exaggerated modern style first introduced by Robert Thorne in 1803, with extremely fine serifs and heavy black strokes reminiscent of Gothic types). A number of newspapers shifted to blackletter nameplates at the very end of the 1700s, for instance, and others switched back and forth to bold or fat-face nameplates. We also noted a considerable amount of experimenting with ornamentation, especially in the 1790s. None of the changes would merit notice among art historians, who look for originality rather than mere variety, but the experimentation did resonate with the political realities of the period. The formative time for the new republic clearly echoed in the emerging form of newspapers.

After 1800, a period of republican austerity appeared to accompany the Republican succession to the presidency. The combination of larger format with more columns made newspapers look very gray, with little contrast. The news matter of the U.S. press would remain gray for a century or so, with some variations. The advertising matter, however, began to grow more daring, a significant change that we probe later (see Chapter 3).

Transitional Period (1810s–1820s)

As the printer's newspaper began to give way to the editor's newspaper, the press adopted elements of a new vocabulary that eventually came to characterize the Victorian formation: bolder type, decorative lines, column rules, and engraved advertising images. These changes reflected the emerging age of romanticism, in which the arts and architecture sought to give form to national aspirations and to mask the unsightliness of the Industrial Revolution (Craven, 1994).

Typographically, the period saw a wide adoption of fat-face modern type, first in nameplates and then in display type (for ads first, then news). That bold modern-style typeface had a simplicity of line and so-called rational geometric inspiration. Throughout the 1810s and into the 1820s the typeface advanced into ads and some headlines of the *Courant* (Figure 2.5). An older, classic type remained as text but elsewhere faded in importance little by little as other forms of display replaced it, producing the effect of real continuity despite other changes.

The extreme thicks and thins of modern-style type — a marker of later Victorianism — also echoed in the ruled lines the *Courant* and other newspapers employed during the period. Slowly the simple, single lines disappeared, replaced in some uses (such as at major shifts in content) by *Scotch rules*, sets of double lines with one thin and one thick.

These changes in the typography and the accompanying ruled lines reflected two important urges. The first, an urge to exhibit contrast, began to link news to one of its manifest values: the unusual as against the expected. Where the monotonic visual vocabulary of colonial newspapers suited the metaphor of a town meeting at which gentlemen deliberated as equals, the new, visible contrast began to project a courtroom metaphor, with editors and partisans as advocates, exchanging assertions and rebuttals. The visual form of news thus registered that a shift in the exercise of power had begun, away from genteel disputation and toward combative popular mobilization.

The second urge, an impulse to decorate, began to link news to one of its latent values: the following of current fashion. Printers and editors (and later, publishers and reporters) defined news in terms deflecting attention away from themselves and toward a world external: the ascertainable fact, the reliable account, and, ultimately, the timeless truth. The gaze of journalism mutated from period to period. Many journalisms have prospered, each subject to the whims of passing style.

Take the example of the fat-face nameplate. The *Courant* was typical in

FIGURE 2.5. A *Courant* front page, for October 29, 1816, shows style during the Transitional period.

introducing a fat face, then reverting to blackletter (at the end of the 1820s). Other newspapers did the same. The *National Intelligencer* in Washington abandoned its fat-face nameplate for a very elegant blackletter, exactly the same fashionable face used at that time in the *Charleston Courier*. Fashion thus entered into every aspect of language and of visual design in newspapers (as it eventually would in other news media) in a manner that gives every change a double function. A fashion commonplace, such as the changing hemlines of women's skirts, can serve as an example. Forms in culture have two aspects, a serious one that gives insight into attitudes about social norms, such as beauty, conformity, and sexuality in the case of women's skirt lengths, and another that is whimsical and quirky. The two aspects exist together, contradict each other, and make fashion interesting. The changes in form during the Transitional period gave newspapers a human face, with foibles and inconstancies, lapses into bad taste, and occasionally a sense of play.

Another precursor of Victorian design emerged with the introduction of ruled lines between columns of type. The custom, which arose in the *Courant* as well as in other newspapers, distanced newspapers from books of a single column. Multiple columns, separated (but visually joined) by rules, had traditionally accommodated such content as holy scripture, scholarly treatises with references, and books in more than one language — all associated with the medieval power of the church and universities. In design terms, column rules further closed off space in the newspaper, giving it a full, complete appearance. Space in colonial newspapers provided a hiatus in visual form, an opening where, for example, a reader might make notations. Column rules closed off space, leaving no holes that formerly opened news to annotation, to a lapse into doubt, or at least to a pause for reflection.

Column rules, like other elements of what would become Victorian design, did not arrive and establish themselves firmly and all at once. They came and went with changes in newspaper design fashion (that value not usually acknowledged) and in wider arts expressions of the national mood. The discernible movement toward these forms over the course of the nineteenth century does provide an index of larger currents in U.S. culture. As its political role and economic clout grew, the newspaper acquired visible forms that tacitly expressed its particular claim to cultural authority.

Finally, the Transitional period saw the emergence of images as a very common element in advertisements, not only at the back of the newspaper but on the front page. The growth of advertising images set a pattern, persistent in newspapers, of design innovation. In the Transitional period, advertising began to follow a new course, diverging from news decisively in its use not only of image but also of type and space. Advertisements became the van of design that news slowly followed.

Transitional style accompanied a series of changes in the uses of the newspaper. In large part, these were driven by the appearance of a new form of political behavior, the rise of the modern system of majoritarian electoral politics. The new political parties of the 1820s and 1830s coopted newspapers, and in the process changed them, both as networks of relationships and as forms.

MASS POLITICS
AND THE EDITOR'S NEWSPAPER

Whatever the relative merits of the two men, George Washington and Andrew Jackson represented different political cultures. The Washingtonian ideal of republican stoicism and disinterestedness trumped the grievances of an always restive body of ordinary men, many of whom remained politically inactive or disenfranchised. The Jacksonian common sense of ordinary folk trumped the pretensions of elites, who were encouraged to withdraw from politics into private life. The Washingtonian culture considered the airing of private grievances in public unseemly, whereas Jacksonian culture acknowledged the general mass of private disaffection as the engine of politics. The era of Jackson expected partisanism, encouraged partisan attitudes, and invented apparatuses of partisan communication.

In essence, the mass politics of the 1820s reconfigured public life as a marketplace. No longer would politics aim to arrive at consensual solutions for common problems through rational deliberation. Instead politics would resolve conflicts through brokered appeals to divergent interests. Democracy (now a good word, having escaped its odium of the 1780s and 1790s) succeeded by achieving a balance of interests. Political parties, as bureaucratic machines for winning office, worked to balance interests because their electoral ascendancy depended on gaining the support of a majority of the electorate. The parties, of necessity coalitional, operated like the marketplace, that other relatively impersonal mechanism for adjusting conflicts of material interests among the different real factions in the public: farmers, planters, merchants, artisans, Germans, Catholics, evangelicals, midwesterners, southerners, slaveholders, and so forth. The apparent fury of mass politics was the sound of two invisible hands clapping.

Behind the rise of mass politics, and behind the transformation of the newspaper associated with it, stood the long and large development that

Charles Sellers (1991) has dubbed the market revolution. Although Sellers's largest claims are controversial, some aspects of the market revolution thesis seem well grounded. On the microlevel, the market revolution meant the intrusion of market considerations into ever more facets of everyday life. People bought more goods in, and produced more for, the market. As a result, they thought more and complained more about the market, and their activities sparked political movements that targeted one or another aspect of the new market regime.

On the macrolevel, the market revolution meant the appearance of a national market. Through a series of contested institutional maneuvers, post-Federalist government produced national systems of transport, banking, and corporate law. The banking system generated the cheap and abundant (and often questionable) paper money that often incited public anger. Andrew Jackson's presidential career prospered through attacks on the Bank of the United States. The legal regime allowed for the easy charter of powerful corporations, understood as fictional persons with all the rights that individuals could claim and immortality besides. Although the United States remained a developing country, it became one where capital could flow and form more easily and in ever larger quantities.

Newspapers promoted themselves and developed within the market revolution. They operated, obviously, as important carriers of commercial information, both in news and in advertising. The rise of market transactions supported an expansion of the newspaper system. As a result, newspapers became more dependent on the market in general and more sensitive to their own specific market appeals. They found themselves, in addition, increasingly in direct competition with other newspapers.

The fact that newspapers competed with each other commercially made it more likely that they would compete politically as well, and particularly in a partisan fashion. Certainly, if two newspapers published in Balderdash, Missouri, both on Saturday because, of course, the mail coach arrived on Friday, then both would compete for the same readers, and neither would have a significant advantage for covering news. In such cases partisan affiliation added a value; each newspaper could lay claim to a different loyal readership. One newspaper, sensibly, would proclaim itself the Jackson newspaper, leaving the other to champion Clay or Adams or whomever.

If, however, newspapers as monopolies could at best yield marginal profits, what would make them profitable in competition? Again, larger economic and political forces helped transform the circumstances of the newspaper. First, the materials of newspaper production, especially paper and type, became cheaper as domestic manufactures grew. Then available advertising revenue increased as more goods came on the market. Luxury goods and other nonessentials, especially, used newspaper advertising to attract new customers. Another important source of advertising income, governments on both the national and the local level, were required by statute to publish laws. Governments customarily hired private printers for that purpose, as well as using the advertising columns of newspapers. Because elected officials decided where to spend money budgeted for publishing laws, printers had an incentive to align themselves with political parties.

As the press became more openly partisan, it adopted new attitudes and divisions of labor, and these engendered new visual forms. As the newspaper embraced a more active notion of its role, it chose a matching label. The newspaper conceived as an advocate named itself the *Advocate*, or something like that, such as the *Enquirer* or the *Vindicator* (Schudson, 1978, p. 17, makes a similar point). Active names weren't new: earlier gossip newspapers had named themselves Bees or Wasps or Hornets, for instance, and plenty of general-interest newspapers had styled themselves Guardians of Liberty or Advertisers or Examiners or Spies. In the Transitional period, however, these active names sponsored an authoritative typography. Each aspect of design in turn expressed the newspaper's newly acknowledged role as political agent and specifically the editor's role as conductor of that agency.

When newspapers became openly partisan, the editor replaced the printer as the face and voice of the press. Unlike a printer, an editor took on a persona. Often lawyers by training and usually members of the party's state or local committee, editors truly authored newspapers, introducing the (still) clipped news items with formulas such as "we include the following important item from the *Clifford Gulch Expostulator*," composing both terse paragraphs and long florid essays of political commentary, and dueling, both verbally and sometimes physically, with competing editors.

Clashes were in keeping with lawyering, then still an unformed profession. Men became lawyers by reading law with a lawyer, then seeking admission to the bar — no law school, no bar exam. Refinement was not necessarily required. Courtroom proceedings — not a daily occasion but a periodic public drama — featured colorful personalities in spectacular combat. Partisan newspapers provided a textual courtroom, another venue for agonistic spectacle. The Partisan formation embraced the courtroom metaphor as its ideal.

Reflecting their roots in the emerging market economy, partisan newspapers borrowed visual elements from advertising matter. Headline forms pioneered in the advertisements eventually found their way into the editorial matter. Typographical variations, which had been limited to fonts of a single typeface in earlier periods, also appeared first in advertising, so that more than one typeface — sometimes a clashing one, in the spirit of the age — became a common element in newspapers. On occasion, the editorial columns also began to run illustrations, once advertisements had led the way. Despite these changes, the newspaper did not abandon its earlier appearance entirely but remained relatively austere.

One particular aspect of the partisan press, the importance of personality, influenced the development of the visual culture for news. Because mass political parties were coalitional, a successful campaign had to recode specific material interests so that the diverse interest groups behind a candidacy would not come into conflict with each other, but would instead aim their antagonism at the opposing candidate. Discordant material interests required mediation through symbols selected for their useful polysemy. In the case of Jackson's reelection campaign, for instance, the Bank of the United States, symbolized as a monster bank, united and energized the divergent grievances of planters, artisans, and farmers without drawing attention to their many significant differences.

The candidate himself furnished the most potent such symbol, and presidential campaigns especially turned to the manufacture of personae. Jackson and his managers anticipated Barnum by creating an aura of almost mythic potency and virtue around their candidate. Jackson's tactics became the template for subsequent campaigners, even those who had to work with far humbler material. The fact that William Henry Harrison and Zachary Taylor could be Jacksonized underscores the plasticity of fame in the Partisan period.

Politicos found one form of celebrity particularly useful: military prowess. Jackson's military credentials became an obvious asset, and Martin Van Buren suffered by contrast. Succeeding elected presidents — Harrison, Polk, Taylor, Pierce, and Buchanan, as well as all the bearded presidents after the Civil War — all presented themselves as soldiers. A certain amount of military iconography consequently found its way into the press.

It was (and is) difficult to create a cult of personality around someone the public has never seen. Most newspapers could not reproduce pictures, but other media circulated woodcuts and lithographs of national leaders. The monthly periodicals of the political parties made a particular point of depicting party leaders, following the obvious logic that voters could more easily develop an emotional allegiance to someone they could see. The modern eye, however, finds such lithographs strangely unmoving: they all look alike. The distinguishing characteristics — the strong brow, or the determined chin, or the brave nose, or some other physiognomic detail that then held cultural significance — escape today's reader, who studies pictures with an eye toward personality rather than character (see Chapter 4).

The typical newspaper constructed the political persona through verbiage. The process followed two paths. First, partisan newspapers printed long speeches by their political heroes. Leaders customarily worked hand in hand with editors to produce dense columns of political rhetoric, in many cases reading proof of their own remarks in the newspaper office. Second, in print but more often in person, the editor pimped for the politico, touting his winsomeness and willingness and thorough lubrication.

These forms of promotion always climaxed in the autumn, when elections drew near. On election eve, a typical partisan newspaper would print little that did not push specifically toward driving voters to the polls. As the election approached, the names of candidates the paper supported would appear in bold type atop the column of editorial matter signaled by the newspaper's inside nameplate. By 1840, these seasonal party ads grew larger, more eye-catching, and more elaborate than even the advertising in the newspaper (Figure 2.6).

Meanwhile, the editorial persona had escaped from its old neighborhood — formulating the opinion matter and reporting some local news — to inhabit every bit of the newspaper. Except for the least urgent and most routine stuff, that is, the front page (a soft-news ghetto) and the commercial information (shipping news, marriages, and deaths), the editor handpicked items that appeared as news in the newspaper. Often these ran in no particular sequence, or in order of something as arbitrary as size, from longer to shorter. By this point, the older geographical arrangement of the news had disappeared, along with the grand narrative of History that animated that pattern.

Typographically, items of news after the Federal period resembled the less innovative ads. A line of italic type, set above or below the event's little square of text, attributed the item to its source, usually copied from another newspaper. Each item customarily had a headline, set larger (only slightly at first), in boldface, and in either all capitals or capitals coupled with small capital or lowercase letters. The headline provided little more than a label or subject title: Monster Whig Rally, for example. Rarely did it include a verb. In this, it resembled the display type in ads, of course.

Very few illustrations appeared in the news matter — even fewer than expected. A notion persists that the introduction of the penny press in the 1830s, a movement sometimes regarded as the birth of the mass media (Tucher, 1994), fueled a drive toward illustration. We observed no such drive. Instead the penny papers used fewer illustrations than did their elec-

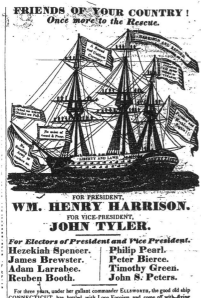

FIGURE 2.6. An 1840 political ad for Harrison and Tyler, from the *Courant*, ran through the month leading up to the November election at the top of the main editorial matter on p. 2.

tioneering counterparts. Most of the illustrative material in fact served the naked partisanship of the mainstream press through the 1850s. Although commercialization expanded illustration in ads (see Chapter 3), the opposite effect held for news, at least at first.

Commercial influences, although present throughout the century, came to the fore in the Imperial period and reached a zenith in the Victorian period, with the integration of the newspaper into emerging national and local markets. We therefore leave detailed discussion of commercialization and the profane expressions of newspaper form to a later discussion (see Chapter 3).

Partisan Period, 1830s–1840s

The early 1830s through the mid-1840s saw a period of relative stability in the visual form of U.S. newspapers. Here the story of the press diverges from the art historical narrative of accelerating innovations in the fine arts and in typography, especially among the graphic arts. Newspapers would reap the benefits of those artistic advances later. What change occurred in the mainstream world of newspapers continued in directions already set in the Transitional period and took the form of increasing refinement in the organization and illustration of the pages. Newspapers continued their pattern of increasing the page size and the number of columns per page. The *Courant,* for example, continued quite constant visually. Its format provides a useful demonstration of how changes occurred without disturbing the overall stasis. As the page size grew, a six-column format persisted, along with the same size of text type. The new format accommodated more content (columns ran 30 characters wider and ten lines deeper per page), enlarging the newspaper's capacity by almost one-sixth, but the underlying typographical character persisted just as did the overarching structure of columns.

Newspapers did show signs of increased refinement. The quality of detailing in all aspects of the news presentation — typography, organization, and illustration — became more intricate. Typical of other newspapers during the period, the *Courant* began to refine its typographic appearance, taking steps that came to the fore in the next period: developing a pattern for headlines, standardizing display type, and introducing bold modern initials in advertisements. In one refinement, the blackletter used for the nameplate became much lighter and more condensed than it had been in earlier versions. Other newspapers abandoned their fat-face nameplates in favor of the authoritative blackletter, rendered with cleaner detail, finer lines, and sharper edges and points, by the end of the period. The precision and regularity of such changes not only reflected the growing sophistication of the printing and typographic design trades in the United States, but also revealed a growing mastery over the new design vocabulary of newspapers as a genre distinct from books.

Several trends in newspapers made manifest the beginnings of the drive to organize. Contents became more clearly grouped, with the emergence of classified advertising separators and a notable growth of subject heads in the news columns. Several of the 1837 newspapers we examined had no headings, but by 1847 almost all did, especially those in bigger cities. The most elaborate scheme, in the *New York Herald,* included a local news digest called City Items, a distinct fat-face type for news (such as Business and Marine Journal), and headings breaking up columns, in a full-fledged system of spatial order. The *Courant* began polishing its organization around 1840, developing its first classifications for advertising, and then multiplied such headings in subsequent years.

Although limited primarily to advertising, illustrations became more common in newspapers, expanding in number especially for standardized cuts. A single back page of the *Courant* of the 1830s contained 19 illustrations, most of them standardized. Other newspapers we examined ran fewer such images, but an 1837 issue of the *New York Herald* included 36 and by 1847 the *Daily Missouri Republican* in St. Louis included 105 cuts of various types, most of them standardized. Occasionally illustrations migrated into the news columns, reiterating the divergence of image from text. For example, in an 1842 news story in the *New York Daily Plebian* presenting a design for a utopian socialist community, two diagrams envisioned the plan and elevation for the new construction (Figure 2.7).

These refinements, coupled with the enlarged format, embodied a climate of partisan debate between opposites. Contrast became the preferred expression of the period. The fat-face initials marking individual ads produced a speckled texture on the pages. Space within tabular material created sporadic gaps in the gray sea of text. On the enlarged pages, the text looked darker and more dense, especially compared to the growing number of illustrations. The Partisan style spoke subtly but visibly of opposites. The expanded format, by making individual items appear smaller, emphasized and lent further authority to the nameplate. With its ever more competent visual form, the newspaper presented itself as if presiding over the give and take of the Partisan period.

NEWS FOR PARTISAN CITIZENS

By the mid-nineteenth century, the impulse of U.S. political development had done much to construct the form of the newspaper. It did so through ideology, through material support, and through tactical mobilization. The upshot was the creation of a visual news culture. The newspaper reiterated and reinforced the emergent ideal, embodying a particular vista on civic culture. In this vision, the key player, the self-reliant voter-citizen, acted responsibly but nonetheless out of self-interest and not just because of duty. Politics was also damned interesting and good clean fun. Such citizens read their newspapers because they found them full of zip and élan, the arguments zesty, the language piquant, and the pace brisk (based on the typical unit, the paragraph, in contrast to the European unit, the essay). Moreover, the content of the newspaper focused on the most compelling characters of the age: leading national politicians, who were also folk heroes. Davey Crockett served as a congressman, after all.

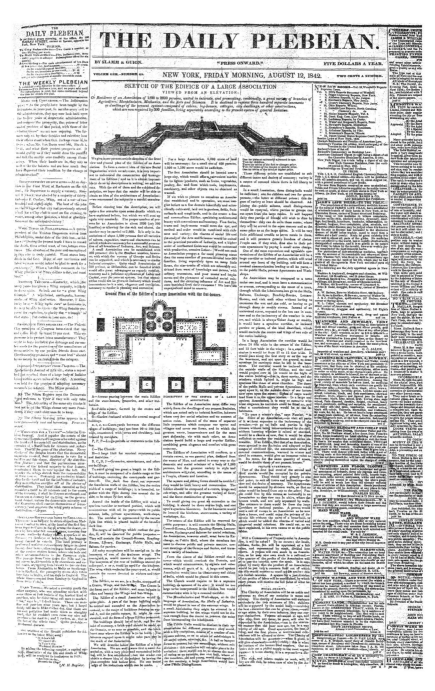

FIGURE 2.7. Illustrations appeared for a utopian community, from the *Daily Plebeian* of New York, August 12, 1842, p. 1.

66

Despite the indifference or even hostility today toward the grayness and apparent uniformity of their pages, newspapers during the first half of the nineteenth century obviously invited readers in. Compared to the colonial press, newspapers of the Partisan period charged little for admission. They did not demand that a reader purchase them religiously or play a privileged part in local business or politics to find them fully satisfying. Foreign visitors by the 1820s consistently remarked on the impressive ubiquity of, as well as on the appetite of common folk for, newspapers. These newspapers, however, stood on the verge of a complicated transformation that would turn them into the Victorian newspapers of the postbellum years.

CHAPTER 3

COMMERCIALIZATION

The Newspaper and the Market Revolution, 1780s–1880s

At the beginning of the nineteenth century the newspaper was about politics. The Revolution and its aftermath had put the newspaper to work as a political instrument, a propaganda tool, and part of the infrastructure of a new public sphere. From the Revolution onward through the nineteenth century, the newspaper remained primarily political. The governments of the early republic recognized its importance and subsidized its expansion, which outstripped both population growth and market support. Its role in politics changed over time, from passive medium to partisan agitator, but in any manifestation it was a political enterprise.

Nevertheless, commercial functions from the outset augmented the political work of newspapers. The ads, of course, provided some financial support, but commerce blended into other aspects of the press. The mercantile class constituted one of the chief audiences for the colonial newspaper. Printers tailored much of the content they published to these readers, including columns and whole pages of shipping news. They also selected much of the European political news they published because it shed light on provincial economic developments.

The Revolution and its characteristic norms of public discourse, however, suggested that the commercial matter remain subservient to the politics in the newspaper. Politics was sacred, the marketplace profane. The republican notion of the public sphere drew a line between appropriate behavior in politics and acceptable behavior in the marketplace. In the market, a realm of freedom and inequality like civil society generally, individuals pursued their personal interests and passions, achieving differential power that often resulted in domination. The public sphere in contrast bracketed and put aside private interests and passions, so that citizens could perform rational deliberations as equals. These two realms, governed by different norms, supposedly balanced each other out, preventing political domination by the economically powerful, and guaranteeing the right of individuals to pursue material and social interests free of government interference.

In practice, of course, the two realms permeated each other and contained contradictions. Male domination in households made women and children subject to the master, defining them as private in essence. The public realm never entirely bracketed off the private situation of women, and minorities likewise experienced diminished status, despite the proposed norm of public equality. Men of great wealth, known as such, could wield power in public discourse as the greater among supposed equals.

Newspapers were supposed to stand astride the division between civil society and public sphere. Advertising and commercial news would provide income that would then underwrite the newspaper's performance as a public forum and information resource. In theory, commerce would willingly and selflessly subsidize politics, and newspapers would effortlessly and even-handedly function both as commercial and political enterprises. Normatively, the political (or sacred) mission of the newspaper was supposed to trump its commercial (profane) needs and opportunities. In practice the two were often in tension.

THE MARKET REVOLUTION THESIS

Sometime in the early republic the marketplace moved to the center of national development. Historians argue over when and why this happened, and what implications it had for national politics. The most influential account of the rise of the market, contained in Charles Sellers's *The Market Revolution* (1991), posits a preexisting subsistence economy, with family farms as the molecular units. These farms, designed to produce enough food to feed a family, also generated enough surplus to barter for other essentials. Local producers, however, provided most of the goods and services a family consumed, and thus very little production or consumption on a farm involved the market.

This durable economic system had built-in contradictions. A functioning family farm required a good deal of labor, and because farmers preferred to use family members, who didn't really have to be paid, each generation produced a much larger succeeding generation. All those children, in turn, wanted their own farms. Where would they get the land? In early America, land came plentiful and cheap, once cleansed of Native Americans. With that resource, the children of subsistence farmers could set up their own subsistence farms. They still needed money to pay for the land, however, and could earn enough only by producing a surplus to export from the local community, that is, for the market. In short, subsistence farming produced demographic growth, which in turn promoted the growth of market relations.

Meanwhile, in cities and towns, the craft shop emerged as the counterpart to the subsistence farm. Run by the traditional rules of their craft, these shops often produced comfortable incomes for their masters, who had risen to positions of independence after long apprenticeships and many years of journeyman work. Like the family farm, however, the molecular craft shop also produced geometrically larger succeeding generations. Any particular shop employed several journeymen and apprentices, each of whom would hope someday to become a master running yet another shop. To acquire the initial investment needed for independence, craftspersons had to sell their labor for wages and then scrupulously set aside a portion of the income. Again, the reproduction of a so-called subsistence system required more market involvement.

In the early nineteenth century, farms and shops began to encounter structural scarcities. The most fertile land became less easily obtained, and other land required greater inputs, such as scarce water resources and longer transport distances. With older shops already occupying the most lucrative locations in cities, additional craftspersons could either crowd in or work further away. Structural scarcity accompanied overproduction of goods. Both farmers and artisans, by continually bettering their efficiency, produced more and more for the market. The opportunities for independence and the prices for goods seemed to contract, leading to the general disaffection that fed Jacksonian politics.

The resulting political and economic pressures drove the market revolution. Structural improvements in communication and transportation, undertaken to accommodate the increasing flow of goods, extended and ultimately nationalized the market economy. The market revolution not only affected businesses but also caused market relations to penetrate ever more deeply into the everyday lives of ordinary people.

People found the market both magical and terrifying. It promised enticements — luxury goods, labor-saving ready-made necessaries, a new kind of equality in consumption, a democratization of the dollar — that many found alluring, even intoxicating (Lears, 1994). It nevertheless heightened risks and threatened people with *downward* mobility. Farmers who went into debt to buy land and plant crops and journeymen who sold their labor on the open market could suddenly find themselves destitute because of bank failures or market downturns that they couldn't even understand, much less do anything about. The popular literature of the period is filled with depictions of the naïve victims of market forces, and the moral discourse trumpeted the dangers of the cities (Reynolds, 1988; Moore, 1994; Lippard, 1844). What the marketplace gave it could always take away.

Some historians are quite dubious about this account of the market revolution. They feel it oversimplifies a complex process, caricatures the economic modes it labels subsistence, and overstates the popular dissatisfaction with the developing economy. Rather than arguing these questions in detail, we can contribute to the discussion by pointing out how much the market-revolution thesis made sense for and how closely it fit the evidence we found in newspapers. Market concerns that were national in implication unquestionably touched ordinary people more and more as the nineteenth century advanced. At some points popular concern with one or another aspect of the market (currencies, prices, debts, tariffs) reached crisis proportions, and throughout the antebellum period a sizable group of intellectuals voiced a consistent theme of anxiety over the marketplace and issues of moral decay and economic justice. Large numbers of people also joined utopian communities to flee the market. National political parties responded to and manipulated all these developments. Moreover, newspapers unquestionably experienced a market revolution of their own and did what they could to promote market development.

Newspapers advanced the market revolution in three ways. Informationally, they promoted market development by spreading news such as prices current and stock quotations, while at the same time promoting internal improvements in transport and communication. Practically, as advertising media, they provided a conduit for promoting the sale of goods and services. Finally, they marketed themselves as goods, as arguably the first branded commodities. Together these functions comprised a process that we might call *commercialization*.

The commercialization of the press augmented but did not eliminate the political press. Partisan newspapers commercialized and yet retained their partisan editorial practices even while surrounding them with all sorts of commercial endeavors. Gradually, however, the emphasis shifted. By the end of the nineteenth century, the commercial functions of the newspaper outweighed its political work (Baldasty, 1993). It could no longer be said with confidence that the newspaper was primarily a political creature.

A dimension of the press had always aimed at the commercial reader. In the colonial era, printers and readers alike assumed that a large share of any newspaper's clientele participated in commerce. Initially, commercial news and public affairs news appeared unsegregated. Most of the material in the paper would address both registers of interest, the commercial and the political, at the same time. Thus the shipping news could wander amicably from details of voyages to news of European political, diplomatic, and military affairs; indeed, colonial newspapers framed much of their original matter as a conversation with a ship's captain. Because presumably every reader would read every item, printers felt no obligation to separate information into domains.

Such segregation became common after the Revolution, in part because of the ideological impulse behind the emerging public sphere, premised on the separation between political affairs and civil society. On a concrete level, newspapers in growing commercial cities like New York and Philadelphia began to target readership segments. In particular, the daily newspaper emerged in both these cities explicitly as a tool for the business class. Consistent with the logic of the public sphere, commercial newspapers represented themselves as personal enterprises, offering their proprietor's name on the nameplate — like *Claypool's Daily Advertiser* in Philadelphia — as a suggestion that the newspaper would serve as a personal adviser or surrogate financial agent for the reader.

As market relations grew, ordinary humble newspapers took up the market-advice function and proudly featured commercial information. One simple reason they did so was supply: markets produced information. The newspapers of the early republic always welcomed news that came in prepackaged form, such as government reports or texts of legislation. The rising national market spawned organizations that produced information of exactly the ready-to-use sort. Newspapers in turn touted their ability to provide up-to-date prices for commodities in many distant markets: pork in New Orleans, cotton in New York, lumber in Chicago. The marketplace also produced a welter of competing currencies, few of which exchanged at face value or managed to prevent ready counterfeiting, and so newspapers carried columns of currency information. Developments in law accommodated the creation of publicly traded mutual stock companies, spawning stock markets that in turn provided newspapers with another staple of economic information.

Economic news had its own form: the table. Newspapers had mastered the visual display of information by the mid-1830s, when many tables in the news ran as long as a full column (the *Chicago American* tax rolls filled four columns on the back page in 1837). Shorter tables and lists covered election returns by town, local currency rates, stock exchange results, and other sundry information. By the 1840s this type of material had increased greatly. An 1847 issue of the *National Intelligencer* ran fifteen different tables, mostly in advertising but also in the business columns.

Tables introduced a radically different form for commercial information. The old form had been called shipping news, which consisted of the prose listing of ships arriving and departing (or "cleared"), presented as running text and paragraphs. Tabulation reformulated the listing of commercial information and gave it predictability and authority: the newspaper offered an organized and simplified account of an abundant and complex world. Tables ordered the text, enhancing the role of newspaper editors as conductors, and also opened up areas of white space (Figure 3.1). The gaps drew attention to the new form, appearing like oases amid the flowing gray of text typography and suggesting freedom for readers to pursue their own economic agendas. The form implied the central role for newspapers as the marketplace of information, offering an array of goods to the autonomous reader-turned-consumer.

Advertising tables implied a similar autonomy, while asserting authority for advertisers. For shipping and other commercial information in the editorial content, the newspaper conductor collected the data and produced a tabulated form. That process ceased to hold for advertising around midcentury. Display advertising began to arrive at the newspaper office already packaged; the newspaper conductor simply provided space for the designs of an external entrepreneur. As a result, dozens of people designed advertising matter for any given newspaper, while only one designed the news. Eventually the advertising sections filled with innovation and the news trailed behind.

THE PUBLISHER'S NEWSPAPER

As the market transformed the press, the newspaper type we have called the editor's newspaper gave way to what we'll call the publisher's newspaper. We derive the name from the fact that, although the editor retained a guiding hand in selecting news matter and still functioned as the chief voice of the newspaper, paramount control had passed into the hands of a proprietor who often played no editorial role. At the same time, the varieties of content

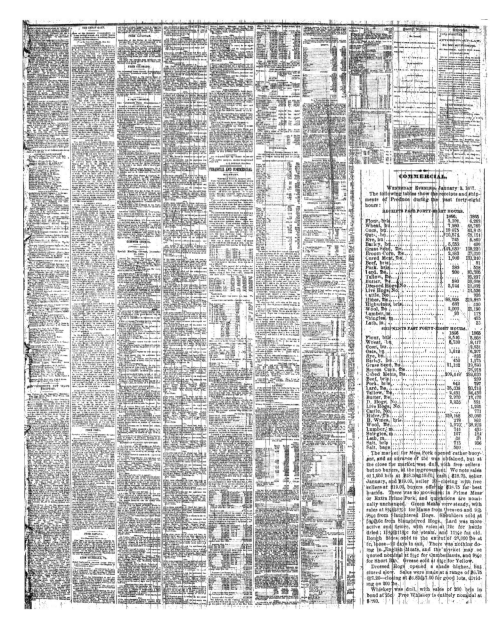

FIGURE 3.1. In the tables from the *Chicago Tribune*, January 3, 1867, note the change in the texture of the page as city and political news (on the left half of the page) yields to financial news (on the right half), which had become primarily tabular in form. The detail lists agricultural prices.

within the newspaper increased, and *pari passu* the number and variety of editorial personnel. The line between newsgathering and manufacturing, which had divided the tasks of editing from printing in the editor's newspaper, became more marked, and the work of advertising, circulation, and finance became relatively autonomous from both editing and printing. The publisher's newspaper, then, consisted internally of a proprietor controlling three different departments: editorial, production, and business. The divisions were still permeable, of course, and often the publisher also held the title of editor in chief. Because politics remained key to the life of many newspapers, the editorial function could still trump everything else. The publisher's newspaper, however, consisted of a more diverse network of relationships that often resulted in multivocal content.

The many voices that would come to occupy the publisher's newspaper stood in stark contrast to the editor's paper, which was univocal, and also to modern newspapers, which tend to submerge voices entirely. For many newspapers, including the always eccentric *New York Times,* the editor's newspaper remained at the center of the publisher's, occupying pages 4 and 5 in an eight-page daily edition, surrounded by other sorts of content in other voices.

For the publisher's newspaper, a chief concern — making everything fit — became the job of the print foreman, who was to production what the editor was to news. The foreman had final say on the allocation of space. Usually this required cutting back or cramming in the content, especially because, except for the very largest metropolitan papers, the usually ironclad commitment to print on a single sheet of paper limited the space available. Thus it was the foremen who would develop the forms comprising what we call the Imperial and the Victorian styles.

Imperial Period, 1850s–1860s

From the end of the 1840s through the mid-1860s, the visual tendencies of earlier periods coalesced into a newspaper form that anticipated and then served the ideology of imperialism common to political and economic endeavors of the time: the mechanization of textiles, founding of the steel industry, building of national railroad links, and amassing of fortunes through business and the Gold Rush. The unifying characteristic of this period was a revisualization of the newspaper as territory. Newspapers enlarged their pages and brought them under a bureaucratic design regime. The press became an engine of wealth, controlled by increasingly powerful publishers. Advertisers likewise used newspapers to seek dominion, albeit indirectly, over consumers. The reconceptualization of the newspaper in the Imperial period clearly displaced many of the earlier evidences of its political mission.

Newspapers generally expanded in format after midcentury, moving from roughly six to eight columns, achieving what editors themselves called imperial proportions. By 1852, the *Courant* page grew large enough to contain an extra column, employing the same number of characters per line and lines per page in the same typeface. The new page could hold at least a quarter more words. The format grew again by almost a quarter in the 1860s (reaching 53 characters per line, 200 lines on eight columns per page, with somewhat smaller text type). The *Courant* typified the period. The *Boston Daily Advertiser,* by far the grandest of the 1857 newspapers we examined, had eight columns. Among the 1867 examples, the *Chicago Tribune* reached a truly grandiose ten columns (Figure 3.2). In the *Courant* the larger page size and greater number of lines and columns produced a predictable effect: text became much denser gray (in relative and in real terms) and nontext items could appear in a greater range of sizes (possible because the columns made the smallest images relatively smaller, typically at a ratio of 1:8 as opposed to 1:6).

Illustration expanded through most of the period. In the 1850s, newspapers presented a range of design style, from mostly text-based (like the Washington, D.C., *Daily Union,* with only a few small illustrations and occasional tables to break the gray type), to mostly image-based. An example of a newspaper with heavy emphasis on images, the 1857 *Peoria Daily Democratic Union,* used large illustrations, towering circus-bill ads, and adventuresome lettering. By the end of the Civil War, newspapers had adopted the image-based Imperial style with surprising uniformity. The most dramatic example that we examined, the 1867 *Daily Leavenworth Times,* contrasted the lively typographic play and generous spacing in advertising to the tightly packed gray text in news columns (Figure 3.3). In their conspicuous display of spatial wealth, newspapers reflected social conditions of the period. At the *Courant* during the Civil War, because of the abundance of timely and urgent war news and also because of wartime austerities, the number of illustrations in a typical issue fell by half, illustration sizes declined, and the ratio of advertising to news dropped below half before rebounding after the war. Advertising then reconquered the acreage of space taken by war news. On the larger pages (equivalent to long-term territorial expansion), economic and political forces left their visible marks.

The increasing capacity of pages accompanied a growth in the modes of visual control. Newspapers of the period imposed more order on the news

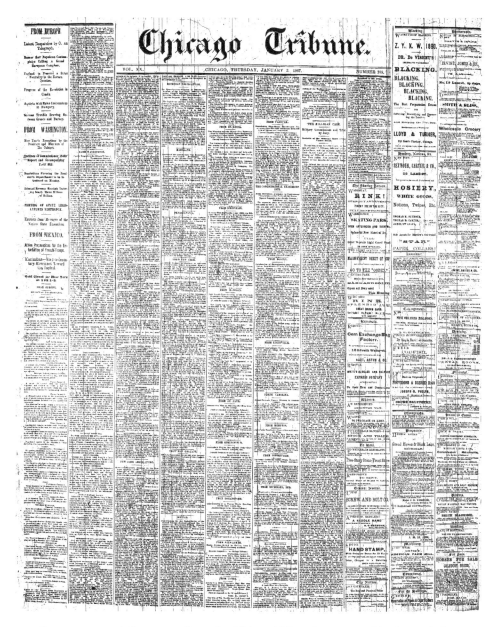

FIGURE 3.2. A front page, from the *Chicago Tribune*, January 3, 1867, shows design of the Imperial period.

FIGURE 3.3. On a page from the *Daily Leavenworth Times,* February 10, 1867, p. 8, note the contrasts between the look of the news matter in the left-hand column and the spacious, varied, illustrated advertising matter.

columns, grouping items together and using subject heads and other labels. The *Daily Union,* a model of editorial organization for its time, included subject headings (such as General News), labels for physical geography (By Telegraph, Local), and markers for political geography (City of Washington versus national, and legislative Congressional versus executive Department News), treated with distinctive typography and decoration. The *Courant* followed a less rigorous but more usual organizing scheme, with vague headings. By 1852 news digests appeared under the title Short Paragraphs (Figure 3.4), with as many as a score of one- or two-paragraph items, each marked by the familiar pointing-finger engraved cut. A variety of logotypes (or illustrated sigs) emerged to identify specific editorial content. The changes at the *Courant* and elsewhere grew out of advertising and reflected notions of bureaucracy, achieving order through ever more specific subdivisions (a topic we return to later in this chapter).

Heightened contrast also enhanced the visual impression of hierarchy. Newspapers drew starker distinctions among news text, illustrations, and advertisements. The space-rich ads stood out ever more starkly against the crowded background of news typography. Variable line-spacing came into common use for news, giving emphasis to the more open areas of type. As a result, the type on news pages grew more dense toward the bottom right of the pages, as an indicator of center and periphery begun some decades earlier now became routine. The placement of content also gave cues concerning geographic and social hierarchy. In 1867 the *New York Dispatch,* for example, assigned a subordinate space for the private sphere (labeled Our Weekly Gossip), and the *Chicago Tribune* placed Foreign and Washington news ahead of Weddings. On the other side of the great divide, ads grew to skyscraper proportions on the page, visually superior to classifieds in their diminutive sizes and more detailed categories.

At the *Courant* these changes produced an overall appearance of dramatic contrast, an effect that extended into typography. In the late 1840s, the variety of type in the editorial contents increased. A condensed, all-capital typeface (a style approaching Latin type, characterized by wedge-shaped serifs) appeared in many headlines, under the nameplate, and elsewhere mixed with the older display type. The blackletter of the nameplate appeared in standing heads such as Marriages and Deaths. Other variations emerged over the next decade, with more exuberant contrasts in the headlines echoing the general tendency in the arts toward eclecticism after midcentury. By the end of the period, the dense, dark text had completely distinguished itself from the assorted headlines and capacious ads and illustrations. The increasing contrast gave a clear impression of visual hierarchy.

d, so numerous, as far as becomes
, so abounding in unlabored felici-
o choice. the epithet so pictured,
ate truth, or the most exact and
ice the human wit can devise—the
bject, if you have regard to the kind
handle—political, ethical, legal, as
is Payley's, or Locke's, or Butler's,
ilton's, of their subjects; yet that
mpleteness of sense, made transpa-
tal waters, all embodied in harmo-
d and poured along in a tide of unso-
apable to be withstood—recall the
row, the tone of voice, the presence
ting of men—recall him thus; and
Mr. Justice Story, commemorating
a may well "rejoice that we have
ge; that we have listened to his elo-
nstructed by his wisdom."

MORNING, NOVEMBER 6.

of the Daily Courant.

e end of the year.............$5,00
advance......................4,50

rs, with privilege of a square..$20,00

Our First Page.

ction matter for the last fortnight has
: the publication of many interesting
DANIEL WEBSTER, which have found
papers since his decease. We de-
ntire first page of this morning's pa-
"readers will find it quite deserving
he articles are—Birthplace and Early
Life—Affection for his Family and
nestics—his Real Estate—Retiring
Fondness for Fishing—A Death Bed
|—his Epitaph—Religious Reminis-
the Evidences of Christianity—Ad-
Alden at the Funeral—Extract from
Choate.

FOREIGN RELATIONS.

neral of Cuba has, it appears, con-
l apologized for his hasty conduct.—
m at one time, or his submission at
avert the destiny that hangs over the
The invasion of Cuba has entered
e as an element into the late election,
candidate and his advisers will not
be outside pressure, that will impel
annexation. Spain may declare war
as she hears of the preparations for
at she cannot prevent the inevitable
nay be inclined to join her, but Eng-
e. The prospect of a four years
le with a customer numbering twen
ll lead her to forget other old allian
ch herself, before she will go to war,
e sale of her manufactures. England
t we can, that a war with her would
r adoption of an "American System."
l not only lose a good customer while
d find at its close that our own manu-
t established on a firm basis, and that
people had been confirmed in self de-
and has the very best of reasons not
us, as the ally of Spain, much as she
ted at our possession of Cuba. She
the more inclined to withdraw her
Central America and on Mexico, and
lves on this continent. It is to be
hat the rapacity of our citizens or the
 g government will not involve us in
ain.

EUROPE.

Congress or of the American People?   Or do they savor
of the Holy Alliance?"

The South.

It is stated as a fact that up to ten o'clock Friday
night, the telegraph lines south of North Carolina were
not in working order and have not been since Monday.
If so ; the returns from Georgia &c., must have been
manufactured for the Northern market.

Annexation of Cuba.

Mr. Walbridge, member of Congress elect from the
Third Congressional District, New York, has issued an
address to his constituents in which he says that he
regards his election as an expression in favor of incor-
porating "the beautiful island of the Antilles" within
the limits of our government as soon as it can constitu-
tionally be done without violence to existing treaties.

Concert This Evening.

THE NEW ENGLAND VOCALISTS give their first Concert in this city, this evening, at American Hall. They
are excellent singers, and present a very attractive and
well-selected programme, consisting of Songs, Quar-
tetts. Choruses, Burlesques, &c. Master CARDELLA as-
sists at the piano. We feel confident they will give an
entertainment every way worthy of the patronage of
our citizens, and trust they will have a full house.

☞ The *Times* of Thursday evening, after alluding
to a paragraph in this paper on the subject, asserts that
the Democratic Hickory Pole in New Britain, ninety
feet in height, was maliciously cut down on Monday
night. A gentleman from that place informs us that it
was standing yesterday.

☞ The report of the Congressional election in New
York stands better for the Whigs than it did. It is now
said that the delegation will be 18 Democrats,14 Whigs,
and one Abolitionist. Last Congress there were 17
Democrats, and 17 Whigs. New York loses one Representative under the new apportionment.

RAIL ROAD RECEIPTS FOR OCTOBER.—Erie, $376,838-
89, an increase of $20,285 89 over October 1851. Hud-
son River, $105,511 11, an increase of $36,473. Long
Island, $18,780 31, an increase of $4,953. Harlem,
about $70,000. Rochester & Syracuse, $116,000. Mil-
waukee and Mississippi, $15.037.

☞ We are requested to state that a Discourse delivered by Rev. Charles Brooks of Boston, last Sunday
afternoon, in the Church of the Savior, (Unitarian) by
request, will be repeated to-morrow (Sunday) evening.
Subject—*Daniel Webster*. Services will commence at
¼ past 5 o'clock.

☞ Alvah Sabin has been chosen Representative in
Congress, in that district of Vermont, where there
was no choice in September. The whole delegation of
Vermont is now Whig.

☞ The novelist, G. P. R. James, has consented to
deliver a formal oration on the character and public
services of the Duke of Wellington, before the British
residents of Boston.

☞ The Brattleboro' Eagle learns that upwards of
10,000 sheep have been sold and driven from the town
of Shoreham, VT., at prices ranging from 50 cents to
$3,50. This unusual sale of stock is owing to the
scarcity of feed.

☞ The second Lecture on the Evidences of Revealed Religion will be delivered in Christ Church, to-
morrow evening. Service to commence at 7 o'clock.

☞ There was collected at New Haven for the Washington Monument, $181.33.

☞ The telegraphic report that Laborde, the Spanish
Consul, had left New Orleans for fear of personal violence, is declared by the N. O. Bulletin to be false.

☞ The amount contributed in Baltimore for the
Washington Monument was $1500 ; in Cincinnati $1210,
not $12,000, as stated in our telegraphic report yester-
day.

cisely money enough at the printing business, the sub-
scriber is satisfied to give up and retire to the poor-
house. Under these circumstances, he is induced to
offer the Saratoga *Republican* for sale. The paper has
a circulation of about one thousand, one fourth of which
may be called paying, and the other three fourths non-
paying patrons. The office has a good variety of job
type and a fair run of work of this description, provided the work is done at the reduced New York price,
and the printers, will take 'cats and dogs' for pay.
This village is one of the prettiest places in the world
for a newspaper publisher. Every body will find fault,
do the best you can, and the editor who pleases himself will stand but a slim chance of pleasing any body
else. The subscription list and good-will of the office
will be thrown in if the purchaser will take the type,
presses, and materials, for what they are worth, and
pay for them, so that there will be no probability of
the present proprietor being obliged to take the establishment back and return to the business.
                                        J. A. COREY.

Saratoga Springs, 1852.

We learn from *The Scientific American* that instantaneous portraits can now be taken on collodion by a
very ingenious French invention. The person whose
portrait is to be taken is placed at some distance off, in
front of the lens, and the operator, while conversing
with him, pulls a trigger. By so doing a newly invented cap (*obturateur*) turns on its own axis, and in its ro-
tary movement allows the light and the image of the
sitter to pass through a hole twice the diameter of the
lens. The portrait is obtained in the fraction of a second, and for quickness can only be compared to elec-
tricity. It is but justice to the inventor of the collodion
(Mr. Bertsch) to state that the rapidity is owing to its
extreme sensitiveness, which rendered it necessary to
use the above instrument. By the ordinary method
the collodion would be spoiled by the light, however
skillful the manipulator, before the portrait could be
taken.

A CURIOUS RELIC.—The Oneida Morning Herald gives
the following clause from the will of Lewis Morris, one
of the signers of the Declaration of Independence. 'It
will be seen,' remarks the Herald, 'that the worthy old
patriot partook liberally of the prejudice which existed
among our honest Dutch fathers against the Yankee
race :'—

"It is my desire that my son Governeur Morris may
have the best education that is to be had in England or
America, but my express directions are, that he be
never sent for that purpose to the Connecticut colonies,
lest he should imbibe in his youth, that low craft and
cunning, so incident to the people of that country which
is so interwoven in their constitutions, that all their art
cannot disguise it from the world, though many of them,
under the sanctified garb of religion, have endeavored
to impose themselves on the world for honest men.
1790, Nov. 23.   LEWIS MORRIS.

Plants in Rooms.

The reason why plants fade so much, is because due
attention is not paid to them. The mere supplying with
water is not sufficient. The leaves should be kept per-
fectly clean. "If as much washing were bestowed, in
London," says Dr. Lindley, "upon a pot plant as
a lap-dog, the one would remain in as good condition
as the other. The reasons are obvious. Plants breathe
by their leaves ; and if their surface is clogged by dirt,
of whatever kind, their breathing is impeded or pre-
vented. Plants perspire by their leaves ; and dirt prevents their perspiration. Plants feed by their leaves ;
and dirt prevents their feeding. For this breathing, perspiration, and food, are fatally interrupted by the accumulation of foreign matters upon leaves. Let any one,
after reading this, cast an eye upon the state of plants
in sitting rooms, or well kept green houses ; let them
draw a white handkerchief over the surface of such
plants, or a piece of smooth white leather, if he desires
to know how far they are from being as clean as their
nature requires.

A Royal Botanist.

There is one king in Europe who is a good practical
botanist, and who must look back upon the hours spent
in the arrangement of his fine herbarium with far more
pleasure than upon those wasted in a vain and retrograde course of politics. The monarch in question is
his majesty of Saxony, who, in his scientific career at
least, has gained honor and respect. Many are the
stories told by his subjects of their ruler's adventures
when following his favorite and harmless hobby ; how,
more than once, astray from his yawning courtiers, he
had wandered in search of some vegetable rarity across
the frontier of his legitimate dominions, and on attempt-
ing to return was locked up by his own guards as a
spy or a smuggler, since he could produce no passport
nor give any more probable account of himself than
the preposterous assertion that he was their king. Fifteen years ago, he made a famous excursion into the
stony and piratical little republic of Montenegro. It
was literally a voyage of botanical discovery, and the
potentate sailed down the Adriatic in a steamer fitted
out with all the appliances of scientific investigation.—

Finally, newspaper nameplates achieved something akin to brand identity. By the 1860s, nameplates had become repetitive, appearing in the first column of news on every page in such newspapers as the *New York Dispatch*. In the Imperial system, the brand name of the press supervised all the visual territory of the news, and editors (and later publishers) in turn supervised the nameplate. Throughout the period, the authoritative and by then traditional Germanic blackletter competed with the industrial and geometrically inspired fat face, until at last the blackletter nameplate became dominant. Only one of our examples, the *Leavenworth Times*, used a modern boldface by 1867. Redesigning the nameplate became a perquisite of the newspaper's leadership. For instance, the *Hartford Daily Courant* of the Partisan period (with an engraved illustration cum scroll) became *The Connecticut Courant* (without the seal) under the new proprietors, Boswell and Faxon, during the 1850s. The changes obscured an essential sameness. The two models of nameplate (like the two typographic competitors, fat face and blackletter) shared the bold inking and dominance of the newspaper front page. Either nameplate grew by contrast on the Imperial pages, providing typographic clarity above the mass of content. Newspapers, as entities in the market, endorsed and lent their brand authority to the events they reported.

Despite the impression that traditional newspapers of the nineteenth century lacked order, elements of modern design did in fact emerge, however slowly. In the *Courant*'s headlines after its mid-century redesign, one of several new typefaces (a condensed face from the transitional school of old-style typography) used caps and lowercase, a combination later favored by modernists to make the headlines much clearer. Changes over the period also jelled into a form that anticipated modern headlines, including a dateline. The contrast of headlines to text resulted in more visual order, a surprising by-product for a period commonly considered disorderly.

The shift to the Imperial ideal rejected the older conception of the newspaper, with the text flowing like a discussion among citizens as found in books. Instead, extensive catalogs of news and ads presented an abundance of items to an audience of consumers, and the newspaper page became re-imagined as territory open to subjugation by bureaucratizing order.

Victorian Period, 1860s–1880s

The Victorian formation crystallized in the period from the late 1860s through the 1880s. Many of the trends of earlier periods realized their culmination: the growth in size and contrast in scale, the dramatic variety in typography and illustrations, and the detailing of ordering and separating devices. Some of these foreshadowed the modern era to come. In aspect, the newspaper took on a regal mien, while in content it observed distinctions between sacred and profane zones.

Newspapers continued to expand in format and moved by consensus to nine columns. The *Courant* grew to its most ungainly size. Column layouts exaggerated the grand format. At times text ran in half columns (in the design equivalent of carving up building lots, paradoxically increasing land values by parceling it out). Each column continued to carry the same number of characters per line, but the longer page now accommodated more (225 lines). Tighter interline spacing (called leading) added even more lines, increasing capacity almost a quarter by 1872 (to 275 lines) and another tenth by 1876 (to 300 lines, although no page ran that tight from top to bottom). The larger pages, more numerous columns, and tighter typesetting resulted in a much denser texture for most newspapers of the period.

The capacity of Victorian newspapers multiplied in other ways as well. The period saw a definitive break with the four-page limit. Newspapers, except leading metropolitan dailies, generally published only four pages through the 1870s. By 1887 other urban dailies ran eight pages, with Sunday editions at double that (small-town newspapers continued at four). In addition, metropolitan newspapers often published two or more editions on weekdays.

These changes opened a vast new landscape to even greater contrast. In the *Courant,* illustrations swelled in size and number, with as many as 100 appearing (mostly in ads) in a single issue of 1868 or 1872, and some ads began to run wider as well, reaching across the width of two columns. Display typography grew larger, so that in 1880 a single word ran as many as fifteen lines deep. The images and display type dwarfed the subdivided columns (effectively increasing the range of contrast to 1:18) and the tiny text, even after the newspaper returned in the 1880s to the earlier, less-crowded leading. Other newspapers also introduced contrast in text typography. The Louisiana *Concordia Eagle* in 1877 ran three different type sizes for text appearing on a single page, and the *Benevolent Banner* of North Topeka, Kansas, ran portions of its news text in boldface.

Variability in typography and illustrations also increased. The fluctuating interline spacing, inherited from the previous period, expanded to produce an accordion effect. At the *Courant* the line spacing contracted and expanded, sometimes in relation to specific content, such as an article opening. In the space that normally held ten lines of type, as many as thirteen lines squeezed in or as few as eight lines spread out. Besides these daily alterations, other design elements changed frequently. The *Courant* mixed in even more typefaces by 1880, and its nameplate design changed every few years, adding elements or words but always set in the strong blackletter. Other newspapers also favored blackletter and tinkered with their nameplates.

Advertisements became more notably designed. In 1877 ads in dailies contained a variable texture and high contrast, although venerable newspapers such as the *Post* and the *Evening Star* in Washington, D.C., remained more staid. By 1887 most newspapers relied increasingly on large, mixed typography, now spanning multiple columns, now stacked down the page. In the *Courant,* many advertising images lost their generic character (typical earlier in the century) and became more planned and self-consciously designed. Even so, the older cookie-cutter designs still appeared. The newspaper found room for more of everything, in ever more varied quantity and placement for advertising as well as news. The element of surprise increased.

The expansion in territory and variety eventually encouraged greater organization. Newspapers of the period learned to use contrast and typographic detail to order and separate contents. Headlines grew to multiple decks listing the contents to follow, a form developed first in advertisements. At the *Courant*, all pages took on unity from the use of running heads (the familiar set of ruled lines across the page top, with the newspaper name, date, and, later, page number, sandwiched in between). Increasingly, stacks of advertising separated editorial content, organized topically. Classified headings also multiplied greatly over the period. Such devices organized content without simplifying the abundance of news.

Many of the elements we found anticipated modern design in some fashion. Besides the modernizing order on the editorial side, advertising layouts moved toward asymmetry (setting type, for example, flush left, with the right ragged rather than justified, a form favored later by modernists). Advertisements in the *Courant* at the end of the period clearly indicated a direction for news. Individual ads made up of tightly integrated units gathered and grouped related imagery and text within a defined space. Topical arrangements, tabulation, segregated ads, asymmetry, unitized space — in short, all the elements of modern design existed, available and present, within the variety of Victorian form. The tenor of the times, however, encouraged the metaphor of the marketplace. Newspapers depicted a world not as subject to the sense-making control of journalists but instead as witness to endless variation and diversity.

As the Victorian period reached its apotheosis, newspapers looked majestic, while respecting sacred and profane precincts. The blackletter nameplate, complete with distinctive type and emblem, crowned the form. Its pages began to mark a distinction between sacred spaces dedicated to news, especially political news, and profane spaces open to advertising. Although such cues suggested a higher status for news, design innovation continued to run from profane into sacred spaces.

All newspapers employed the vocabulary of Victorian design, but used degrees of contrast along a range, from the most reserved to the most emphatic. Those devoted to news (sacred), such as the Washington, D.C., newspapers, assumed a reserved look at one extreme. At times they even removed advertising (profane) from the front page, as did the *Chronicle* in Milledgeville, Georgia, and the *Concordia Eagle* in Louisiana. Those at the emphatic side, such as *The Rocky Mountain News,* used every extreme of contrast and scale. They lavished space, always at a premium, only on the affluent (profane) advertiser, in an organization reminiscent of the marketplace, where stalls present types of goods and activities (news and classifieds occupying close quarters, compared to display advertising).

Readers, as projected out from the Victorian form of news, played a primary role as consumers, and even political events occupied a position in the market. The Victorian newspaper became the arbiter of market boundaries within its broadsheet domain. In the controlling metaphor, abundance won over attempts at order, and miscellany in commerce stood out against the growing hierarchy in news.

PATTERNS OF VISUAL CHANGE

In these opening chapters, we have described three types of newspaper and five periods of design. We organized this description according to two analytically separable but overlapping historical impulses, politicization and commercialization. *Politicization* refers to the integration of the newspaper into emerging political forms and systems; *commercialization* refers to the integration of the newspaper into emerging market forms and systems. Politicization played a key role in creating the editor's newspaper, and commercialization did the same with the publisher's newspaper. The point of transformation from one newspaper type to the next occurred when commercial forces rose to the ascendant. Earlier newspapers presented themselves with a sense of civic purpose that, although retained subsequently, had to find a place within an increasingly market-oriented project. Editors made newspapers for voters, publishers made them for purchasers.

The transformation represented deeper currents, reflected in the direction for design change followed in the Imperial and Victorian periods. The descriptions we have already offered, however, in which styles succeed each other in apparently linear fashion, may not make those currents readily apparent. To highlight the more complicated trajectory, we offer in the following sections several continuous histories that track specific aspects of design styles, beginning with advertising and moving to news matter.

Advertising consistently acted as the leading edge in visual innovation. As the press served to expand the market revolution, it depended in fact, if not at first in spirit, on the creative energies of advertisers. Merchants and their advertising agents, with the encouragement of type founders and wood-type houses (which carved wood blocks to produce larger type, or more elaborate illustrations), felt the urgency of the market and would take visual risks to get noticed. On the editorial side, newspapers lagged behind but ultimately followed suit. All the markers of newspaper organization — headlines, topical segmentation, tabular matter, lists, classifications — and all the characteristic visual signs for news — logos, sigs, display type, space, pictures — developed first as advertising devices and only subsequently found their way into news matter.

According to the simplest account of the birth of Victorian newspaper design, in the beginning printers had bookish ideas. Then, in the early republic, a design distinction appeared between news and advertising matter. On the ad side of the wall of separation, innovation flourished. Experiments both in inviting attention to specific items and in organizing the total body of ads for ease of browsing yielded a host of visual techniques. Finally, when newsworkers began thinking about making the editorial content more appealing to readers, they borrowed techniques from advertising. Although basically true, that account gives the misleading impression of smooth progress. It was more complicated than that.

Advertising, sparse in the first colonial newspapers, had come to occupy a large share of space by the time of the Revolution. On average, throughout the age of the four-page newspaper, ads occupied between one-third and three-quarters of total space, with the norm at about one-half. At the beginning and the end of this period, printers and publishers isolated advertising at the end of the newspaper, on the back pages, with the most recent ads appearing just after the main original editorial material on pages 2 or 3.

During the intervening years (the 1790s through the 1860s) ads appeared on the front page as well, because, as we already noted, editors reserved the inside pages for the most important matter. Breaking news colonized the front page only in the 1870s, except among a narrow class of metropolitan dailies where the change started earlier.

Advertising occasioned design creativity, and in fact the elements of newspaper design not borrowed from book design came from ad design. The development of advertising design did not, however, follow a straight line. Instead, the pattern of change over time followed a three-beat rhythm. First came a phase of expansion and experimentation, followed by a phase of regularization and consolidation, and then another phase of experimentation that ultimately yielded the genres of newspaper advertising familiar in the twentieth century.

These three phases of advertising development corresponded roughly to the overall rhythms of newspaper development. The opening phase of experimentation coincided with the period we call Federal and with the type we call the printer's newspaper; the consolidation phase coincided with the Partisan period and the editor's newspaper; and the final experimentation phase coincided with the Imperial and Victorian periods and the publisher's newspaper. We found the pattern of development apparent across a wide range of advertising forms: typography, headline styles, ornamentation, illustration, and white space.

Typography

In the colonial press, advertisements appeared in the same type as everything else in the newspaper, and a reader might, upon a first casual glance, mistake the ads for news. Gradually advertising came to acquire a different appearance. Several techniques — setting initial words in caps and bold, for instance, or setting lines of type in different sizes — emphasized particular elements, such as the items for sale or the identity of the sellers. By the Revolution, ads at a glance announced themselves as distinct from news.

In the Federal period, some ads began to use enlarged capital-letter initials, a device borrowed from book design. By the Partisan period, the device had become generic, as ads beginning Wanted, or For sale, marched down the columns in close formation, presenting a shimmering army of W's and F's to the eye (Figure 3.5). At the high point of the Partisan style, virtually every ad in the newspaper included an enlarged initial somewhere. The use of initials provided the most characteristic design trait of the style.

The initials emphasized not the internal hierarchy of the advertising

FIGURE 3.5. A detail from an advertising page from the *St. Louis Republican,* January 6, 1847, p. 3, shows several common elements of advertising in the Partisan period, particularly enlarged initial capitals and monopoly ads. Note the generic runaway slave, lower left.

pitch but instead the external relation to other ads. In many cases, for example, the enlarged character was a number, as in "100 hats for sale" (a practice that would make no sense today). Rather than emphasizing some content specific to the ad, the enlarged initial number or letter signaled a classification. And in fact the style of the high Partisan period became associated specifically with the classified ads. Meanwhile, other devices developed to mark the unclassified display ads, especially retail ads for products, stores, and services.

Headings

By the Revolution, advertisements routinely ran under large, centered headings. In the Federal period, display lettering ran three to five times the size of the rest of the advertising type. The headings also introduced variety into ad typography, often appearing in bold, italic, or all capital letters and from time to time in a contrasting typeface. At first a heading rarely included the words today's reader might expect. They tended to emphasize the generic rather than the specific, much as the enlarged initials did. Gradually the emphasis in headings moved to the particulars of the ad: the merchant, for instance, or the article for sale.

In the mature Partisan period, however, heading size and use both diminished, apparently for practical and stylistic among other reasons. Most advertising composition still took place in the print shop, and printers had to fit ever more ads into a restricted space. Such practical pressures encouraged them to use smaller type. Printers also seemed to prefer the neatness and predictability of identically styled advertising, which provided the kind of regularity so valued in vernacular design. Stylistic preferences thus reinforced the move to small headings.

In the transition to the Imperial period, headings again became aggressively innovative: larger, more specific, and more typographically varied. Newspapers had begun to lose job printing to the wood-type poster houses that emerged by midcentury, and the demand for such work grew along with the railroads, touring circuses, and vaudeville acts (Meggs, 1998). The large and varied typography of wood-type posters led the way to greater emphasis in newspaper advertising. Many of the most assertive ads came from populist retailers, who used large type to shout out how CHEAP! their goods were (Figure 3.6).

Ornamentation

Two sorts of ornamentation (other than illustrations) passed in and out of fashion through the long period. One employed ornamental varieties of display typography, and the other decorative borders. Advertisements used novelty typefaces as a form of illustration, sometimes in a heading and sometimes in the body or text area. In the *Hartford Courant* of 1844, for instance, the text areas of several ads for dentists all used reverse type (white letterforms on a black field). Ornamental headings really took off during the Imperial period, when the production of advertisements moved outside the newspaper print shop. External design sources proliferated after the technology of stereotyping developed.

Stereotyping, a process for casting a replica of a typeset text or page from which to print an image, had a surprisingly important impact on the printing trades. The process allowed printers to free up their limited set of

FIGURE 3.6. Ransom's hysteria over low, low prices appeared in the *Hartford Courant,* October 29, 1864, p. 4.

cast-iron letters without losing work they had already set in type. Printers could cast multiple copies from one typeset original. In newspapers, stereotyping primarily affected advertising. For an ad created in-house, the printer could produce a stereotype of an ad or a column of ads, then break down the original to reuse the type for other tasks. In a more important use, advertisers could design an ad independently, make multiple stereotypes, and send each one out to a different newspaper. Even more significant, stereotyping allowed advertising agencies to produce entire pages filled with advertisements from their clients, and then take out a full page in various newspapers.

Stereotyping encouraged ornamentation in both type and borders. A newspaper in effect drew on the type collections of many print-production houses, and the resulting pages sported a greatly increased variety. Merchants also took part, encouraged by wood-type manufacturers to send in a sketch for a new typeface, from which the production house would create an entire font. Similarities in ornament appeared across newspapers, as agencies placed their stereotyped advertisements widely in the press, especially in major urban newspapers. Advertising for some things, such as for patent medicines, lent themselves to the new, national marketing (Laird, 1998). Particular novelty typefaces then became associated with certain products or product categories (Figure 3.7).

Borders, the other common type of ornamentation, developed slowly. In the early republic, printers often separated one advertisement from another with a simple ruled line (actually a thin strip of metal that sat type-high between the end of one text and the next heading). The common unit of ad space, called the *square,* defined a chunk of column as deep as it was wide (pretty much as you'd expect). It made sense to set off a square with rules. As squares — subject to the pressures already described — shrank to thin rectangles in the Partisan period, printers retained horizontal rules, clearly vestigial, without the generous spacing above and below. Later borders responded just as display typography did to the growth of stereotyping and advertising agencies. Type production houses created catalogs of elaborate curlicue borders and would produce others on demand. By the Imperial period, many more borders in ever more ornate patterns appeared in newspapers (Figure 3.8).

Illustration

The growth of illustrations also followed a wave-like pattern. In the Federal period, illustrations were few, quaint, and usually generic. The work required

FIGURE 3.7. National product ads often included decorative type, along with elaborate illustrations and logos, as in a detail from the *Concordia Eagle*, April 7, 1877, p. 4.

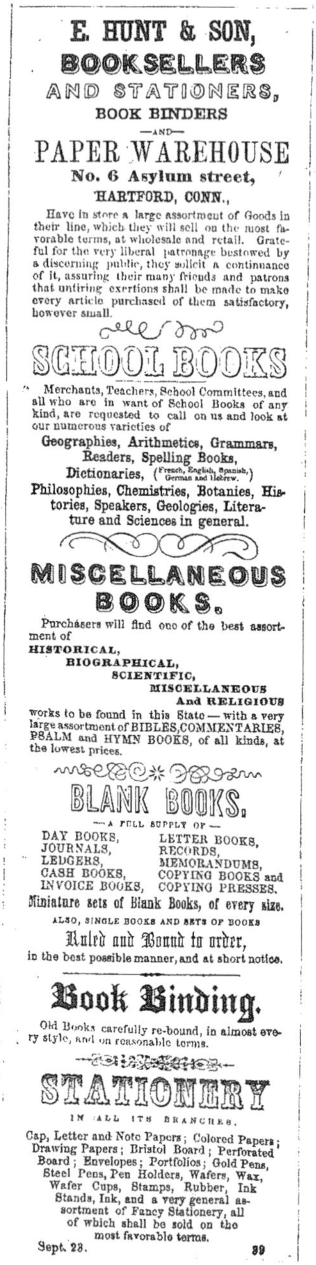

FIGURE 3.8. Note the decorative borders in the E. Hunt & Son advertisement from the *Hartford Courant,* October 23, 1852, p. 1.

to produce a woodcut for printing took time and increased expenses. The cuts required particular wood stocks and skilled labor, which when unavailable resulted in crude renditions. Printers still engaged in experimentation for clients willing to pay for making a visual impression of the unique — the grandness of a place of business, for example, or the character of a merchant, performer, or professional.

Once cut into wood, an illustration had a limited but still useful life that allowed printers to run their experimental cuts numerous times. Some designs proved popular, and the life of illustrations increased as type founders produced them in metal. Slowly illustrations became more routine and far more generic, resulting in what we have dubbed *monopoly* illustration. The preferred cut for a House for Sale ad, for example, a generic engraving of a house, looked eerily like the little red hotels found today in the board game Monopoly. Shipping ads had a similar engraving of a sailing ship; railroad ads had one of a train; horse ads, a horse; and, most jarring to our eye, notices of runaway slaves had a desperate little fugitive in silhouette (see Figure 3.5). At the height of the Partisan period, virtually all other illustrations disappeared, leaving only monopoly images to grace the advertising matter. Little houses and horses and ships and slaves marched single file down the columns.

The repetitive images amounted to a de facto organizational device that classified advertising headings eventually replaced (although not entirely). Innovation then returned to newspaper illustrations. In the Imperial era, the unique illustration came back in force. Presumably designed outside the newspaper print shop, the individually created images gave a distinctive look to advertising, especially for large retail outlets. The process of stereotyping also gave the press the luxury of many different illustrations in competing styles, and identical advertisements for a national product could run in many newspapers (Figure 3.9).

White Space

In the colonial era, white space ran evenly distributed throughout the newspaper. Each visual element appeared in an envelope of space. The practice followed that of serious book printing, in which interline spacing and generous margins marked a style of discourse suited to the intellectual. Romances and other private reading had developed their own distinctive look with much less space (typecutters first developed italic type, with the letters slanted to fit more tightly together, for such light reading matter).

In the Federal era, the envelopes of white space shrunk to the point of

FIGURE 3.9. The more elaborate ads are stereotyped, as shown in a detail from the *New York Dispatch,* March 10, 1867, p. 4.

disappearing from news matter but flourished here and there in advertisements. It was not uncommon for spacious ads to break out of the rigid single column and spread into a second one. In the Partisan period, however, advertising matter turned tighter and grayer as space came at a premium.

The course of spatial change subsequently divided into two paths, one for classified and another for display advertising. Classified ads squeezed into reduced spaces, with the text set smaller on less interline spacing. The enlarged initial letter on many ads produced a salt-and-pepper look, although the overall result became grayer, especially after monopoly illustrations went into decline. In contrast, retail ads grew not only in size but also in spaciousness through mid-century. The use of white space particularly marked the advertising by nascent department stores, such as Wanamaker's (Figure 3.10). In the Imperial period, such display ads began to apportion space differently, applying it as an external frosting that separated the retailer and its products with a sometimes generous buffer zone.

The new designs produced a lumpy pattern of space in newspapers, in contrast to the more even consistency of earlier periods. Some display advertisements continued to employ the circus-poster style of design, interspersing mixed types with irregular slabs of space, next to other ads filled to the brim with increasingly elaborate illustrations and ornaments. News matter developed the same unevenness, with the accordioning text described previously. Besides connoting the great variety of wares in the market, such high contrast emphasized the wealth of those advertisements that could luxuriate in space, giving respite to the weary reading eye and inviting consumers to share the wealth (by spending).

CLASS AND ORDER

The goods and services advertised in newspapers from the colonial era to the Partisan period aimed almost entirely at upscale readers. Ordinary folk did not buy ready-made clothing, much less the finery that merchants and shopkeepers advertised; nor was property dealing common. Even though many everyday folk owned some property, they tended to hold onto what they could acquire. Acquisition, trade, and consumption occupied primarily the elite classes.

As time went on, the goods and services offered in advertising became steadily more common, and the appeal increasingly emphasized cheapness rather than distinction. The whimsical images in advertisements of the Federal period soon gave way to a more down-to-earth task: showing the type

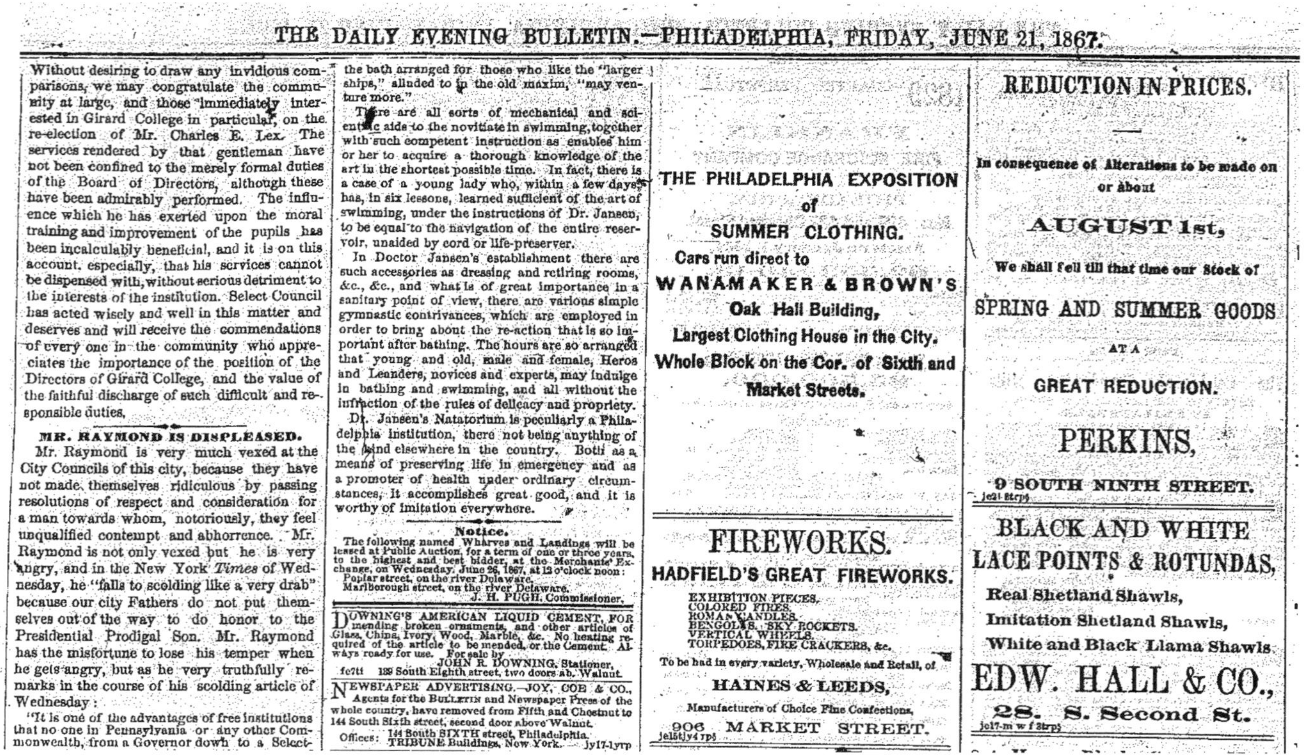

THE DAILY EVENING BULLETIN.—PHILADELPHIA, FRIDAY, JUNE 21, 1867.

Without desiring to draw any invidious comparisons, we may congratulate the community at large, and those immediately interested in Girard College in particular, on the re-election of Mr. Charles E. Lex. The services rendered by that gentleman have not been confined to the merely formal duties of the Board of Directors, although these have been admirably performed. The influence which he has exerted upon the moral training and improvement of the pupils has been incalculably beneficial, and it is on this account, especially, that his services cannot be dispensed with, without serious detriment to the interests of the institution. Select Council has acted wisely and well in this matter and deserves and will receive the commendations of every one in the community who appreciates the importance of the position of the Directors of Girard College, and the value of the faithful discharge of such difficult and responsible duties.

MR. RAYMOND IS DISPLEASED.

Mr. Raymond is very much vexed at the City Councils of this city, because they have not made themselves ridiculous by passing resolutions of respect and consideration for a man towards whom, notoriously, they feel unqualified contempt and abhorrence. Mr. Raymond is not only vexed but he is very angry, and in the New York *Times* of Wednesday, he "falls to scolding like a very drab" because our city Fathers do not put themselves out of the way to do honor to the Presidential Prodigal Son. Mr. Raymond has the misfortune to lose his temper when he gets angry, but as he very truthfully remarks in the course of his scolding article of Wednesday:

"It is one of the advantages of free institutions that no one in Pennsylvania or any other Commonwealth, from a Governor down to a Select-

the bath arranged for those who like the "larger ships," alluded to in the old maxim, "may venture more."

There are all sorts of mechanical and scientific aids to the novitiate in swimming, together with such competent instruction as enables him or her to acquire a thorough knowledge of the art in the shortest possible time. In fact, there is a case of a young lady who, within a few days, has, in six lessons, learned sufficient of the art of swimming, under the instructions of Dr. Jansen, to be equal to the navigation of the entire reservoir, unaided by cord or life-preserver.

In Doctor Jansen's establishment there are such accessories as dressing and retiring rooms, &c., &c., and what is of great importance in a sanitary point of view, there are various simple gymnastic contrivances, which are employed in order to bring about the re-action that is so important after bathing. The hours are so arranged that young and old, male and female, Heros and Leanders, novices and experts, may indulge in bathing and swimming, and all without the infraction of the rules of delicacy and propriety.

Dr. Jansen's Natatorium is peculiarly a Philadelphia institution, there not being anything of the kind elsewhere in the country. Both as a means of preserving life in emergency and as a promoter of health under ordinary circumstances, it accomplishes great good, and it is worthy of imitation everywhere.

Notice.

The following named Wharves and Landings will be leased at Public Auction, for a term of one or three years, to the highest and best bidder, at the Merchants' Exchange, on Wednesday, June 26, 1867, at 12 o'clock noon:
Poplar street, on the river Delaware.
Marlborough street, on the river Delaware.
J. H. PUGH, Commissioner.

DOWNING'S AMERICAN LIQUID CEMENT, FOR mending broken ornaments, and other articles of Glass, China, Ivory, Wood, Marble, &c. No heating required of the article to be mended, or the Cement. Always ready for use. For sale by
JOHN R. DOWNING, Stationer,
fe7tf 139 South Eighth street, two doors ab. Walnut.

NEWSPAPER ADVERTISING.—JOY, COE & CO., Agents for the BULLETIN and Newspaper Press of the whole country, have removed from Fifth and Chestnut to 144 South Sixth street, second door above Walnut.
Offices: 144 South SIXTH street, Philadelphia. TRIBUNE Buildings, New York. jy17-1yrp

THE PHILADELPHIA EXPOSITION
of
SUMMER CLOTHING.
Cars run direct to
WANAMAKER & BROWN'S
Oak Hall Building,
Largest Clothing House in the City,
Whole Block on the Cor. of Sixth and
Market Streets.

FIREWORKS.
HADFIELD'S GREAT FIREWORKS.
EXHIBITION PIECES,
COLORED FIRES,
ROMAN CANDLES,
BENGOLAS, SKY ROCKETS,
VERTICAL WHEELS,
TORPEDOES, FIRE CRACKERS, &c.
To be had in every variety, Wholesale and Retail, of
HAINES & LEEDS,
Manufacturers of Choice Fine Confections,
906 MARKET STREET.
je15tjy4rp

REDUCTION IN PRICES.
In consequence of Alterations to be made on or about
AUGUST 1st,
We shall sell till that time our Stock of
SPRING AND SUMMER GOODS
AT A
GREAT REDUCTION.
PERKINS,
9 SOUTH NINTH STREET.
je21 3trp

BLACK AND WHITE
LACE POINTS & ROTUNDAS,
Real Shetland Shawls,
Imitation Shetland Shawls,
White and Black Llama Shawls.
EDW. HALL & CO.,
28 S. Second St.
je17-m w f 3trp

FIGURE 3.10. Wanamaker's ads were pioneering in their modernism. Note how this one stands out not just from the news matter but also from the other, more traditional ads appearing in the Philadelphia *Daily Evening Bulletin*, June 21, 1867, p. 5.

of product (almost always in generic form). The visual landscape of the newspaper filled with prefabricated images in the Partisan period, hailing ordinary people to the categories of consumer products on the market.

Unlike the undulating course that formal aspects of design followed, class appeal in advertising experienced a fairly direct, linear development. At first glance, the linear trajectory of class appeal might seem unusual, but it does square with common sense. The intrusion of ordinary folk into the ranks of advertisers at first encouraged a kind of republican humbleness and uniformity in ads. As a result, we can add class appeal to the considerations (practical and stylistic) that encouraged the simplification and routinization of advertising styles in the Partisan period.

Although individual designs declined, by the end of the Partisan period such illustrations began to present not only goods for sale but product endorsements, portraits of consumers, and architectural views of stores or factories. In an incipient form of narrative, advertising engravings even showed the new consumers how they should act. In 1847, for instance, the Milledgeville, Georgia, *Federal Union* included a scene in which consumers find a store and appear in various poses in the act of shopping (Figure 3.11).

In the Imperial newspaper, advertising also aimed to conquer consumer emotions, serving the interests of business: to attract attention and motivate consumption by keying to the needs, fears, and desires of readers. In the *Courant,* a typical advertisement for impotence elixirs would announce "Manhood restored." The happy product user made an appearance, along with the comforting faces of authoritative figures giving endorsements, such as a Dr. Christie, who embodied scientific and fatherly trust. Other ads played on consumer fears, asking, for example, "Are you insured?" The pitch often contained a narrative of consumption that targeted the least secure classes.

At the end of the Victorian period, many display ads in the *Courant* appeared as already described: a separate, self-contained entity, with its elements gathered in a tight unit at the center of a spacious territory. The advertising looked much as it does today (and offered some products still on the market, such as Royal Baking Powder or Baker's Chocolate). The growth in display ad proportions clearly contributed to the grandness of the newspaper but also to the centrality of commerce in its visual form. The market revolution thus pushed advertising toward narrative and to emotional appeals long before the invention of a psychology of advertising described elsewhere (Marchand, 1985; Trachtenberg, 1990; Goodrum & Dalrymple, 1990; Craig, 1992).

So far our discussion has dwelt mainly on the level of the individual ad.

FIGURE 3.11. J & E Saulsbury display not just their store but also their shoppers in action in a detail from the Milledgeville, Georgia, *Federal Union*, December 7, 1847, p. 4.

Another linear pattern of change occurred in the overall organization of advertising matter. It became increasingly segregated from news matter and increasingly subdivided internally, and this segmentation was announced in increasingly clear and pragmatic terms.

We have already noted several aspects of the increasing variation in genre and categorization. By the mature Imperial period, a retail store ad had a certain look, while a House for Sale ad had a different look. The commercial content had settled into the general divide between display and classified advertisements. The organization of advertising matter, however, went deeper than that. In the early republic, newspapers arranged the ads mainly by age, drawing a distinction between new and old ones. Because printers set their rates to accommodate advertisers willing to pay for multiple insertions, newspapers filled up with old advertising (evident from the date of first insertion commonly included in each ad). Printers set aside a special zone, usually near the prime space for original editorial matter, for new ads. The distinction between new and old mattered more for printers and advertisers than it did for readers, of course. Someone in the market for a new set of chairs would care about the chairs, not the age of the ad, but new advertisers would be pleased to see their chairs showcased. The printer would find it convenient to set all the new matter at once and then move it farther back in the newspaper as older items dropped out. Such considerations retarded the movement to a more systematic organization of ad matter, but only for a while.

By the Transition period following the early republic, organization under topical heads had become common in ad matter. This innovation appeared in response to an increase in the number of ads, reaching a threshold at which the typical reader would no longer look at every item. In the Partisan period, the nearly universal topical heads customarily sat atop most advertising columns. The heads, usually set in blackletter, differed markedly from whatever topical heads appeared in news matter. As the Partisan period yielded to the Imperial period, the blackletter type disappeared, but the heads became only more routine and pervasive.

Meanwhile, the display ads, those occupying the most space and leaving the most white space, clustered together, sometimes on the front page, sometimes in the space formerly reserved for new ads, and sometimes on the back page. Display advertising sought a mass audience looking for cheap goods or entertainment. At the end of the century, such clusters of advertising would begin to attach themselves to particular news departments; in the twentieth century they would drive the segmentation of the newspaper into sections devoted to specific interests, such as sports, homemaking, cars, and business.

TOPICAL SEGMENTATION IN NEWS

Early newspapers had a fairly consistent notion of how to divvy up the news. They did it geographically, by point of proximate transmission, not by point of origin. The newspapers seem a little opaque about this, because at first glance geographical indicators look like datelines, which today tend to convey the point of origin. Most frequently, however, newspapers until the Federal period used geographical indicators to indicate the place where the printer got the news, not the place where the news happened. An item in a New York newspaper under the geographical head Boston might actually deal with matters in the Caribbean or the Maritimes. The heading indicated proximate transmission, denoting an item copied from a Boston newspaper.

Early newspapers presented what they called clipped items of news in geographical order, beginning first with news from European papers, then from the Americas, then from domestic locations. This organization approximated the experience of a news reader in a coffeehouse, presumably, one who would begin with the newspapers from the metropolis, that is, London, then move closer to home.

The European focus to the news considered most important came from a sense of History. History was the coherent drama of collective human development, and the protagonists in that drama were the European states. The news matter was supposed to consist of the episodic account of History. At the end of each year, newspapers often put together a summary of the workings of History in verse form and included it in the annual New Year's Day carriers' address to patrons. The "News-boy's Verses" of the *New York Gazette* for 1763 are typical, summarizing the European military and diplomatic maneuvering behind the ongoing colonial warfare:

> To bless the Realm great PITT arose,
> Sagacious, wise, and just
> The Dread and Curse of Britain's Foes,
> Whose Pride he's laid in Dust.
>   . . . .
> Among the Tales his Papers told,
> The following may be found:
> The Russian Empress, fierce and bold,
> Lies mould'ring in the Ground (News-boy's Verses, 1762).

From time to time the scene of History moved. During the Revolution, America became a primary rather than a secondary location for news (Merritt, 1966). Subsequently national politics became more a plot than a subplot of the drama of History. Nevertheless, the scene of History usually remained European, portraying the superpower conflict between France and England, for example, as the driving force behind much of the political struggle of the Federalist era (Wiebe, 1984).

By the turn of the nineteenth century, then, the news was organized geographically and according to a grand narrative of History. The different newspapers we looked at made this organization explicit to varying degrees. In one typical case, the leading newspaper of a growing frontier town, the *Pittsburgh Gazette,* had three large topical heads in its news matter: Foreign Intelligence, American Intelligence, and Pittsburgh. A final column headed By Yesterday's Mail complemented the main headers. (The advertisements in this and most turn-of-the-century newspapers used the same typeface as the topical heads in news matter, giving the visual impression that each ad was its own department.)

One might expect this pattern of news organization to become more elaborate over time, eventually arborescing into the departments of the newspaper common today, but that is not what happened. Instead the geographical order of the newspaper gradually diminished. This happened when the organizing grand narrative, History, which had sustained the newspaper's geographical sense, dissolved. In its place, a lesser notion of historical importance attached itself to domestic politics, which defined one pole of the news worldview that today we call public affairs, and segregated this sphere from another pole of news that we might call the everyday.

The grand division between the historical and the everyday undergirded the newspaper, which gave it typographical expression. Beginning in the Federal period and reaching maturity in the Imperial period, newspapers began to present regularly recurring news matter in departments such as Financial, Markets, Courts, Married, Died. Grouped together, the departments often came at the end of the news matter. Typographically they resembled advertising more than news (surprisingly, to a reader today). In the 1840s these departments usually had blackletter heads, the same typography used for topical heads in advertising. In contrast, news headlines tended to run in the typeface used for news text. Everyday events thus occupied profane, private ground, along with advertising. Meanwhile, the sacred public realm had been colonized by the persona of the editor.

The editor replaced the printer as the news selector at the same time that partisan interests replaced History as the driving force behind public affairs news. The tidy geographical organization of public affairs news was displaced by a decentralized welter of intelligence about political matters. Items in the main news section still appeared under the newspaper nameplate or dateline (on page 2 or 3), but they were now more self-consciously hierarchical and more consistently broken up into freestanding units of a single paragraph. By the 1840s such paragraphing had become a distinctive practice of U.S. newspapers. Elsewhere in the Western world, editors preferred the essay; the frenetic Americans considered this long-winded and installed the compact and punchy paragraph as the preferred unit for both commentary and news. Typically, each edition offered several columns of paragraphs meant for reading in one long string. The top items usually engaged in editorial jousting. The remaining items, usually clipped from other newspapers, appeared in order of decreasing significance and decreasing size. Editors attributed such borrowings either in an italicized line above or below the text or in an introductory sentence written in the editorial we: "We find the following useful information in the Portland Argus."

In the prime news space, topical heads appeared, but had remarkably little uniformity. One could easily imagine a standard set of news departments, such as U.S. Congress (used frequently in the Partisan period, particularly for news universally copied from one or two Washington, D.C., newspapers), Diplomatic Intelligence (rarely used), North American Affairs (also rare), and a few others. In fact, newspapers customarily made up topical heads ad hoc. Instead of having regular departments, they occasionally assigned a topic to particularly long or important pieces of news. An item on trade in the Caribbean might acquire a topical head like Free Trade, but would never become a department. Instead, under a miniature of the newspaper's nameplate, the prime news appeared homogenized into a single unnamed department and processed by the voice and persona of the editor.

The editor's page was the product of a particular system of news distribution. Editors put their paragraphs and pages together out of other newspapers that circulated within the system of free postal exchange (Kielbowicz, 1989; John, 1995). News during the Partisan formation thus read like a compendium of newspapers, all filtered through the editor's voice. That filtered digest began to change with the introduction of a succeeding system for distributing news: the telegraphic wire service.

In the editor's newspaper, items were haphazardly attributed. Sometimes editors made a point of mentioning an item's source, but just as often they might fudge it, pretending to have had more direct access to an item than in fact they did. Even more typically, the editor simply would not care particularly about attributing an item. In the age of postal transmission, with the wide and gratis sharing of news items, saying where an item had originated had little importance.

Attribution accelerated as news became commoditized. In the new era of telegraphy, editors bought and sold transmitted news as a commodity. The latest news no longer arrived free and equal through the mail. Telegraphic news cost money and initiated a distinction between newspapers that bought it and others that waited to copy the news in the old-fashioned way. Newspapers therefore acquired an incentive to label their news as telegraphic. Columns headed By the Electric Telegraph (or something like that) became universal in mainstream dailies by the end of the 1850s, easily dwarfing in significance their immediate predecessors, columns headed By the Latest Mails.

The various forms of byline attribution appeared simultaneously. Most bylined stories remained anonymous, hiding behind a generic attribution, such as By our special correspondent. In a sense, the attribution worked as an extension of the statement of ownership that editorials under the newspaper masthead would make. What the editorial form was to the politics of the partisan press, the special correspondent's byline or pseudonym was to the publisher's newspaper. In the latter half of the nineteenth century, correspondents, whether anonymous, pseudonymous, or named, provided regular voices and personae. Such matter (like the editorial matter) ran segregated from the telegraphic news that eventually overtook it, until in the modern newspaper the correspondent became a reporter sending stories over wires rather than a letter writer sending commentary through the mail.

Telegraphic news in the Imperial and Victorian periods became the premier content of newspapers and had its own formal characteristics. For practical reasons, telegraphic news tended to brevity. If editors preferred the paragraph and correspondents the column, the telegraph preferred the line. By the 1870s, the miniaturization of content had reached an extreme, and mainstream dailies contained columns titled something like Sparks, comprising very short items arrayed in order of increasing length. Set in tiny type and ranging from a few words to a few lines in length, the items taken together formed a kind of shadowy pyramid.

Telegraphic news columns also adopted the form of stacked headings that originated in advertisements. From advertising, so-called deck headlines moved into news before the emergence of telegraphy. In the 1840s editors used deck headlines for printing up digests of European news carried by steamships. Telegraphic content came in a similar digest form, and it became customary to run the items under a series of stacked headlines (Figure 3.12). The items in a telegraphic digest would of course be multifarious. Instead of extruding them and giving each its own headline, the newspaper left them all piled together and put a corresponding pile of headlines on top of them.

FROM EUROPE.

Latest Despatches by O.. an
Telegraph.

Rumor that Napoleon Contem-
plates Calling a Grand
European Congress.

England to Preserve a Strict
Neutrality in the Eastern
Question.

Progress of the Revolution in
Candia.

Austria Will Make Concessions
to Hungary.

Serious Trouble Brewing Between Greece and Turkey.

FROM WASHINGTON.

New Year's Receptions by the
President and Members of
His Cabinet.

Outlines of Commissioner Wells'
Report and Accompanying
Tariff Bill.

Resolutions Favoring the President's Impeachment to be Introduced on Monday.

Internal Revenue Receipts Yesterday Nearly Three Millions
of Dollars.

MEETING OF STATE LEGIS-
LATURES YESTERDAY.

Extracts from Messages of the
Various State Executives.

FROM MEXICO.

Active Preparations for the Em-
barkation of French Troops.

Maximilian---His Involun-
tary Movement Toward
the Capital.

Gold Closed in New York
at 132 1-2.

FROM EUROPE.

BE OCEAN TELEGRAPH.

GREAT BRITAIN.
Liverpool, January 1.
The steamship Hecla, from New York (Inman line),
13, has arrived.

VOL. XIX.

FIGURE 3.12. Headlines were stacked as they came in on the telegraph, as this detail from the *Chicago Tribune*, January 3, 1867, p. 1, demonstrates.

The headlines acted as an outline of or table of contents for the digest that followed. Later, newspapers adapted the deck headline form for use on long and highly significant single items.

By the Imperial period, many features of a new segmentation for news had already appeared. In the Victorian era, the segmentation would become more standardized (although hardly recognizable as such to readers today). The Victorian period based topical segmentation on production routines and not on content. Its subdivisions included the editor's news, the telegraph's news, the essayist's news, and the advertiser's news, all of them organized sequentially. In most dailies, as we already mentioned, the editor's news occupied the inside pages (pp. 2–3 in a four-page edition, pp. 4–5 in an eight-page edition). By the 1870s, page 1 had become the front page, where the most compelling of the telegraphic news appeared. Soft news, fiction, poetry, religious material, and the other elements of the essayist's news drifted toward the back pages, along with local events, financial matters, crime, and all the other features of the everyday. Advertising filled in the cracks, sometimes up front, sometimes in back, but always clearly demarcated from news matter, and always now divided between mass retail and classifieds.

NEWSPAPERS AND READERS

Newspapers always marketed themselves, but colonial and revolutionary era newspapers did so with restraint. They understood their audiences as very restricted, either socially and demographically (colonial newspapers were for the elite only) or topically (revolutionary newspapers were about politics). Like subsistence farmers, early printers did not anticipate tremendous growth and did not eagerly seek out new paying customers. Because they published a weekly edition, they expected (grumpily) that far more people would borrow a copy than pay for one, and they worked under the impression that each copy had about ten readers (Leonard, 1986). The pattern of readership encouraged them to emphasize the durability of their newspapers by using regular and predictable dress. The fact that each edition looked pretty much like every other one reminded readers of the reliability of the newspaper establishment.

The market revolution changed the newspaper. It encouraged the press to publish daily by increasing both the flow of news and the available readership. It also encouraged publishers to think of readers as paying customers. As publication became more frequent, as the price of materials dropped, and as advertising gradually subsidized more of the production costs, it became more possible to sell newspapers as disposable commodities to individual users. Of course, the tie to advertising revenue involved a further shift in attitude toward readers. Publishers would be concerned to attract readers whom advertisers wanted to reach, readers with disposable incomes and habits of consumption. Newspapers looked for readers in a buying mood.

The market revolution encouraged the press to sell itself in new ways, and newspapers began to market and promote themselves aggressively, both to advertisers and to the public. To the public, newspapers claimed to offer the latest news, the most colorful and interesting miscellany of interests, the most gratifying window into the social and cultural world. To advertisers, newspapers claimed to offer the largest and most compliant readership.

The new Victorian organization of the newspaper signaled a change in the way newspapers hailed their readers. The partisan press hailed them as citizen-voters, although it also carried advertising matter entirely unconcerned with the sacred world of public affairs. The Victorian press hailed readers as both citizen-voters and everyday Americans (in the editorial pages) and as consumers (in advertising pages). As time went on, newspapers became increasingly adept at hailing specific categories of consumers. Advertising matter would shepherd news matter into demographically coherent departments aimed at women, youth, sports fans, or businessmen. The full articulation of this segmentation awaited the development of the modern newspaper.

PART II

THE ROLE OF PICTURES

A PATIENT RAILROAD TRAVELER.

Thomas Nast, "A Patient Railroad Traveler," *Harper's Weekly*, March 14, 1874, p. 244.

Playful Commerce

Family portraits in the nineteenth century began to show newspapers in the hands of fathers and heads of households. The best-known example, *The Tilton Family*, an 1837 watercolor by the folk artist Joseph H. Davis, balances the father and his newspaper, books, and writing tools with the mother and her child, pet, and flowers (see Zboray, 1993, p. 88). The two sides of the composition contrast the tools of public (masculine) life with those of private (feminine) life. In the hagiography of the Victorian era, a newspaper in the hand indicated the presence of a publisher (in Mathew Brady's portrait of Horace Greeley, for instance), the knowledge of the man of affairs, and the domination of the patriarch (as in Thomas Nast's illustration, "Col. Juggins Reading the *Somerville Star* to his Wife"; see Leonard, 1993, p. 388).

In this Nast cartoon, a newsboy, one of the ubiquitous icons associated with newspapers, walks away (to the left), while a railroad traveler peers out from under a mass of goods distributed en route: snacks, an envelope and booklet, along with newspapers. The traveler is the patient victim of abundant manufacture and distribution, and the newspaper is again a source of frustration. The boy has given him a taste of his own merchant-class medicine, and the reference to the iconic newspaper-as-power gives the frame its comic touch. Of course, serious images of newspapers on the railways also appeared during the period (see, for example, the publicity image reproduced in Leonard, 1993, p. 319), as rail travel attempted to associate itself with the icons of the ruling classes. The newsboy served as a countertype, the merchant class writ small.

The children who regularly appear in nineteenth-century illustrations of newspapers draw attention to the relation of the press to power and the powerful. One 1812 children's book illustration, for instance, shows a dog in formal dress alongside a monkey reading the newspaper by candlelight (*Pompey*, 1812). The dog pounding a bed warmer with a spoon is all noise and nonsense, offering an ironic comment on the news the monkey reads. More commonly, childhood figures embodied a realm of play in contrast to the world of affairs. This opposition, usually understood as the contrast between the home and the world, is all the more compelling in some illustrations because it is inscribed *inside* the home. An engraving of a domestic scene from the 1840s shows a father with his spectacles on his forehead as he leans forward to watch his four children play with a blanket broadsheet so large that the oldest boy stands on a chair to hold up one end, the next eldest kneels over the top edge and holds on, while a girl crawls across an expanse of newsprint columns, and the youngest peers out from the bottom end (Alden, n.d.). The lifted spectacles indicate the suspension of the proper use of the press, suggesting that the appearance of the blanket sheet, a novel form of popular newspaper, marks a historical rupture in the uses of literacy. The normal uses are depicted in a stock scene in children's books from the latter half of the century: the child at play with a cat, while a father sits in the background reading the newspaper. Sometimes the father pauses to observe, or he may simply ignore the child (*Prints, 1865*).

These pictures of reading fathers suggest that if newspapers were supposed to be adult, they were also supposed to be male. Although images of women reading newspapers appeared in nineteenth-century art, the form clearly aligned with masculinity well into the twentieth century (see the examples in Leonard, 1995, especially the suffragist who holds the paper and dominates her husband). This habit was iconic and not ethnographic. In fact, by midcentury women had become great readers of newspapers (Zboray & Saracino Zboray, 1996b), although little in the editorial matter of the mainstream press would indicate that. The illustration regime, like the overall form, has always had less to do with facts on the ground than with an imagined world more or less removed from those facts.

CHAPTER 4

CIVIC PICTURING

The Regime of Illustrated News, 1856–1901

Technology so far has been a background player in our story. From time to time a new technique (like stereotyping) or an institutional development that exploited technologies in a new way (such as woodcut houses that produced ads) appeared on stage. On occasion a major systematic change (like the telegraph) involved new technology, but at no point did technology drive the changes we have discussed. Instead it acted as a tertiary force, providing the props and backdrops for broad sociocultural factors like politics and economics and for the design sense of printers and publishers.

The pace of technological change picked up by mid century, and with it the amount of attention paid to technological forces in descriptions of news and of newspapers. It became common (and remains so among some historians) to talk about the development of news as a series of revolutions in the tools of publishing and to talk about the power of the press as coming directly out of these new tools. According to common sense, television ended the war in Vietnam because of its qualities as a visual and domestic technology: it showed dead bodies in people's living rooms, and people made the government stop the war. In that one simple sentence lies a set of arguments about communication and media effects. The tools (the camera's eye) dictate both form and content, and predictable results follow.

In its purest form, this habit of thought has the entire modern world flowing from new machines. The steam engine and the dynamo produced raw power with even greater efficiency, enabling the railroad and the telegraph to pump goods and data through the social system at ever greater speeds, nurturing the new industrial factory and the new industrial school and the new middle-class home, and hence the modern individual, a centered subject in a changing society full of choices to be made.

Picture technologies occupy a special niche in this narrative. Before the nineteenth century ordinary people had few pictures and had no real way of knowing what distant people and far away places looked like. By the end of the century photography and new techniques of photo reproduction promised to provide realistic pictures of anyone or anything anywhere in the world. Surely this was a tremendous change.

Thinkers have made much of the new picturing technology. Taking a cue from Walter Benjamin (1969), many see the age of mechanical reproduction as marking a fundamental rupture in art, ending the era of concrete physical uniqueness and finally allowing the occasion of a hyperreal world of simulacra. Others, following Foucault, see photography giving rise to a new scopic regime (Crary, 1990) in which picturing technologies allow increased surveillance and discipline. The diverging positions have opened a fertile region of controversy, and scholars debate what they call the ocular-centrism of the modern era and the importance of picturing technology in creating so-called prosthetic memory (Jay, 1993; Lury, 1998).

In any version, photography as a technology played a most revolutionary role. It sparked an internal revolution that extended from the broadest social practices and institutions to the deepest seat of individual subjectivity. It birthed the modern sense of self.

In Part II we examine the history of news practices with these issues in mind. We find that, well, things were complicated. The line between photography and other kinds of picturing was quite blurred, as was the line between realism and its opposites, romanticism and impressionism. We find the modern, but not coming out of the camera per se. And we find that photojournalism's complicated history raises questions about its legacy.

Photojournalism, it is often assumed, came out of the camera full-armored like Athena out of the head of Zeus. This is certainly not the case. Contrary to the received history, in which all techniques and styles of news illustration lead toward the photograph at the summit of journalistic representation, research underscores the contingency of photographic styles and usages (see Chapter 5). That photography might wed permanently with news was not obvious in the Victorian era. Its adoption or rejection depended not on technical barriers but on its usefulness to the existing regime of news illustration, dominated by typography, and its capacity otherwise to express the routines of news work. Available technology sometimes limited the styles and usages of photography, but this limiting was just that: a limitation. It did not amount to a phototechnological determination of the project of journalism.

Within the larger regime of news illustration, moreover, photojournalism appeared tardily. Beginning in the 1830s, in Great Britain and the United States, newspaper and magazine publishers began to experiment with the use of various kinds of illustrations. This experimentation preceded the successful introduction of photography in the form of the daguerreotype in 1839 (Anderson, 1991; Brown, 1993). The numerous technologies available to illustrators included woodcuts and wood engravings, various forms of metal engravings, and lithography. Eventually these combined with photography, but much as it was talked about as supremely realistic and unauthored, as an epochal invention, a radically different and discontinuous tool of illustration, photography was used simply as one tool among many.

The key figure in this regime of illustration was the artist. Every news illustration had to be composed and rendered by an artist of one sort or another — usually either a sketch artist, an engraver, or both. These artists were journalists, like the textual journalists of the printerly and Victorian newspapers, and they fell into the same categories: correspondents and scavengers. Their jobs were the same as the textual journalists: to provide intelligence about distant and important people, places, and events, and to provide a fulsome and engaging miscellany of deviant goings-on.

This chapter analyzes the regime of illustrated news in the United States in the period from the late 1850s to the assassination of President McKinley in 1901. The period begins with the establishment of the first successful illustrated newspapers in the United States and ends with the full implementation of the photographic halftone. Culturally, it corresponds to the rise of a realist ethos, both in art and literature and in the social sciences (Orvell, 1990; Michaels, 1988). In journalism, it corresponds to the growth of a sense of literary professionalism that produced the great muckraking reporters, and also to the birth of press clubs, trade periodicals, and other institutions that would support the emergence of the occupational ideology of objectivity (Schudson, 1978; Wilson, 1985). In terms of the media system as a whole, the period begins with a largely partisan newspaper press and with a largely genteel range of nationally circulated magazines, and ends with an industrialized newspaper system employing an increasingly routinized pattern of news production and with a new range of mass-circulation popular magazines (Baldasty, 1993; Ohmann, 1996). Meanwhile, the readers of the print media had become more and more socialized into the "land of desire" that the advertisers in the media were helping to create (Leach, 1993; Lears, 1994).

In this chapter we look at two illustrated periodicals, *Leslie's* and *Harper's,* easily the most important of the genre. They share many similarities: both were printed in New York City, both appeared weekly, both circulated nationally, both were founded in the mid- to late 1850s, and both came of age during the Civil War. As we shall see, both also used similar techniques of illustration for similar content, but they also differed in important ways. *Leslie's* insisted that it was a newspaper and maintained an emphasis on breaking news. It was the mainstay of the company that produced it, and sought out a large, heterogeneous readership (its circulation varied from around 50,000 to around 200,000, with higher peaks for dramatic issues, like assassinations, because much of its circulation was in single-copy sales; see Brown, 1993, ch. 1). *Harper's* was published by the nation's leading book publisher. It aimed at a more genteel audience, was more concerned with literature and the arts, and recycled its illustrations in its other publications, notably novels and a monthly magazine. Where *Leslie's* was a newspaper, *Harper's* styled itself "A Journal of Civilization," a self-nomination it took seriously. We base our comments in this chapter on a sample of representative issues from each taken at five-year intervals (1856, 1861, 1866, and so forth).

TECHNIQUES OF ILLUSTRATION

Nineteenth-century printing found picture reproduction challenging (Carlebach, 1992). The basic technical difficulty was getting an image onto a material that could be locked into a printing form along with textual material. More than a dozen discrete solutions were found for this one problem. Of these, woodcuts and later wood-engravings were the favorite media for printers of news illustrations. Both, of course, required the hand of an engraver. Both also required a supply of suitable wood. *Leslie's* pioneered routines for both requirements (Brown, 1993, pp. 48–59). The preferred wood for engraving grew in trees with trunks no larger than six inches in diameter, too small for a full-page or even a half-page engraving. The solution for *Leslie's* was to machine the wood into uniform blocks two inches square, then bolt them together to form a smooth block of any desired size. This allowed for a routinization of the hand of the engraver as well. The outlines of a picture were engraved on a large composite block by a head engraver, then the block was broken down and the pieces distributed to specialist engravers, who worked simultaneously. The various engravers had specific skills — one was good at faces, for instance, and another at architectural details — so that a complex division of labor was built into the routine.

The composition of an engraving followed a similar routine. Artists in the field — sketch artists and photographers, among others — would collect images. Then in house a chief artist would select among these pieces. Some, such as portraits of individual statesmen, would be engraved from one image or photograph. Others, such as large-scale depictions of events, would be composed from a large number of individual drawings and combined into one continuous scene. These sometimes formed two-page panoramic center spreads. The chief artist or engraver would often affix a signature on these, in effect introducing the chief artist into the company of editors like Horace Greeley, cartoonists like Thomas Nast, and the pseudonymously bylined correspondents of major news organizations as journalistic personae.

This process made illustration in the newsweeklies collective and routinized. Each illustration required the skilled intervention of several artists, in addition to going through a process of editorial selection and, often, composition. The artists' eyes and hands ensured that the illustration would have clarity and would convey a meaning of some sort, but this was applied art. Its production was mechanized to an extent that permitted predictable manufacturing schedules and allowed the (believable) claim to authentic representation. A reader of *Leslie's* or *Harper's* could expect in each issue to see illustrations on about half the pages, and those illustrations presenting themselves as news would have their origin in "Nature," that is, they would have been drawn or photographed at some point from life.

The illustrations, then, were quite a bit like the text that accompanied them. They almost never stood without comment (the exceptions being cartoons and editorial icons, themselves forms of commentary). Usually the text amplified and explained the illustration. A typical example is "The Port of Genesee, Lake Ontario" (*Leslie's*, July 5, 1856, illustration on p. 53, text on p. 54). The picture by itself remains fairly mute: "Look at the pretty boats!" The text tells you more: "Our beautiful picture of the Port of Genesee is from an ambrotype by Whitney of Rochester," meaning it is reproduced from a photograph. Here, and throughout the history of *Leslie's*, a photographer typically is named, whereas a sketch artist rarely is. The photographer has an identity as a technician, we surmise, whereas the sketch artist, as a journalist, was meant to be anonymous. The text goes on to recount how recent engineering projects, especially the construction of one-half mile of piers, have made Genesee a key port for Lake Ontario traffic:

> There is here a pleasant and thriving village, called 'Charlotte,' which is yearly increasing in importance, owing to its lake position and connection with Rochester by means of a Railroad, eight miles in length, and also to

the fact that, from this point the steamers, forming an international line, arrive and depart daily during navigation, for Toronto and other Canadian ports.

That's what all those pretty boats are up to! This text tells the reader what one would see if the illustration could be in color and in motion — that is, it amplifies the visual experience — but it also tells the reader what the picture means. It presents elements that could not be depicted no matter what tools were available.

Often the relationship between text and picture was reversed. In these cases, the picture amplifies aspects of the text, adding emphasis or emotion to what is already a full textual account. This is the rare case for the illustrated newspapers. Usually the paper was composed on the basis of what pictures became available; rarely, though notably in cases of monumental news such as an assassination, were illustrations found for a specific story. In the above example, the availability of an ambrotype of Genesee "suitable for engraving" drove the content, not any breaking news about Genesee.

No matter what the specific relationship of picture to text, the two elements were understood in the same way. Both were representations of real persons, places, and events, but neither was unmediated; both were authored, whether the author had a persona or not. The attraction of news depended on telling a good story, anchored in real events to be sure, but not merely reflecting them. Text and picture both were held to standards based on the facility with which they advanced a narrative.

The regime of illustrated news did not point to photographic realism or to any other notion of unmediated realism. Instead, it insisted on clarity and lucidity. The images were expected to be articulate, not independently, of course, because the typographic text was usually indispensable, but certainly when amplified or contextualized by accompanying verbal reportage. Photographic realism was irrelevant to this kind of storytelling, a conclusion supported by the fact that neither *Leslie's* nor *Harper's* highlighted the photographic aspect of visual reportage nearly as often as we expected. Engravings that are obviously done from photographs were usually not distinguished from others done from sketches. This blurring of lines occurred not because the technological limits of early photography stymied journalists. When the aim is to present a grand landscape upon which Human Ingenuity takes on Nature (the setting in imagery for many stories in text, to be discussed later), the long exposure times required for photography hardly represented a limitation. The artist's eye and hand were needed to help the text tell stories and make arguments and limn characters, and not just to transfer photographic images into newsprint.

GENRES OF ILLUSTRATION

Illustrated newspapers presupposed that their readers read daily newspapers. They therefore conceived of their own function as complementary. The daily newspaper would cover breaking news, allowing its reader to monitor the day's events. The illustrated newspaper, appearing weekly, would build on the literacy generated by the daily newspaper, and allow the reader to have a vicarious experience of distant and important people, places, and events. The *New York Tribune* would tell people what happened at Lincoln's inauguration, for instance. *Leslie's* would then give its readers a visual sense of what it was like to be there. In this way, the illustrated press was a form of travel literature — a popular form of nonfiction at the time illustrated newspapers were invented. Leslie himself acknowledged this in an editorial in 1873 ("Illustrated Journalism," August 23, quoted in Brown, 1993, p. 131). Noting that daily newspapers provided verbal descriptions of events, Leslie points out that these are visually vague — from such accounts "a hundred artists . . . will produce a hundred pictures each unlike the others." What his illustrated paper proposed was to provide an authentic visual image that fixed in the public mind *Leslie's* picture of the event. There was some sleight-of-hand in this argument, obscuring (while acknowledging) the artistry of illustrated news. Like all journalism, the project took its authority from events "out there." Illustrated news promised the sort of picture that one would have come away with had one actually been at the event — clear, with the force of memory. Readers could trust that the image actually represented the event because the artist had been physically present (even if only after the fact, as was often the case with breaking news). Illustrated journalism thus intended to intervene between readers and the world, and provide them with an artificial archive of memory images — a primitive form of total recall of the sort that scholars today ascribe to later visual media (Lury, 1998; Moeller, 1999).

The subjects of illustrations throughout the period we studied were the sorts of things that a sophisticated traveler might experience. We might denominate the subjects briefly as prominent people, the wonders of nature, the built environment, and noteworthy events. We might further divide the category of events into those of national political or military significance — the assassination of McKinley, or the battle of Bull Run — and those of more social interest — sporting events, for example. All of these categories represented "real" things. In addition, illustrations often presented images that were symbolic or iconographic. *Harper's* included the cartoons of Thomas Nast, as well as frequent illustrations for fictional material. (*Leslie's* carried serial novels in every issue through the bulk of its career, but these were almost never illustrated; *Leslie's* also carried few cartoons.) And both publications occasionally featured allegorical illustrations.

They conveyed this subject matter through a complicated arsenal of illustration techniques. We identified seven modes of illustration in the two illustrated papers, here listed roughly in the order of their importance over the period: sketches, drawings or "fine drawings," photographs, cartoons, editorial icons, maps, and technical drawings (see Table 4.1).

All of these modes appeared in editorial content and often tied to specific types of content. The sketch, for example, belonged to breaking news but also to fiction. Cartoons belonged to editorializing and entertainment. Advertising also employed many of these modes, but favored technical drawings for representing products and the more fully rendered drawings for representing scenes of the consumption, marketing, or manufacture of products. Of course, the tie was not as physical as it would become later. Illustration could appear anywhere without regard to the placement of the related text (see, for example, the illustration of a statue of Nathan Hale on p. 504 that refers to the story of its unveiling in *Harper's,* July 4, 1891, p. 494, and note that the story does not refer back to the illustration).

These various modes did not move in an evolutionary continuum from drawing to photography, as one might expect, but were used side by side in an array. The different techniques complemented each other; they did not colonize or displace each other until the end of this period, when photography finally displayed imperial tendencies. The course of change cannot be summarized as the emergence of photography or the development of photographic realism — that is too neat and proleptic a narrative. The things represented and the modes of representation shifted over time in a complicated pattern. Instead of a shift in technique alone, we discerned a shifting notion of subjectivity that accompanies a shifting notion of didacticism, along with a shifting notion of the relationship of the individual to the polity. At the outset, the regime of illustrated news showed prominent personages as public symbols, attending to the grandeur of institutions and the built environment on a ground of natural splendor. At the end, it showed people regardless of their position of authority as indexes of ordinary life, closely

TABLE 4.1. MODES OF ILLUSTRATION

Forms used in the illustrated newspapers, listed in the order of importance and described

Sketches   emphasizing irregular shading, deep shadow as from ink washes, and the position rather than the edges of forms; all loosely drawn at first from life or eyewitness accounts, and later from photographs, but containing signs of the human hand, such as smudging and scribbling

Drawings   (or "fine drawings") emphasizing precise tonal shading and perspective; drawn much tighter as a finished artistic work, with greater detail and surface finish that disguised overt evidence of the artist's hand

Photos   emphasizing fine detail in a limited range of gray tones, with shading in regular, repetitive patterns, all in a clean, mechanical rendering; at first reproduced as engravings, later as halftones

Cartoons   emphasizing outline rather than fill, which is limited to relatively small areas: showing human forms with the tendency to caricature

Editorial icons   emphasizing silhouette and shape, rather than outline or tonal value, giving the impression of woodcut and scratch-board techniques; project the allegorical and symbolic

Maps   emphasizing varying degrees of line, to show position, in plan; sometimes also tonal shading, to show what things look like, in elevation

Technical drawings   emphasizing outline and surface contour, rather than tonal shading and shadow; great detail at the points of human interface, such as knobs and handles

observed in a range of emotional expressions and fleeting gestures meant to reveal an interior landscape of thought and feeling.

BUILT VERSUS NATURAL ENVIRONMENTS

The built environment was one of the favorite themes of the first illustrated newspapers. This fits in with a sense of the mission of illustration to effect the virtual travel of middle-class readers. They could tour the great buildings of the world in the pages of *Harper's* and *Leslie's*. Early images emphasized the monumentality of human civilization (feats of engineering, architecture, and city planning), with people depicted as textures occupying the foreground like the grass growing around permanent structures. At first the structures seem to grow organically out of the natural landscape. In a travel story, "A Railroad Pleasure-Trip to the West," *Harper's* shows the growing city of

Cincinnati, Ohio. Cityscapes like this one (Figure 4.1) attest to the permanence of the built environment growing out toward equality with the overarching hills or surrounding waters. The simple quantities of space the two occupy in the picture plane reveal an interesting play that suggests a hope for growth (and ultimate dominance) by human constructions over the natural world.

Even great men were small in relation to the products of material culture. The emphasis on one or another was accomplished through techniques of composition, in which the elaborate vaults of a ceiling dominate the image showing men in Congress (*Harper's*, December 12, 1857, pp. 792–93). A dramatic example of this is Lincoln's inauguration picture, with the mass of humanity clearly dwarfed by the Capitol building and the flag, which symbolize the republic (March 16, 1861, pp. 168–69). Lincoln himself is smaller than the Capitol statuary and some of the closest spectators (a point we return to later).

A later moment of celebration for the built environment was the 1876 Philadelphia Centennial Exposition, or world's fair. Especially for *Leslie's*, whose proprietor was president of the exposition board of commissioners, this was an occasion for rhapsodic treatment of the progress of human control over the forces of nature. The narrative of progress was made to dovetail with the political commemoration that the exposition enacted: the career of U.S. representative democracy and the career of industrial progress intertwined. So in one issue, on July 22, 1876, the center spread features a grand Fourth of July procession, in which orderly crowds of people traverse an urban panorama — Union Square in New York City — while a later spread of illustrations features the Wilson Sewing Machine Co. of Chicago, Illinois (engravings of the corporate headquarters and the factory, done from photographs, and another engraving of the exhibit in Machinery Hall of the exposition, done from sketches). *Harper's* similarly emphasized the buildings (July 22, 1876, p. 593).

The power of nature emerges later in the nineteenth century and takes a place as the only equivalent of (and perhaps the superior to) these human monuments. From the initial tourist views of Cincinnati, Ohio; of Jefferson City, Missouri; and of other western towns, the imagery becomes more expansive. Consider, for example, later aerial perspectives, whose acts of consummate imagination show human constructions marking the face of nature. The railroad system of Boston (Figure 4.2) shows a vast landscape contained by the system of tracks. In this sense, maps become the conceptual tool of empire; they were a staple for military coverage as well as for stories on the western expansion.

The destructive power of nature over human construction comes to

CINCINNATI, OHIO.

FIGURE 4.1. A travel story shows the growing frontier city of Cincinnati, Ohio, from *Harper's*, July 4, 1857, p. 428.

FIGURE 4.2. A view of the railroad system of Boston shows the entire region subdued by the network of tracks, from *Harper's*, July 8, 1871, Supplement, pp. 636–7.

the fore in various disasters involving weather and ships and especially in coverage of the Great Chicago Fire. An artist takes the aerial view published in the previous week's issue, and obliterates much of the city in black billows of smoke interrupted by tongues of flame (*Harper's*, October 28, 1871, pp. 1008–9; cf. October 21, pp. 984–5). The text exclaims: "The pathetic sketch by Mr. Reinhart, printed on our front page, conveys a more graphic idea than can be expressed in words of the privations and sufferings endured . . ." (p. 1011).

A particularly revealing example of change over time in styles of illustration is the treatment of humans in physical activity and sports. Images of annual regattas were a regular feature of the illustrated press. Initially the mechanisms and objects dominate the action, with images of the sails against the ocean and sky. There are no participants, but spectators look on, and their depiction turns the occasion into a social and not a sporting event (see, for instance, the onlookers in *Harper's*, July 7, 1866, p. 420). In the *Leslie's* drawing, "Regatta of the New York Yacht Club" (Figure 4.3), the sails of the competing boats appear in the background, pictured against the cityscape, while in the foreground the shore is occupied by fashionably dressed ladies and gentlemen. The spectators appear in the exaggerated and stylized poses of painting, and the engraver highlights some elements — such as a pair of handsome, bonneted women — while leaving others only sketchily realized. In this case, the related text is devoted almost exclusively to a list of the boats and the times of their finishes (pp. 276–7).

These presentations of the spectators for sport continue (see *Harper's*, July 4, 1891, p. 492), but increasingly they are accompanied by presentations of the human body. For participants, sport moves from the action of man-made mechanism against the barriers of nature, delighting onlookers, and into another definition, in which the human body competes, and perhaps increasingly against not nature but other bodies. The change parallels the emergence of the notion of the body as a human motor, one of the originating metaphors of modernity (Rabinbach, 1990). In *Leslie's* 1896 coverage of a rowing team competition against Oxford in England (Figure 4.4), a series of photos of the rowing techniques of the various teams are interleaved with text to form a detailed commentary. Here the illustrations show men in action.

THE CIVIC GAZE

The evolving coverage of affairs like boat races indicates a more general shift in the way events were depicted. The change seems rooted in a reformula-

REGATTA OF THE NEW YORK YACHT CLUB JUNE 2D.—NEARING THE LIGHTSHIP.—SEE PAGE 275.

FIGURE 4.3. In a drawing of a sporting event, the sails of the racing yachts appear in the background, from *Leslie's*, July 8, 1871, p. 273.

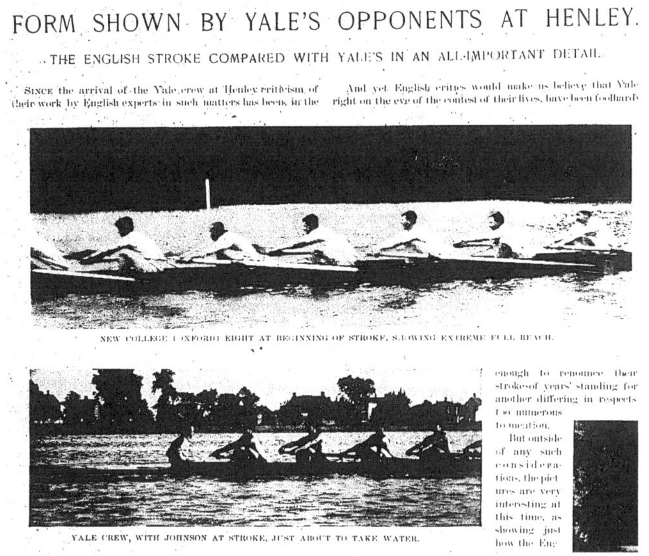

FORM SHOWN BY YALE'S OPPONENTS AT HENLEY.

THE ENGLISH STROKE COMPARED WITH YALE'S IN AN ALL-IMPORTANT DETAIL.

SINCE the arrival of the Yale crew at Henley criticism of their work by English experts in such matters has been in the

And yet English critics would make us believe that Yale right on the eve of the contest of their lives, have been foolhardy

NEW COLLEGE (OXFORD) EIGHT AT BEGINNING OF STROKE, SHOWING EXTREME FULL REACH.

YALE CREW, WITH JOHNSON AT STROKE, JUST ABOUT TO TAKE WATER.

enough to renounce their strokes of years' standing for another differing in respects too numerous to mention.

But outside of any such considerations, the pictures are very interesting at this time, as showing just how the Eng-

FIGURE 4.4. In coverage of a rowing team competition, a series of photos showing techniques interleaf with text, in a detail from *Leslie's*, July 9, 1896, p. 28.

tion of the subject position of the reader or viewer. Initially subjectivity takes the position of spectator. That is, images represent incidents as viewed by a citizen not directly involved but paying close attention at a distance. These most assuredly are not ordinary or common viewers but privileged ones, who look from among the ranks of better society upon (and who at times look down on their social inferiors in the middle ground separating them from) the great men and events being depicted (see, for example, *Harper's*, July 6, 1861, p. 426). Most often the faces clearly visible are of social peers, as examples from the coverage of the Civil War demonstrate. In the "Grand Review of General McDowell's Corps d'Armee, etc.," the soldiers stand in an ordered mass receding into deep perspective, while their leaders occupy the central ground on horseback (*Harper's*, July 6, 1861, pp. 424–5). The largest figures are the well-dressed onlookers in casual poses, some of them in admiring clutches around military officers, their faces turned toward the reader.

This privileged subjectivity was reinforced by the technique of composition. Sketch artists, acting like correspondents, composed images. They gathered visual impressions as they walked around an event, then used them to construct a composite scene. This scene would compend the various detailed images that the artist had sketched in such perambulations. In the case of depictions of groups of important men — for instance, a meeting of the U.S. Senate — recognizable faces seem to float on a flat surface of bodies and architectural details. Another example of this style of drawing (Figure 4.5), is a *Leslie's* two-page illustration of Garfield's inaugural ball.

This positioning of the subject as privileged and perambulatory was well suited to narrative illustration. In their depictions of events, the illustrated newspapers often combined sketches that were temporally adjacent into one illustration, allowing for the telescoping of sequential occurrences into a single, supposedly instantaneous depiction. *Leslie's* depicted Garfield's shooting, for instance, in a two-page illustration (Figure 4.6) that shows the look of surprise on Garfield's face as the bullet hit and before he collapsed, the look of concern on the faces of bystanders, and the apprehension of the assailant — a temporal range that would have covered about a minute of actual time and could never have been captured by a camera. This drawing was based on the sketch artists' interviews with people on the scene; the journalists themselves had not been present but arrived two hours after the shooting.

The position of subjectivity changed quite dramatically. By the turn of the century, subjectivity floats in the air around great events — a fly on the wall, not connected to any identifiable social or political subject. The emphasis has moved from a public (being those with the franchise) to a more generic "public view" available at closer quarters, revealing emotion in the moment and emphasizing the human face and body frozen in action or reaction. When *Leslie's* illustrated McKinley's assassination, the age of the photograph had arrived. Although it published dozens of photographs of McKinley in action, and of other figures associated with the administration, plus a haunting portrait of the assassin, Leon Czolgosz, behind bars, *Leslie's* made no attempt to illustrate the shooting itself. The nearest thing, a shot of the scene of the shooting, used an X to mark the spot where the deed was done. The viewers of these photographs could experience an emotional response to the depictions of human moments, but they could no longer read the president as a monumental personage or the image as a story unfolding before them, the citizenry as public witnesses to grand spectacle.

FROM PERSONAGE TO PERSON

Another dimension of the pictures shows the shift from personage to person best: the tenor or mood conveyed, most evidently in depictions of people.

FIGURE 4.5. Separate drawings of the scene and portraits of notables fuse (not entirely seamlessly) in an illustration of Garfield's inaugural ball, from *Leslie's,* March 19, 1881, pp. 52–3.

WASHINGTON, D. C.—THE ATTACK ON THE PRESIDENT'S LIFE—SCENE IN THE LADIES' ROOM OF THE BALTIMORE AND OHIO RAILROAD DEPOT—THE ARREST OF THE ASSASSIN.—FROM SKETCHES BY OUR SPECIAL ARTIST'S A. BERGHAUS, AND G. DURAN.

FIGURE 4.6. One composite illustration renders multiple moments, including Garfield's shooting, the reactions of bystanders, and the capturing of the assailant, from *Leslie's*, July 16, 1881, pp. 332–3.

128

Initially, each leader occupies the picture plane as a *personage,* that is, as a relatively fixed set of traits that spring from social class, race, position of power, physiognomy, style of dress, and personality. Illustrated journals appeared when notions like animal magnetism and phrenology were current. The vogue of illustrated journalism coincided with the age of Darwin. Common sense at that time affirmed the importance of genetics and physiognomy to character, and even race reformers like Frederick Douglass assumed without much questioning that there was a science to the relationship between race and behavior. Ordinary people, then, were usually depicted according to physiognomic stereotypes (for an extended discussion, see Brown, 1993, ch. 2, also see Lalvani, 1996). Ordinary people, however, were rarely if ever the subjects of portraiture; they appeared in crowd scenes, usually sketched, or they appeared as the appendages of machines and buildings. Portraiture was reserved for leaders, and to depict them as personages meant something more than mere racial or physiognomic characteristics.

The president and other political leaders (and their wives) were personages who moved into view but did not change; their poses remained stiff and their gestures, if any, theatrical signs. Again, this mode of depiction is not divorced from technique. Most portraits were engraved from photographs, which initially required that the subject maintain a fixed position for several seconds of exposure time. However, these facial expressions and poses were also stiff because the sitter and the photographer arranged them so: more casual poses were technically feasible and were used for lesser persons. Equally fixed were the accompanying texts, verbal descriptions of character, presenting a record of the personage's career and an account of his or her values, allegiances, and characteristics. Fixity was the point; the image was supposed to present the essence, the distilled character, of the personage. Even in sketch art, the brow, nose, and mole of Lincoln are as set as the faces of buildings presented elsewhere, as can be seen in "Presidents Buchanan and Lincoln Entering the Senate Chamber, etc." (*Harper's,* March 16, 1861, p. 165). Emotions are formulaic, like the masks of drama and comedy.

The fixity and materiality of the personage, even the character of great men, is quite alien to the photographic age. One index of this is a series of engravings following Garfield's death (Figure 4.7), rather gruesome depictions of his corpse being autopsied and embalmed. No matter how intrusive the camera eye may be said to have become, such illustrations — so intimate and seemingly unconnected to the public interest — are unthinkable today. They relate more closely to the medieval concept of power invested in the king's body. They could illustrate only something larger than any mere person. Indeed, ordinary people usually appeared relaxed and unposed (Figure

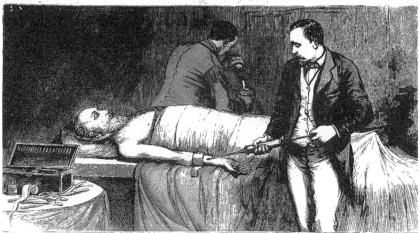

EMBALMING THE BODY OF THE DECEASED, ON THE MORNING OF SEPTEMBER 20TH.

FIGURE 4.7. "Enbalming the body . . ." is one of a series of grisly engravings showing Garfield's corpse being prepared for burial, from *Leslie's,* October 8, 1881, p. 85 (cf. p. 92).

4.8), while elsewhere men of substance took theatrical poses (see, e.g., Figure 4.3, on page 123).

By the turn of the nineteenth century, the mood had changed utterly, because now even great people were possessed of emotional lives that were fleeting and existed on a background that was no longer so clearly fixed and monumental. *Harper's* shows McKinley after his inauguration in portrait (Figure 4.9), not as the grand personage as in previous presidents' portraits, but in a private moment of reading and reflection. The era that produced Freud and Einstein, in which an invisible world came under the gaze of the new sciences, thus found cultural expression in the illustrated press.

Images meant for amusement or commentary did not follow the same course, remaining largely untouched by the realist ethos. The illustrations accompanying fiction consistently emphasized the characters in the stories as characters. Cartoons likewise always emphasized persons and did not shift from personage to emotional person, because they remained focused on the realm of satire. In *Harper's,* an 1861 cartoon called "A Dust-Storm in Broadway," showing two figures in vignette (March 16, p. 176), does not differ that greatly from the vignette in an untitled cartoon from 1896 (July 19, p. 696).

HARPER'S WEEKLY.

A JOURNAL OF CIVILIZATION

Vol. XV.—No. 774.]   NEW YORK, SATURDAY, OCTOBER 28, 1871.   [WITH A SUPPLEMENT. PRICE TEN CENTS.

Entered according to Act of Congress, in the Year 1871, by Harper & Brothers, in the Office of the Librarian of Congress, at Washington.

THE GREAT FIRE IN CHICAGO—GROUP OF REFUGEES IN THE STREET.—Drawn by C. S. Reinhart.—[See Page 1010.]

FIGURE 4.8. Ordinary people appear in informal poses, unlike the usual depiction of men of substance, who appear in theatrical poses, from *Harper's,* October 28, 1871, cover.

WILLIAM McKINLEY, PRESIDENT OF THE UNITED STATES

FIGURE 4.9. McKinley after his inauguration is depicted not as the grand personage but in private contemplation, from *Harper's*, March 9, 1901, p. 247.

THE MOMENT OF CHANGE

The year 1890 may be taken as a watershed, a moment of change in the practice of illustrated journalism, in much the same way as it marked a change in periodical literature more generally. By 1890, a new genre of middle-class mass-market periodicals, led by Edward Bok's *Ladies' Home Journal*, had embraced a realist ethos, preparing the way for the great muckraking journals founded in the next decade. Photography was, of course, the picturing tool most congenial to the realism of the new periodical literature. The landmark moment in the marriage of social realism, journalism, and photography was the publication of Jacob Riis's *How the Other Half Lives* in 1890.

The illustrated journals were caught up in these changes. In *Harper's* in 1891, people appear for the first time arrested in motion (Figure 4.10), usually larger than the monuments near them. Note the slicing off of the rider's horse in the foreground, in clear echo of the fleeting moment as originally visualized in the art of impressionism (such as Edgar Degas's *A Carriage at the Races* of 1873). By 1891, the stock regatta image is gone, replaced by an intimate view of people inside a boat watching the much smaller regatta in the distance. People are also the center of imagery meant to cover the inauguration of a cold-storage facility. Interestingly enough, these changes occur just when type and image begin to have a different, much more fluid interplay, with type wrapping around images (an effect that occurred much earlier in advertising). In 1896 the images of battle scenes finally begin to show people in action; no longer does the coverage focus on the physical objects of war, as it did during the Civil War.

Travel coverage is an especially valuable indicator of the shift to realism. More than any other kind of reporting, it shows how *we* — the *we* of elite, civic society — see the world, and in the 1890s what we usually see are faces, costume, and gestures from faraway places. This focus on surface representation and fleeting subjectivity is true of the new sports photos as well, where, as we have noted, the human figure — sometimes in motion — has replaced the equipment as the center of pictorial attention. Even so, sketch art and drawings continued to be used, both for purposes of explanation and as a way of reporting with a point of view. In short, a change has taken place, and it is dramatic, but the old continues to coexist with the new.

Coverage of McKinley's swearing-in ceremony in 1901 is emblematic of this shift. The illustrations are realistic, and his portrait (described earlier) is not the standard monumental pose but a moment of contemplation. A new regime of typography has also taken over, with hierarchical clarity in type (gray text, heads made darker or larger to pop out, distinctive display type — all elements of the emerging modern style). Even the illustration of the president-elect passing through the Capitol, despite the old way of showing the building and the bodies with portrait-heads stuck on them, has people in motion (*Harper's*, March 9, 1901, pp. 260–1). Although this is a drawing, it nevertheless clearly indicates that the goal of imagery has changed.

Meanwhile, in the photographs after 1890, there is an abandonment of

VOL. XXXV.—No. 1802.
Copyright, 1891, by Harper & Brothers
All Rights Reserved

NEW YORK, SATURDAY, JULY 4, 1891.

TEN CENTS A COPY.
INCLUDING SUPPLEMENT.

THE GRANT MONUMENT TO BE ERECTED IN CHICAGO.—Drawn by T. de Thulstrup.—[See Page 494.]

FIGURE 4.10. Images of people first appear arrested in motion and larger than the nearby monuments, from *Harper's,* July 4, 1891, cover.

134

the art of storytelling and a reversion to the lifeless portrait images of the 1860s. This had been the case throughout the introduction of photography in these publications. In Civil War engravings, those taken from photographs reproduce a very narrow range of grays, their interest lying primarily in their novelty, not in their content. In the *Leslie's* and *Harper's* coverage of the Great Chicago Fire, the stunning images are the sketches and drawings. One of these the editors tout (as quoted previously) — despite the presence of photographs on the adjacent page — for good reason. Consider two *Harper's* engravings in that week's issue (both titled "Chicago in Flames"), one from a sketch (well to the front of the magazine) and the other from a photograph. In these examples, the photograph (Figure 4.11a) emphasizes precise mechanically rendered details, producing a composition in which the flames seem incidental. The sketch (Figure 4.11b) pits the flames against the fleeing crowd in a V-shaped composition that uses the buildings in silhouette as the wedge between the two living flows. If the photos were always the more artless of the illustrations, then the era of press photography marked a triumph of artlessness, as well as the demise of an earlier notion of picture-enhanced storytelling. It is evident that the producers of illustrated journals had misgivings about this adventure in naïveté.

Editors understandably questioned and delayed the use of images that were clearly inferior in their narrative range. In the 1896 *Leslie's* example cited previously (Figure 4.4, page 125), the Yale rowing competition photos are once again not as lucid as drawings would be. The same is true in the coverage in *Harper's* of McKinley's death. The drawings capture candid moments, but the photographs have an unskillful, snapshot quality. There is a wonderful retrospective in the same issue (September 21, 1901, pp. 952–3), showing depictions of the deaths of Lincoln and Garfield. In the 1865 engravings, people appear as specks beneath the man-made ceiling and draperies as the casket lies in state, and again as mere texture covering the hills and beneath the trees at the burial. Even the more closely rendered citizens in the foregrounds are dwarfed by the monumental man-made and natural world. On the facing page, reproductions of the 1881 Garfield pictures are much the same, with arches, canopies, and hills dominating, but a candid quality is emerging, although tiny details are blurred in favor of focusing the scene. But the images of McKinley depend on photography and as a result revert to older forms, with small people dwarfed by large buildings. Instead of the old monumentality, the photograph reduces everything to minute, dull, and inarticulate detail.

CHICAGO IN FLAMES—BURNING OF THE CHAMBER OF COMMERCE.—[SEE PAGE 1010.]

FIGURE 4.11a

CHICAGO IN FLAMES—THE RUSH FOR LIFE OVER RANDOLPH-STREET BRIDGE.—FROM A SKETCH BY JOHN R. CHAPIN.—[SEE PAGE 1010.]

FIGURE 4.11b

CAUSES AND CONSEQUENCES

The new regime of realism embodied in photography is not a culmination of a process of development. A whole new regime fundamentally recast the role of illustration. After this revolution, photography, explained in the terms of realist ideology, became understood as the zenith in a long drive toward true fidelity, toward the capture of the real, unmediated by human artistry. This implied the simultaneous demotion of sketches and drawings, which in the twentieth century no longer get credited with authenticity and become instead mere art. The condition for the rise of photojournalism, then, was the rejection of the regime of illustrated journalism, with its obsolescent (and perhaps too republican) collusion in the explicit artistry of storytelling.

Why the disappearance of the regime of illustrated news? Its fate was not simply determined technologically, by the superiority of photographic reproduction. The historical evidence cannot support that interpretation. To a certain extent, the failure of illustrated journalism was brought about by changes in media ecology. It became increasingly difficult for the illustrated weeklies to compete with the daily press. In the 1890s, papers such as Pulitzer's *World* and Hearst's *Journal* and the *Chicago Daily News* carried illustrations like those in *Leslie's* but on a daily basis and more cheaply. Newspapers effectively absorbed the franchise of the illustrated weeklies. The scale of newspaper manufacturing made it simpler and more efficient in the 1890s for a daily to print a photo than to create an engraving from it, thereby justifying the investment in photographic technology.

The larger cultural environment also realigned the real with the technical, obscuring the centrality of human mediation. We reject the notion that photographs were simply inevitable because they were more truthful than engraved or woodcut illustrations. Nevertheless, along with new ideas about the unconscious and about the possibility that invisible physical forces could be somehow seen and measured by machinery, the rise of photo-as-realism did interfere with the ability of *Harper's* and *Leslie's* to proclaim the fidelity of their sketches. Illustrated journalism had a choice. It could adhere

FIGURE 4.11. Of two engravings that *Harper's* ran on October 28, 1871, both entitled "Chicago in Flames," the one from a photograph that appeared on the top of p. 1012 (Figure 4.11a), emphasizes mechanical detail, but the one from a sketch that ran near the front of the issue, on p. 1004 (Figure 4.11b), composes the flames and the crowd.

to art, or it could imitate its photographic competitors. Adhering to art had come to mean divorcing art from the notion of the real, and illustrated journalism since its founding had married artistry to authenticity. Trapped in this contradiction, the illustrated papers imitated their more powerful competitors and eventually failed.

What consequences flow from the loss of the regime of illustrated news? As a result of its marriage with realism, press photography embraced a notion of reportage that required the effacement of authorship. If photographers simply operate the machinery revealing reality, they cannot be held accountable for what the camera exposes. Unlike artists and authors, who hold responsibility for their vision of the world, photojournalists are witnesses and bystanders to events ostensibly beyond their control. Thus the realist regime effectively removed any clear lines of responsibility, hiding news work in what has been called the fog of documentary force.

Realism in art welcomed into the canon of imagery the depiction of ordinary life, as opposed to great scenes from history, mythology, and literature — a move that preceded the shift we observed in the illustrated papers. In ordinary parlance, the real, of course, is what exists no matter what folks think of it. This obdurate sense of realism springs from naturalizing conceptions of its rock-hard substantiality — as in Gustave Courbet's *The Stone Breakers* (1849) — as well as from its origins as the incursion of the exotic other, the ordinary (read: the lower classes) ruled inadmissible into the canon of greatness for centuries but thereby rendered fixed and immutable. Journalistic realism, at the receiving end, projects an audience that can neither blame journalists nor take effective action in the public sphere. Thus the regime of photojournalism contributes to a sense of powerlessness and fatalism in the face of intractable social problems (Barnhurst, 1994). Certainly a kind of visual intelligence disappears when readers forget about the authored artistry of pictures and succumb to what philosophers call naïve realism.

A more important loss was the disappearance of an implied model of citizenship. The new regime divides the reader or viewer from the world in ways normatively distinct from those of the old regime. Journalism driven by narrative carried along in its wake the reader, who anticipated sequence, emplotment, and resolution. Realist press photography trades away temporal narrative in exchange for other things, such as immediacy and emotional impact. Photojournalism is exciting and startling, but by doing more it may, in fact, do less to bring readers into the storytelling of news. Illustrated journalism projected the comforting belief that pictures can amount to a form of travel, annihilating time and space, and offered vistas of great occurrences and personages. This removed a form of social distance even while reinforcing the notion of greatness. Those illustrations of Garfield's autopsy and embalming brought him close to the reader, but also reinforced the idea of the president's body as a symbol of state. The viewer became an insider elevated to the citizen's vantage point. Seeing the president in ordinary moments of emotion obliterates both social distance and the civic posture, while calling for raw sentiment: he is not a hero but a friend. The camaraderie that such candid photographs imply is false, however; we can feel his pain but cannot touch him or ask him to touch us. The republican ethos of citizenship is thus lost.

CHAPTER 5

THE PRESIDENT IS DEAD

Pictures and Journalistic Values, 1881–1963

Unlike the illustrated weeklies invented to focus on the particular strengths of and enthusiasm for pictures, U.S. daily newspapers followed a long-standing tradition built on a foundation of text. In typographic journalism, pictures were interlopers. Their entry into daily news is usually retold as a battle to overcome technical barriers, in which photojournalism eventually emerges triumphant. Viewed from another perspective, the entry of pictures occurred in parallel with other shifts in form and meaning for news reporting and for newspapers. Although not usually viewed this way, the triumph of picture journalism also points to broader changes in U.S. culture.

In this chapter, we propose a close examination of news reports and pictures over time to trace the changes in text as photojournalism took control. Did reporters turn away from some tasks, such as detailed visual description, as photographs began to take over that function? To answer that question, this chapter explores the role of visual information from the perspectives of both text and pictures. It tracks the various trends and phases in the introduction of pictures and examines the mutual redefinition of picture and text as one aspect of the development of professional journalism.

NEWS PICTURES

The history of news pictures has had many retellings, principally by photojournalists themselves but also by art historians and critics and as a footnote to larger histories of photography. We have summarized these elsewhere

(Barnhurst, 1994). The most common account foregrounds technology, especially the slow progress of inventors and scientists toward two creations: the portable camera and the halftone. A small camera capable of working at high speed with ambient light became the prime tool of the photojournalist. The halftone, as a physical means to translate the continuous tones of the photograph into solid blacks and whites, became the tool of newspaper publishers. In this story, all roads lead to modern photojournalism. The visual side of the press goes largely ignored before the two technologies of pictures emerged; prephotographic visual reproduction is viewed as a stunted or embryonic stage of photojournalism.

A more sensitive telling identifies three periods. The first was typographic culture, in which newspaper editors misunderstood pictures as versions of paintings and resisted their entry into news pages (Hicks, 1952). To be reproduced, images first had to be remade by engravers, who inhabited a stratum below painters in the hierarchy of pictorial art.

The second period accompanied the emergence of the graphic newspapers, such as the *Mirror* in London, the *Daily Graphic* in New York City, and *ABC* in Madrid, around the turn of the century. Daily journalism of the era established a sort of apartheid, in which text and pictures coexisted as separate but (perhaps) equal content (Baynes, 1971). During this period halftones became a practical reality, although the pictures usually could capture no more than a single shot of static scenes or people in stiff poses (as the large cameras and explosive flashes required). For publication, pictures were corralled into their own neighborhoods by fences of frothy lines, borders, and decorations.

Modern photojournalism, the third period, emerged by the 1930s as pictures finally gained the status of content, fully integrated into the journalistic enterprise. Newspapers bragged about their pictures, the latest and newest, in the same way they trumpeted their news scoops. New cameras allowed candid photography to capture action and emotion, and these became the primary values of news pictures (Szarkowski, 1966). Photographs gained respect as seemingly objective documents, and editors would no longer permit retouching or decorating the image. Press photography acquired an aura of objectivity, as if it were unauthored.

We speculate that the development of news pictures had an impact on textual journalism. As photojournalists came to depict events in apparent immediacy, they may have deprived reporters of some authorial functions, freeing them for other tasks. This chapter seeks to explore the relationship between text and image. Did verbal descriptions of scenes, actors, and events decline as news photography emerged and acquired the capability to show places and persons in action? Did the forms and styles of presentation of pictures also evolve in relation to changes in verbal reporting?

News pictures developed in markets where two broad categories of daily newspapers reigned. Typically, pictures were introduced into a particular market by an innovative newspaper, often a start-up, often part of a chain (the Hearst newspapers were especially important). These pioneers were often more demotic in character than their older competitors. The competitors would respond to the invasion of the market by adopting some of the techniques of the invader and adjusting some of their other practices. They might, for example, begin to use pictures and then slowly adjust their reportage.

To observe both sides of journalism over time, we selected one from each category of daily newspaper: the inevitable *New York Times* and the more interesting *Chicago Daily News*. The *Times,* once even grayer, was notable for its completeness of coverage as well as for its stylistic conservatism. The *Daily News,* somewhat less voluminous, was more innovative, especially in illustrations. It was demotic, whereas the *Times* aimed for an elite readership. Any patterns of change common to these contrasting newspapers likely occurred elsewhere as well.

PRESIDENTIAL DEATHS

We chose to examine news coverage of presidential deaths in office, an opportune choice because such deaths occurred at regular intervals: James A. Garfield died in 1881, William McKinley in 1901, Warren G. Harding in 1922, Franklin D. Roosevelt (FDR) in 1944, and John F. Kennedy (JFK) in 1963. Unlike inaugurations and other political or state occasions that have already been studied (Schudson, 1982), presidential deaths come closer to a core definition of *news*: the unexpected and startling as against the routine.

By choosing to examine the deaths of presidents, we avoided the difficulty of considering the truthfulness and reliability of the reports. The Victorian newspaper paid little attention to sources, attribution, and verifiability. Reporters sometimes told stories as if they'd witnessed them when they had not. They did not hold modern notions of objectivity based on facts. But when a president dies, journalists confront events of great historical moment, much too important to treat lightly or with too much invention, regardless of their practices for less important stories.

The death of a sitting president, this biggest news imaginable, inspires the most comprehensive reporting by the best available correspondents and artists, who cover developments in the greatest possible detail. At the same time, the deaths occur on what might be described as a beat — and the most important one at that. The news media are sure to be there ahead of time, with their resources in place to cover events fully.

In another sense deaths in office might seem a counterintuitive example for examining change. The oldest, most senior staffers would also be the least likely to adopt new styles based on new definitions of reporting. Subject matter of such weight and seriousness would tend to dampen innovation, encouraging reporters to resort to the tried-and-true. As news events, the deaths provide the most understated, conservative estimate of the process of change.

Reporting on presidential deaths is highly comparable over a long period. Events follow a standard story line. Each death, whether by assassination or by natural causes, features similar characters: a grieving widow, a team of doctors, a cabinet, a successor. Each puts these characters through similar paces: the swearing in of the successor, an elaborate funeral, the journey to a final resting place. Each death motivates reflection on the past — the dead president's career and previous presidential deaths — as well as anticipation for changes in the personnel and policies of the federal government. Each offers the occasion for representing the people: the people in the business districts of cities, hearing and telling the news; the people bordering the streets to witness the funeral procession; the people lining the railroad tracks to watch the funeral train go by; the people pausing in the middle of their daily routines, stunned by grief, eager to touch greatness, morbid with desire to see the presidential corpse.

In sum, the death of a president is shocking and devastating. It happens at the epicenter of journalism, raising all sorts of fears and doubts about the security of society and the continuity of the nation. It demands a seriousness and thoroughness from journalists, who record each detail as faithfully as possible, fully conscious of their role in history. The event follows consistent dramatic tableaux. It is unmatched as a moment to contemplate the meanings, purposes, and definitions of journalism.

Our study focuses narrowly on the life of each story, from the first report of the president in danger to the "final resting place." In the case of Garfield, that was too long. Months of inept doctoring intervened between his shooting by disgruntled office-seeker Charles Guiteau and his actual death. Fortunately, as newspapers grew thicker and more fulsome, the story's life got briefer. FDR and JFK died suddenly and were buried quickly.

Even in a study limited to two newspapers over relatively short periods of time at roughly twenty-year intervals, a mountain of coverage remained. Our final analysis included more than a thousand pages of text and hundreds of images. We entered the material from two perspectives, through text and through images. Through the images, we examined the trajectory of form over the period and across the presentation of the emerging stock narrative of events. This perspective revealed the ways pictures interacted with the surrounding text. Through the text, we examined recurring visual motifs in the stories themselves. These motifs led back to the images as the relationship of text to pictures changed over time and between newspapers.

THE VERBAL REPORTS

At the outset, the variety of description and relation was all relatively lay. The reporter aimed to describe events so that readers could place themselves at the scene of the action. Reporters tended to notice things they imagined a reader would notice and find significant, and they tried to convey the emotional force of these significant details. Reports of presidential deaths emphasized dramaturgy, demeanor, and visual detail. Long narratives were frequently constructed like scenes from a contemporary novel, with extended descriptions of the faces and emotional states of key figures and lengthy catalogs of, say, the people present at a scene or the floral arrangements around the catafalque. One particular way of relating detail, *walking description,* gave an account of the visual impact of a scene as told by an observer strolling around it. This form was used, for instance, to describe the mourning scenes in city streets.

Over time, much of this initial repertoire fell into disuse. Detailed descriptions of floral arrangements became redundant in the age of the photograph, as did descriptions of the emotional state of the widow. Dramaturgy and walking description, along with the stance of the author, declined as well. These narrative modes did not advance the new role that reporters adopted.

For a time, breaking news became formless. In some *New York Times* reporting and much of the *Chicago Daily News* coverage by the turn of the century, breaking stories consisted simply of a pile of Associated Press (AP) bulletins arranged in reverse chronological order (Figure 5.1). One example concerning McKinley's "sinking spell" entered into the lore of the *Times*: Tommy Bracken, a night clerk working in the newsroom long after the reportorial staff had left the building, put together an overnight report from

FIGURE 5.1. In a stack of heads corresponding to a pile of wire service reports, arranged in reverse chronological order, note that the items do not cohere into a continuous narrative, from the *Chicago Daily News*, September 13, 1901, p. 1.

the wire service dispatches. "Tommy and the composing room and the pressroom crews worked until daylight, adding A.P. matter as fast as it came in. They put out three editions, all told, before sunup" (Berger, 1951, p. 141). The anecdote illustrates a relatively unedited manner of reporting breaking news, a raw updating that disappeared into television coverage in the 1960s, as newspapers yielded the function of alerting the people to TV.

Instead, reporters increasingly turned to news analysis. They probed the implications of events surrounding the death of the president, usually by means of quoting experts or officials. Such news often used the future tense and typically ran under a byline. The story engaged readers not by putting them at the scene of the action but by supplying the tools they needed to imagine the truth behind the facts, the structure underlying the action. The photographer took on other tasks: describing physical appearances, conveying emotional states, and supplying dramaturgy. These all share the present tense. Photography also took on much of the memory function of news, crystallizing current events — abbreviating them for memory — but also relating past events (merely by reprinting).

VISUAL MOTIFS

The process of change did not occur independently in either verbal or picture reporting but emerged from the interaction of the two. This process can best be seen by looking at recurring motifs that rely c⁻ conveying a visual impression. Reading images together with accompanying text made several motifs immediately apparent.

One was the cross-country train ride. The tradition began with Abraham Lincoln and continued for all but one of the deaths in office. Garfield and McKinley died after being shot and doctored in Washington, D.C., and Buffalo, New York, respectively. They had funerals in Washington, D.C., then went by train to northern Ohio for burial. Harding, also an Ohioan, carried the train ride to extremes. He died in San Francisco, trained to Washington in a cross-country marathon, and then went on to Ohio. All three took the same route from Washington across the mountains and mining country of West Virginia through the manufacturing region around Pittsburgh and into the rolling cornfields of Ohio. Roosevelt died in Warm Springs, Georgia, had a quick ceremony in Washington, D.C., and then took the train ride to New York State for burial in Hyde Park. Kennedy, breaking the tradition, flew directly to Washington for burial across the Potomac in Arlington.

Other common motifs were the grieving widow, the team of doctors, and the body of the president. The spouse of any president automatically becomes a public figure, but always of a particular kind: an icon of spousehood, required to live out the dominant notions of what a woman of her class ought to be. Especially at the point of death, the widows, while scrutinized and storified, have typically remained mute. By contrast, the team of doctors speaks with authority. Notably, the president's personal life, although always thickly populated, is represented in death by the lone figure of the wife, while his lonely body is represented through the multiple voices of a medical team. The doctors insert their expert vision into the public gaze, for which the president's corpse and his widow's grief are twinned objects.

The oath of office is yet another motif. In every case, the administration of the oath is dramatic, especially in contrast to the festive and elaborate ritual that typically accompanies the president's inauguration. The fact that the oath of office in such cases is an emergency measure makes it all the more exciting. Unlike the president's death, which must occur in presidential surroundings, the swearing in of his successor can happen anywhere. Teddy Roosevelt, who succeeded McKinley, was hiking in the Adirondacks when the news came and took the oath after a hurried trip to Buffalo. Calvin Coolidge, who succeeded Harding, was sworn in at the family farm in Vermont by his father, who happened to be a notary public.

A final motif might be called the news of the news. In each case, the story was itself another story: the way the news spread like a contagion through the public, the way the newspeople themselves covered it. Ironically, while the observer disappeared from the news report, the newspeople made of themselves yet another story. These motifs provide opportunities for divining what tasks the news in its various manifestations was expected to perform.

THE VIEW FROM THE GRASSY KNOLL

A stricken president is always a big story. In 1881 the shooting of Garfield was told as an eyewitness account, full of dramatic detail. Similarly in 1901, when anarchist Leon Czolgosz shot McKinley, an anonymous report in the *New York Times,* typical of the reporting style in that era, described the action after the shots rang out:

> There was an instant of almost complete silence, like the hush that follows a clap of thunder. The President stood stock still, a look of hesi-

tancy, almost of bewilderment, on his face. Then he retreated a step while a pallor began to steal over his features. The multitude seemed only partially aware that something serious had happened.

Then came a commotion. . . . ("President Shot at Buffalo Fair: How the Deed was Done," September 7, p. 1)

In this typical piece of reportage, the story is told like a story. It flows in a narrative from beginning to end, following the sequence of events, at least after a brief summary lead. It is, moreover, written with the same range of observation found in a novel. The reporter feels free to report authoritatively on the mental and emotional states not just of the crowd but of the president himself. To bolster his assessment, the reporter records the details of demeanor, such as McKinley's pallor, with the confidence of a novelist, on the one hand, and of an eyewitness, on the other. The fullness of detail in this four-column report implies at every point a reporter physically present and quite near the president at the moment of the shooting.

This kind of reporting has a clear task in mind: to re-create the scene of the crime for readers. Doing so is a subjective venture: the reporter offers an experience of events for the reader's appropriation. The report could not work if reporters limited themselves to verifiable facts and sourced observations. No way exists to verify "a look of hesitancy" or the multitude's merely partial awareness of the gravity of the moment. The reporter is telling the reader that this is what *the reporter* observed. Giving readers a compendium of others' observations would not have re-created the event for them, although a reporter might think that he or she was supplying the raw information to do so.

By contrast, the deathbed descriptions show the limitations of the fact-telling mode. Reporters actually witnessed none of the deaths, though they were always nearby, and always in a pack. Here, an anonymous eyewitness tells the story of Garfield's death:

Long Branch, Sept. 19. — At 10:35 o'clock, Dr. Boynton was sitting in the office of the Elberon Hotel talking with some newspaper men about the case. Suddenly a man's form appeared at the side-door and beckoned to the Doctor, who sprang to his feet and went outside. He returned in a minute and said, "The President is now sinking very rapidly." At the same time throwing up his hands with an expressive motion. A dispatch was instantly sent to the West End Hotel, and in less than a minute 40 carriages filled with newspaper correspondents were dashing through the darkness in the direction of the Elberon. Hardly had Dr. Boynton disappeared than Capt. Ingalls, the commander of the guard, ran across the lawn. . . . In the meantime the newspaper men had swarmed into the hotel. For a short period they were compelled to remain in suspense. Then, at 10:33, Mr. Warren Young, the Executive Secretary, appeared. . . . He was surrounded by the eager crowd, whom he scattered like chaff by the announcement, "It's all over. He is dead." Back at break neck pace the carriages flew over the shockingly bad road, and in less than five minutes a hundred dispatches were flashing the news to all parts of the country and the world. ("The First News of the Event: How the Newspaper Correspondents Got the Announcement," *New York Times,* September 20, 1881, p. 1)

The story available for first-hand report consists of little more than "they told us this and we ran there, then they told us that and we ran back here so we could tell you." Their physical absence did not prevent reporters from trying to re-create the deathbed scene with the same dramaturgy as a first-hand account, but they had to rely on others for details. The same *Times* correspondent described the death scene in a verbatim transcript of the doctors' press conference and followed up with a catalog of the people present, including an unattributed quotation from one of them:

> Mrs. Garfield sat in a chair shaking convulsively, and with tears pouring down her cheeks, but uttering no sound. After a while she arose, and taking hold of her dead husband's arm, smoothed it up and down. Poor little Mollie threw herself upon her father's shoulder on the other side of the bed and sobbed as if her heart would break. Everybody else was weeping slightly.

Unlike the stories of the initial attack, these deathbed scenes did not usually succeed as dramatic accounts for two reasons. Not being present at the time, the reporters had to piece together the event from various sources and therefore had trouble conveying the experience of a first-hand observer. In this example, the source, expected to describe everyone's actions, does give a fairly compelling rendition of two of the actors, Mrs. Garfield and her granddaughter Mollie, but leaves everyone else "weeping slightly." The *Chicago Daily News* report of Garfield's death ("It Is Ended: The Death-Bed," September 20, 1881, p. 1) used contrasting excerpts from the *Times* and the *New York Herald,* consisting primarily of a catalog of those present: family and cabinet members, servants and doctors. This is only the cast. When it comes time to set the cast in motion, all they do is watch.

Even physical presence may not have allowed the reporter to overcome the banality of these deaths. All death is banal, but these deathbed scenes were extraordinarily lacking in drama or meaning. The dying presidents themselves said nothing memorable. Garfield's dying words were "It hurts." McKinley, according to the *Daily News,* said, "Good-by all, good-by! It is God's way! His will be done!" before lapsing into incoherent mutterings, thought to be snatches of the hymn "Nearer My God to Thee" (Staff Correspondent, "Whole Nation in Grief," Extra, September 13, 1901, p. 1). Harding, who died while his wife was reading to him from an article full of praise for his leadership, uttered these unmemorable dying words: "That's good. Go on. Read some more." (Associated Press, "Death of President Comes Suddenly as Wife Reads to Him," *Daily News,* August 3, 1923, pp. 1, 3). FDR, who usually rose to the occasion, managed only "I have a terrific headache" (Associated Press, "Last Words: I Have a Terrific Headache," *New York Times,* April 13, 1944, p. 1).

In the Kennedy assassination, the photographic images of the shooting along with the endless simultaneous television coverage displaced the firsthand authored account. The moment of death was captured and conveyed first in photographs and then in stills from Abraham Zapruder's film. These canonical shots were perhaps not as lucid as one might suppose. They are not as graphic as the verbal descriptions of bystanders, for instance; nor are they as compelling as the photographic images of the various funeral observances to follow.

Moreover, while the photographic images displaced the verbal, they did not eliminate it. Both the *Times* and the *Daily News* reports of Kennedy's death were full of eyewitness accounts, by both reporters and bystanders. These carefully label the observer's subjectivity so as not to be authorial in the old sense. The single most gripping piece is an omniscient, objective account of the emergency-room action when the president was brought in. The reporter was not in the room and does not proclaim an authorial presence, but in the best tradition of objective narrative composes a story full of drama and action, mostly involving the furious and heroically competent efforts of the medical team, culminating in the tragic moment when the First Lady bids the body good-bye:

> Electrodes from the machine were attached to Mr. Kennedy's left arm. But the green pinpoint of light on the scope did not waver the tiniest fraction of an inch. . . .
>
> Mrs. Kennedy stood up. Two White House aides stood on either side of her. She walked toward the cart where her husband lay. The aides stayed outside.

At the foot of the cart, Mrs. Kennedy stopped. The President's feet were flush with the end of the cart, uncovered by the sheet that had been pulled over his face.

Mrs. Kennedy reached out, touched the right foot then bent down and kissed it. Then she walked along the cart and stood by the President's right shoulder. . . .

The priest turned the sheet down.

Mrs. Kennedy bent over and kissed her husband's right cheek. Then she picked up his right hand, held it in both of hers, and pressed it to her left cheek resting it on her husband's chest her head on it, as the priest intoned, in Latin, the last rites. (Bruce Miller, UPI, "Team of 15 Doctors Strove to Save Kennedy at the Hospital," *New York Times,* November 30, 1963, p. 10)

This story gets told so well because of the authority of doctors. Because the setting is medical, the aura of science provides an incontestable verity despite the story's absurdity: all the action is performed on a body that all of the doctors agreed had already died before they started. The medical setting also allowed the detachment necessary to convey such intimate details.

Doctors were present as interpreters or exhibitors of the president's corpse in all these deaths. In Garfield's case, the illness was so protracted that the team of doctors, quoted on a daily basis, became well known, almost like O. J. Simpson's legal team. So naturalized was the medical discourse that it comes as a shock to read a simple eyewitness description of the corpse:

The body is so greatly shrunken that artificial means had to be resorted to give the clothes an appearance of fitting. In addition to the natural shrinking from his illness, the operations connected with the autopsy has left the body in an even more emaciated state. A plaster cast was taken of his face yesterday, as well as of his right hand. In taking the cast of the hand it was somewhat discolored, so that his hand will not be seen. The effect of the oil used upon the face prior to taking the cast disfigured the features somewhat, and slightly altered the color of the face, so that the appearance is very much less natural. ("The Last View," from the *New York Evening Post,* in *Chicago Daily News,* September 21, 1881, p. 1)

The reports about McKinley's corpse also featured remarks on decomposition. By contrast, the presence of doctors allows one to forget that a corpse is gruesome. In the more recent deaths reporters refrained from describing the corpse. In Kennedy's case, reports repeatedly referred to his living appearance: his youth and vigor, his smile and stride. In the emergency-room story, JFK is just a body made available for observation by doctors. The real drama comes from the evocative description of the very much alive Jac-queline Kennedy hailing this body as a dead person.

THE GRIEVING WIDOW

In all the deaths, reporters paid unwholesome attention to the First Widow. They anatomized her grief for the edification of the nation, applying the same values over time. She underwent scrutiny for the proper balance of emotion and self-control. Expected to grieve, even to make a display of grief, she also had to maintain her composure and conduct the complicated fu-neral arrangements with skill and grace. Ida McKinley was too emotional. Weakened by a recent illness, under medical care, and thoroughly drugged, she could not fully participate in the funeral activities. Florence Harding, perhaps, and Eleanor Roosevelt, certainly, were too controlled. Roosevelt's obsequies were too abbreviated and Harding's too protracted for optimal grief. Anyone presiding over a four-thousand-mile funeral train ride with her husband's corpse would pace her grieving too slow. In the middle of a world war, FDR's corpse could not be gotten out of the way quickly enough. Jackie, though, was just right: the most beautiful, the most capable, and the most tragic of the widows.

Reporters' attention to decorum seems indecorous. In the earlier deaths, they sounded like gossips describing the widow — not common gossips but especially pompous and disingenuous ones. Here is the *Times* on Mrs. McKinley:

> For an hour this morning she remained watching the body. . . . Dur-ing that hour she gave herself up wholly to her grief. While the short fu-neral service was progressing in the Milburn home, although she remained in her room surrounded by members of the family and friends, her paroxysms of grief were pitiful, and her lamentations almost unceas-ing. . . .
>
> Secretary Cortelyou, when asked by a reporter for the *New York Times* this evening whether there was any truth in the oft-repeated statement that Mrs. McKinley had become to a certain extent mentally irresponsible through the administration of drugs and opiates, replied, "It is an infa-mous lie." (Special to the *New York Times*, "Mrs. McKinley's Grief Is Un-controllable," September 16, 1901, p. 2)

"And have you stopped beating your wife?" As intrusive as this scrutiny seems to today's reader, it was every bit as proper in its context as descriptions of floral arrangements and decomposing corpses, and arguably less intrusive than the camera's eye.

Later reports were less moralizing and less intimate. Although one can read between the lines that reporters considered Mrs. Roosevelt too cool a widow, they clearly did not scrutinize her grief in the same way they scrutinized Mrs. McKinley's. Similarly, Mrs. Kennedy was incessantly photographed and equally copiously described, with constant reference to her fortitude and dignity, and provided a conduit for the nation's grief. But the reporters did not gossip. The emergency-room story, quoted above, gives an account of her actions which is heart-rending yet does not pry into her psyche. It simply registers a series of ascertainable facts. The pictures were the gossips, but the pictures were not as eloquent.

There appear to be six categories of pictures or picture content associated with the widows. The first to emerge was the portrait. Mrs. McKinley was first represented in portrait in the *Chicago Daily News,* once (next to the president's portrait) when news broke of his being shot and then again (near her successor as First Lady) when he died (Figure 5.2). A portrait of Mrs. Harding appeared once in the *Times,* alongside Grace Coolidge on an interior page. The *Daily News* also published a close-up of her, taken from a file story rather than a formal medium shot in portrait style.

Portraits appear to have a conservative or traditional place as icons of the women in their official roles. Thus they disappeared from the *Daily News* but continued on in the *Times* until Mrs. Roosevelt, who on the first day of coverage appeared in a page-4 studio shot — this was the last formal portrait of a First Widow. Portraits thereafter gave way to action shots in news style, such as the close-up of Mrs. Kennedy at the moment she received the folded flag from the coffin (*New York Times,* November 25, 1963, p. 3).

A second, much more important, kind of imagery showed the First Lady accompanying her husband during the events leading up to his death. It first emerged during *Daily News* coverage of McKinley in the form of a September 13, 1901, sketch of his wife leaving the Milburn residence in Buffalo after he appeared to be surviving the assassination attempt. Such images became stock coverage with the death of Harding. His wife appeared in the Rotogravure section of the *Times* on August 5, 1923, in half a dozen shots of their trip to Alaska, the strain of which was blamed for his falling ill (Figure 5.3). The *Daily News* also ran two of the shots on August 3. It was by far the most extensive visual representation of the First Lady in any of the deaths until Kennedy's, when his wife appeared again and again in pictures of the limousine just before and after he was shot. A first wave

FIGURE 5.2. Ida McKinley appears in portrait, from the *Chicago Daily News,* September 14, 1901, p. 2.

of these came from the wire services, a second wave came from the snapshots bystanders took, and a third wave came from the home movies acquired by *Life* magazine. A scattering of pictures also recorded her at a series of political events earlier the same day, in each case smiling with her husband or others.

The third kind of First Lady image illustrated stories of the presidents' political lives. Mrs. Harding appeared in shots with her husband campaigning as a candidate and also arriving at the Executive Mansion after the inauguration (*New York Times,* August 3, 1923, p. 3). The *Daily News* showed Mrs. Roosevelt in a family shot as they traveled to Chicago, where FDR would accept his party's nomination (Figure 5.4). Mrs. Kennedy appeared in a *Times* portrait of JFK with his parents after winning election. She also

FIGURE 5.3. Photos of Florence Harding with President Harding on a trip to Alaska, from the *New York Times,* August 5, 1923, appeared in the rotogravure section.

BOUND FOR CHICAGO TO ACCEPT NOMINATION — Mr. Roosevelt and
members of his family flew to Chicago when he accepted nomination for presidency
in 1932. Standing beside the then governor of New York are (left to right) Elliott
Roosevelt, Mrs. Eleanor Roosevelt and John S. Roosevelt. In the center is Bobby
Baker, who came to say good-by. (Associated Press Wirephoto.)

FIGURE 5.4. Eleanor Roosevelt appears on a campaign trip with Franklin, from
the *Chicago Daily News,* April 13, 1945, p. 5.

appeared in a file picture of her husband's swearing in. Such pictures participated in the general move toward narrative in photojournalism, with the
wives playing the role of minor characters or props in stories about a rising
political star.

The fourth and most important pictorial coverage of the widow
showed her during the various funeral rituals. This type of picture first ran in
the *Times* coverage of Harding's burial in Ohio and provided the only current shot of Mrs. Roosevelt in either newspaper. The coverage of Mrs.
Kennedy began as she accompanied the coffin to Washington. The *Times*
showed her with the Johnsons; then boarding the hearse, her stockings still
stained with blood; and finally with Robert Kennedy — all on the first day
of coverage. In the *Daily News,* such images began when she appeared on
Sunday, first accompanying her children outside the White House (Figure
5.5), and then kneeling at the casket in the Capitol Rotunda (from normal
and bird's-eye views). The *Times* showed these images as well as pictures of

FIGURE 5.5. Jacqueline Kennedy is shown with her family during mourning in a photograph from the National Archives and Records Administration.

her with her children during the eulogy and later upon their leaving the Capitol. The Monday funeral services and burial at Arlington saw her in various views in both newspapers, entering and leaving the cathedral and standing at the graveside. The newspapers repeated each other, relying on images from wire services, and the *Daily News* repeated the image of her kneeling at the coffin — the first from United Press International (UPI), the second from the AP.

The extent of coverage suggests the growing reliance on pictures for describing the grieving widow. The space given over to these images, which had already been seen in other papers, on television, and even in the newspaper's own pages, shows how central to the narrative they were considered. They also suggest that the invasive curiosity characterizing earlier reports in the text eventually got transferred into pictures. Photojournalists in their roles as paparazzi could capture every moment of Jackie's grief, every gesture and facial expression, seemingly without responsibility. The picture itself swallowed up any responsibility for humane treatment or respect for privacy.

Another, less important, type of image of the widow illustrated the personal life of the deceased president. This started late, with an image of Mrs. Roosevelt at her wedding, which ran on page 5 the first day of the *Times* coverage in a group of pictures illustrating FDR's life. In the case of Mrs. Kennedy, both newspapers showed pictures of her on her wedding day. Both also published a more recent shot of her and the family at Easter. (These follow a longer tradition of showing the president in various intimate moments, with children or a family dog, for example.)

The sixth, and final, type of image showed the widow engaged in the political life of her husband's successor. These appeared only in the case of Mrs. Kennedy, who figured prominently in the pictures both newspapers ran of Lyndon B. Johnson swearing the oath of office in the airplane on the Dallas tarmac (see Figure 5.12, p. 172).

In general, then, the First Widow emerged slowly, first as an icon in portrait but quickly as an actor, present and witnessing the events leading up to her husband's death and then, most prominently and extensively, as the image of grieving. Pictorially, that role did not take on its full importance until the assassination of Kennedy.

WHEN LILACS LAST

The funeral sequence following the president's death is always a journey through a national landscape. Usually it has been a physical journey through a geographical mosaic. In Kennedy's case, there was no long train ride; still, the mosaic was represented as a kind of metaphorical journey. Lining the route are the people. The funeral journey always calls for descriptions and depictions of the variety of people that, although increasingly divided by race, class, region, age, religion, and political persuasion, are united now by grief into one People.

In a sense, the reporting of a president's death was for a century an extended gloss on Walt Whitman's "When Lilacs Last in the Dooryard Bloom'd," written on the occasion of Lincoln's death. Here he depicts the breaking of the news:

Now while I sat in the day and look'd forth,
In the close of the day with its light and the fields of spring, and the farmers
     preparing their crops,

In the large unconscious scenery of my land with its lakes and forests,
In the heavenly aerial beauty, (after the perturb'd winds and the storms,)
Under the arching heavens of the afternoon swift passing, and the voices of
    children and women,
The many-moving sea-tides, and I saw the ships how they sail'd,
And the summer approaching with richness, and the fields all busy with labor,
And the infinite separate houses, how they all went on, each with its meals and
    minutia of daily usages,
And the streets how their throbbings throbb'd, and the cities pent — lo, then
    and there,
Falling upon them all and among them all, enveloping me with the rest,
Appear'd the cloud, appear'd the long black trail,
And I knew death, its thought, and the sacred knowledge of death.

Whitman begins and ends with the observer. In between, he builds a vast and varied landscape, a large and disparate social world, and a booming, throbbing economy — a naked nation with millions of stories now all interrupted by a cloud of death.

The same ingredients played in all the verbal descriptions of the presidential deaths. First, the initial news, striking like a thunderbolt, interrupts daily activity and hails everyone into the same story. With Garfield's and McKinley's deaths, newspapers were the prime media of diffusion. It was the custom for daily newspapers to maintain streetside bulletin boards where they could post the latest news. In the case of breaking news, street vendors hawked issue after updated issue as extra editions. The following example from the *Times* places the newspaper itself at center stage when describing news of McKinley's death:

> [news of the shooting] was duplicated on the bulletin board of the *New York Times*, and a few moments later on the boards of every journal on Newspaper Row. The casual passer-by glanced at it, stopped, rubbed his or her eyes, and read again. After that, like the shifting grains of sand in an eddying stream, the crowd gathered along Park Row . . . , and many hundreds hurried off to tell it to their fellows. . . .
>
> A little later and the great down-town buildings began to empty their hordes of workers for the day, and then City Hall Square became a great sea of upturned faces, shifting and eddying in a struggle to get nearer the bulletin boards. . . . ("How the News Was Received in New York," *New York Times*, September 7, 1901, p. 2)

Here the faces are all the same, although the anonymous reporter does note women in the crowds. They flow like water: a sea of faces, an eddying stream.

But they are faces — not until the Kennedy death did we find the crowds described as ants.

Newspapers at first positioned themselves as one with the people. Just as the people mourned and wore black, so too did newspapers. With Garfield, the only visual evidence of grief was the column rules turned, so that the back side of the lead castings printed wide vertical bands. These appeared only once in the *Daily News* (Figure 5.6) and twice in the *Times,* when he died and when he was buried. The *Times* also composed one portion of text, the order of the funeral procession, in the shape of an urn. All these were particular or local expressions, as when an individual decided to wear a black armband or a company draped its storefront in black.

McKinley's death saw a change in the turned rules. They appeared only on the first day in the *Times* and not at all in the *Daily News,* when they were replaced by other signs of mourning. At the *Times,* the heavy rules shifted to the page edges, becoming a thick border with rounded corners that ran for six consecutive days. The *Daily News* turned to decoration, showing the deceased surrounded by elaborately drawn frames carrying representations of such objects as black ribbons for grief, laurels that might symbolize either divine selection or victory (Figure 5.7), and federal eagles in a particularly warlike rendition, perhaps evoking the Spanish-American War (see September 18, 1901, p. 1).

These signs slowly disappeared through the following presidential deaths. The *Daily News* used turned rules only on the day of Harding's death, and employed none of the decorative symbols after McKinley. The *Times* likewise used turned rules throughout the edition announcing Harding's death. Since the time of Roosevelt, the heavy borders appeared, if at all, only surrounding the deceased's portrait. Instead, advertisers picked up the custom after Roosevelt died, some of them enclosing their space in the *Times* in heavy mourning rules. A few included an In Memoriam message, but many announced that the store would close on the official day of mourning designated by presidential proclamation. The custom persisted into the Kennedy era, although not universally. Many advertisements running next to coverage of Roosevelt's death announced their cheery spring fashions and offers. The Kennedy coverage ran with similar advertising geared to the holidays. This sort of juxtaposition had always existed, but in the emerging social map of the modern newspaper it provided a jarring reminder of the older form of news, with its unrelated elements jostling for space.

Over time, descriptions of the initial spread of the news changed with the media of diffusion. News of Harding's death was the first heard by radio,

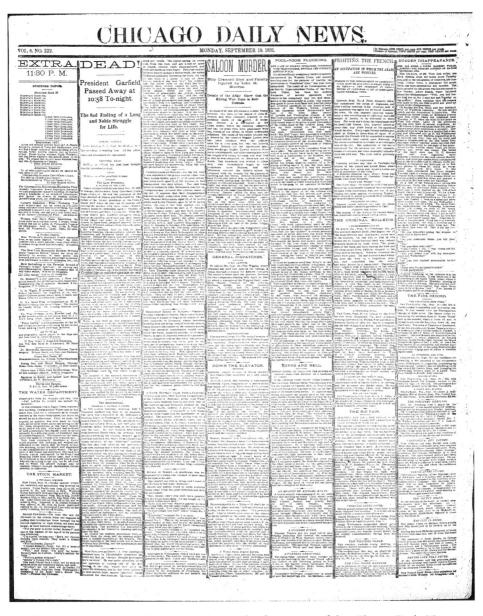

wing to a slight illness, but seemed in | eral years I went to Chicago, where I re- | and wanted to meet me. So I was then in- | afternoon arrested three men suspected of

FIGURE 5.7. President and Mrs. McKinley's portraits appeared with an ornate border in the *Chicago Daily News,* September 7, 1901, p. 1.

and news of the Kennedy assassination was the first via television. With each new medium, the spontaneous crowds of the era of contagious diffusion diminished further. In 1963 people learned of the assassination in a variety of private and semiprivate settings: in their homes and cars, in their offices and schoolrooms. This still left many nonspontaneous occasions for the people to assemble as spectators before the great national drama of mourning. Initially such gatherings were depicted as decentralized, with the rites of mourning occurring all over. With Garfield's assassination, major newspapers carried reports from every city in the nation. Over time that changed into a national audience watching events in Washington and perhaps in one or two secondary locations, and the grief of leading men replaced public expressions of mourning.

After Garfield's and McKinley's deaths, cities literally draped themselves in black, making a visible display of mourning. The black banners on buildings were foregrounded in verbal descriptions, through the technique of walking description. Here is how the *Daily News* described Canton, Ohio, on the eve of McKinley's burial:

> In Tuscarawas Street, from one end to the other, business houses are hung heavy with crape and at intervals huge arches, draped and festooned in mourning colors, span the route of the procession. . . .
>
> One of the arches is in from of the Canton high school. . . . The school is draped and in every window is a black-boarded portrait of the late president. In this thoroughfare, too, are two large churches, one of which was regularly attended by Maj. McKinley. . . . At each corner of the edifice and above the big cathedral are broad draperies deftly looped, each bearing a large white rosette. (Staff Correspondent, "Mourn in Home City," September 18, 1901, p. 1)

In walking description, a visible field is set in motion by the observer, who wanders around gathering impressions. This manner of reporting had a coherent and compelling visual impact. Engravings from photography do not really accomplish the same thing. Photographs of draped buildings, especially in a black-and-white halftone reproduction, have little immediacy. Sketches can do better, by both highlighting the significant (and not necessarily simultaneous) details and posing figures in didactic positions — marveling at the billowing crepe, for instance, in the engraving that accompanied the foregoing excerpt ("From a sketch made by a staff artist for *The Daily News*," p. 2), or striking exaggerated postures with cartoon-like facial expressions, as in "All Chicago Mourns" (*Daily News,* September 14, 1901, p. 2).

Over time, the mourning came to be depicted photographically, and symbols of mourning such as wreaths and floral arrangements became frequent subjects. For Harding's death, the *Daily News* showed a floral arrangement along with a shot of a draped doorway (August 4, 1923, p. 3). Two days later a wreath being sent by the city of Chicago got its own portrait, flanked by inset mug shots of the mayor and the commissioner who would convey it to Washington (Figure 5.8). A *Daily News* picture during observances for Roosevelt showed flower arrangements piled around the casket (April 14, 1945, p. 8), just as during the Harding rituals.

These representations of grief eventually disappeared. No draped facades or doorways appeared prominently in photographs after FDR's death, which marked the last notable appearance of floral arrangements. In the Kennedy coverage, neither of these signs of mourning played a significant role. They appeared instead only as minor details in the background.

THE DAILY NEWS, MONDAY, AU

BURST
CORTEGE

t 7 A. M.;
Likely to
s Away,

ing the passage
train through
s of thousands
ke posts along
'o render silent
ecutive of the

ately ten hours
due, dozens of
vantage points
hen the cloud-
rning drenched
Pekin. Weath-
red that similar
intensity, might
the day.
n was so severe
uthern sections
dequate and in
r ran curb to
ns to wade in
of water.
s Sounded.
ounded in quick
ig summer rain
basements and
vestigating with
'ound a wet and
ure penetrating

d 37th street,
In low, half a
heavily deluged
several thousand
r the district on
Prairie avenue

Sufferer,
nel, always a

THE CITY'S FLORAL TRIBUTE TO DEPARTED CHIEF OF STATE

ACTING MAYOR MARTIN J. O'BRIEN (UPPER LEFT) AND COM-
MISSIONER A. A. SPRAGUE, WHO WILL PLACE WREATH ON
FUNERAL TRAIN; SCENE IN FLORISTS' ESTABLISHMENT AS
J. A. CRAIG FINISHED EMBLEM OF WHITE FLOWERS.
[By a staff photographer of The Daily News.]

HARDING TRAIN ARRIVES

tribute to a great personality," said Mr.
Shedd."
Churches all over the city and sub-

"GREY TOWE
STIR U. (

New Anonymor
pery with Atta
pus Fi

At the Universit
dents, alumni and
members are engag
trying to identify th
characters presented
"Grey Towers"
novel published this
book concern. It pr
expose, done from
University of Chica
author, who is a forr
lish at the Midway s
her innuendoes, alleg
at her former colleag
Disguises are very
barbed references are
at campus personal
anonymous author
campus puddle with
And the splash she h
from comment in uni
already been prodigi

Satirizes Cam
In what has bee
highly disgraceful n
has presented malic
at least twenty uni
personalities. No on
president to junior l
those satirized are I
Linn, Dear Edith Fo
M. Lovett, Former
Dean Marion Talbot
Robertson,
Many slight tidbits
being quoted from
around the campus.

FIGURE 5.8. Chicago contributed to the floral arrangements for Harding's funeral, from the *Chicago Daily News,* August 6, 1923, p. 3.

Photos, although in some ways better than words for depicting grief, make
poor substitutes for many of the other standard visual images in reporting.
Photos cannot do walking description, for example. What photographs lack
is a moving locus of subjectivity.

The occasion for walking description became less compelling over
time, as newsworthy mourning was redefined. In the early deaths it was decentralized, and the reaction of the people was the news. The local character
of even national events gave impetus to walking description. News slowly
abandoned the local definition of political life in favor of larger domains.
Gradually, mourning became defined by the official statements of prominent men, clustered at first in the nation's capital, then later in the capitals of
the world.

Increasingly, grief when a U.S. chief executive died in office became
internationalized. The deaths of Garfield and McKinley, especially, but also
of Harding, inspired local stories and story angles with the pictorial coverage

limited almost entirely to places such as Buffalo and Canton. The rise of
U.S. international power made the event a worldwide story, but the availability of photographs may also have held sway. Plenty of international responses appeared in the earlier textual coverage, but these moved into the
pictures only after Roosevelt died. The *Times* showed three shots in a representative cluster: Churchill in London, several gendarmes in Paris, and a
some "Filipino residents" gathered around a newspaper front page showing
the news (April 14, 1945, p. 3).

The mourners who merit detailed pictures have always been important
people, dignitaries usually shown in full-length images (long shots) upon
their arrival or during their march in procession, but sometimes shown in
closer images from the waist up, with more facial detail (medium shots).
Such imagery began in *Daily News* sketch art after McKinley died. Senators
and cabinet members dominated the early pictures, but more international
dignitaries appeared in pictures with each successive death in office.

The role grew for the military as intermediary in the public grief. An
honor guard first appeared surrounding the catafalque in *Daily News*
sketches of McKinley's rites (Figure 5.9). The *Times* did the same thing photographically in coverage of Harding. The presence of the military became a
dominant theme in pictures of Roosevelt. An honor guard and the pallbear-
ers from military ranks figure among the multiplying signs of the president's
role as commander-in-chief. The most notable sign, a riderless horse, first
appeared in news coverage when Roosevelt died during wartime. This
symbol (dating from the era of Genghis Khan, the newspapers said) com-
memorated the loss of a leader in battle. The horse (at one time killed and
buried, according to news accounts, to accompany the fallen leader into the
afterlife) was led riderless after the bier. Its stirrups carried the boots, turned
backward, of the dead man, and his saber pierced the saddle. The symbolism
made sense to reporters during World War II, and perhaps the mood of gar-
risoned cold war encouraged similar military imagery during the Kennedy
funeral.

The way they deciphered this arcane historical knowledge also highlights the growing tendency of reporters to act as interpreters. The reliance
on the military as the intermediary for public grieving arose as other aspects
of the content shifted away from the individual and toward institutions,
groups, officials of every sort, and expert sources. These groupings in themselves provide a sort of interpretation, in the case of presidential deaths suggesting a nation fortified not only against grief but also against the danger
grief represents to the continuity of the state.

Pictures helped forward the move toward symbolic groupings. The

oy-
nt?
on-
: to
:ton
ient
.ed
the
en-

the
isul
an
illy
rith
ma
ted
sia.
ier.
im-
t I
few
iat-

ble
ias
a
ur-
nat
us-
itic
:an
iys
vas
me
ent
out
ier
ipy
a
ate
ent
ent
ing
St.
out
ree
ily
id-
iok
ind

les
of
uld
is-
ier
ur-
iey
ias
iol.
of
us-

od,
ian
rn-
all
;ht

do
is-
gh
ell
ny
en
ad

p-
kt,

---

sion it was decided that a voluntary subscription should be taken up. Just $3.57
was found in the hat after the meeting,
and this was forwarded to Emma Goldman.

The citizens of Elgin are indignant, and
to-day a committee waited upon all the Elgin bakeries and demanded the discharge
of those who had contributed to the Emma
Goldman "defense fund" upon penalty of
systematic boycott.

Hurt by Gas Explosion.

As the result of an explosion of coal gas
that had accumulated between the end of a
boiler and an outer covering of brick in the

Canton, O., probably will remain at home.
Hurried meetings are being held to-day to
arrive at decisions upon that point. Owing to the present overcrowded condition
of Canton the citizens of that place have
protested to the various railways entering
there against carrying any more outsiders
within their gates.

That protest has been heeded by the
roads. Notices from the Central Passenger association have been sent to the various bodies that had asked for special trains
on which to make the trip. The notices
state that all special rates will be re-
fused and give the explanation.

Notice to the public of the attitude of the

Senator Clark said to-day that he re-
gretted that he was unable to get to Washington in time to attend the ceremonies
there. He was in Salt Lake City at the time
of the assassination and then hearing the
president would recover did not learn of his
death until he reached Butte. Said the senator:

"I was a great admirer of President Mc-
Kinley, of his character, gentleness and af-
fectionate characteristics. He was to my
mind a man of the most marked ability and
his loss is to be greatly deplored. When the
senate convenes I look for the enactment of
legislation that will at least have for its
object the suppression of the anarchists.
They are, it seems to me, allowed too much
freedom of expression. While I believe in
the utmost freedom of speech, something
will have to be done to curb this class. The
immigration laws of the country should be
changed and restricted so that all Europe
cannot use the United States as a dumping
ground for its criminals. I believe that
President Roosevelt will give an admirable
administration and I am certain that he will
be strong to a marked degree in the west."

WOULD ERECT MEMORIAL ARCH.

**A. H. Revell Suggests a Permanent
Monument to the Late President.**

Erection of a memorial arch at Washington, D. C., to honor the memory of President McKinley has been proposed by A. H.

Hearse bearing the dead president's body to the funeral train at Buffalo.
Scene in front of the Milburn residence, Buffalo, when President McKinley's body was removed.
REMOVAL OF PRESIDENT M'KINLEY'S BODY FROM BUFFALO.
[From photographs taken on Monday, Sept. 16, by Oscar A. Simon & Bro. for The Daily News.]

basement of the Illinois Central railway station at Van Buren street to-day, Nels Olson,
janitor at the station, was severely burned and

railways upon the subject was indicated in
a letter from the Central Passenger association sent out for publication and reading:

Revell and has met the approval of many
citizens with whom the project has been
discussed. At an informal gathering yes-

FIGURE 5.9. The military has a presence at McKinley's rites, from the *Chicago Daily News,* September 17, 1901, p. 1.

166

public itself appeared in crowds almost exclusively at first. The *Daily News* showed them in Buffalo as McKinley's body was removed to Washington: the masses, the streetscape, the military officiating (September 17, 1901, p. 4). Crowds (Figure 5.10) appeared in Washington at the Rotunda and during the procession, and finally at the cemetery. The *Times* picked up this approach later, as it covered Harding, showing crowds in Ohio and Washington (August 11, 1923, p. 2), as well as along the train route (August 12, pp. 3–4), a scene that also appeared in the *Daily News*. With the death of Roosevelt, the *Times* began to show a representative mix of crowds. In one cluster of four shots, crowds that gathered at Warm Springs, Georgia, and Hyde Park, New York, stood for geographies. Crowds in local coverage likewise represented places. In New York City, where Uptown and Downtown, East Side and West Side, differ in the social geography, the *Times* selected various groups in sundry locations, such as a memorial service on Seventh Avenue. The *Daily News* showed some of the same wire service crowd scenes, along with the usual throngs at the Capitol and along Constitution Avenue in Washington. Such shots continued without much change in the Kennedy coverage.

The images of citizens mourning document the process. Although most mourning was accomplished through medium and long shots of dignitaries (setting aside for now the special case of the widow), medium and close shots of ordinary people emerged slowly over the period, beginning with coverage of Roosevelt. Newspapers sought to illustrate how the masses felt the death personally, and so besides showing mourning acts en masse, they began choosing emblematic examples of the personal loss. In the *Daily News* these examples took on two forms. The first pictured a group of college students, with each individual fully identified in the caption and with each face clearly visible (April 13, 1945, p. 9). This form of representation, emphasizing the personal identity and grief of ordinary citizens, occurred only with the death of Roosevelt. A second form hid the identity of the emblematic individuals. In the next day's coverage, after showing the crowds around the Capitol, the *Daily News* ran a medium shot of several women from the crowd (Figure 5.11). Of the two clearly visible, one covers her face with her hand, and the other wears an engulfing hat. The caption did not identify either beyond the phrase "women weep openly" and a reference to the crowd. This kind of generalizing of personal grief became the norm for pictures of ordinary mourners.

The *Times* did not pick up the practice until Kennedy's death. On the first day of coverage, it showed a close-up of "a woman" mourning, her hand over her face, with no accompanying identification (November 24,

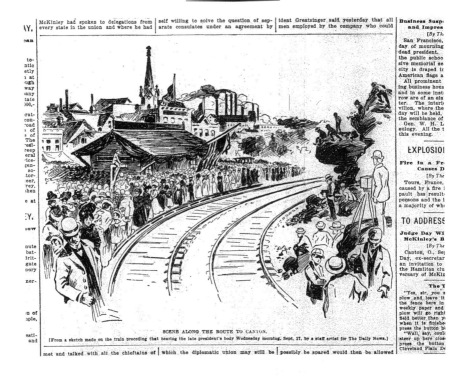

FIGURE 5.10. The crowds appear along the route of McKinley's funeral train, from the *Chicago Daily News,* September 19, 1901, p. 4.

1963, p. 5). On the second day it showed a Harvard student, weeping into his hands, on the steps before a crowd leaving the campus memorial service (p. 11). In subsequent coverage, the *Times* showed medium shots of commuters, of black children, of nuns, and of Catholic boys — all with emblematic expressions and gestures of grieving, but none identified beyond the group affiliation. The *Daily News* took the form even further, running a stack of seven pictures, all uncaptioned — mostly women with their hands over their faces or comforting one another. The full column of images formed a chimney of grief bearing the headline "And his people wept . . ." In early coverage of presidential deaths, the text described men weeping openly and copiously. As grief moved from the text into pictures of the public, usually only women, children, and students appeared in the act of breaking down in tears.

The same process also occurred in verbal descriptions of the people. Besides being described as crowds, they now were described also as individ-

WASHINGTON — (P) — The Metropolitan Police estimated the largest crowd ever assembled in Washington—between 300,000 and 400,000 — saw President Roosevelt's body borne today from the Union Station to the White House.

valued at $1,046 were taken by burglars from the home of Edward Goldman, 3230 Eastwood av., yesterday.

Albany Park police said the burglars forced a rear window while the family was absent.

fuses.

At the Douglas Aircraft plant, 10 minutes were devoted to a program over a public address system. Several thousand workers heard the program in the assembly hall.

CAN'T HOLD BACK TEARS—Women weep openly as the flag-draped coffin containing the body of President Roosevelt passes by on its way to the White House for funeral services. Crowds began forming before 8 a.m. to witness the somber procession, during which many women fainted from emotional exhaustion.
[Acme Telephoto.]

FIGURE 5.11. Women reacting to news of FDR's death, from the *Chicago Daily News,* April 14, 1945, p. 4.

uals occasionally, given voices but not names. In general they remained a category:

> At a crowded bar-lunch room at State and Kinzie Streets, laborers from a nearby construction project gasped as the announcement of the death came over a radio.
>
> A husky Negro workman knocked a glass of whiskey from the bar, said "for God's sake," and rushed out the door.
>
> Women at a table burst into tears. All was silent except for the radio announcer's voice. (Special to the *New York Times,* "People Across U.S. Voice Grief and Revulsion," November 23, 1963, p. 11).

More and more, of course, reporters put themselves in the place of the public, either by writing about the reaction of the press corps (as in Tom Wicker's "Kennedy and Reporters," *New York Times,* November 24, 1963, p. 12) or by writing of their personal responses.

THE CIRCLE UNBROKEN

The oath as a moment of action could not be photographed until the advent of portable cameras in the 1920s and 1930s. That sort of candid shot did not appear in coverage of any of the presidential deaths until Roosevelt. Newspapers could have shown the oath in sketch art but did not. This interesting omission suggests that the oath did not become an icon until recently.

Until FDR's death, then, the oath of office had been described verbally and was a preeminent occasion for dramaturgy. When McKinley died, Teddy Roosevelt, his vice president and a famous outdoorsman, was hunting in the Adirondacks. Messengers tracked him down and hustled him to Buffalo, the city where McKinley had been shot and where, after six days of counterproductive medical attention, he had died. There, in a private home, Roosevelt took the oath:

> It was in the subdued light that filtered through cathedral windows in the great front parlor of Ansley Wilcox's home at 641 Delaware avenue that President Roosevelt bowed his head and said: "I swear."
> There was a hush as deep as the silence of death when the ceremony was concluded and the new president, cool and calm as a statue, kissed the bible and taking up a gold-mounted pen signed the formal oath of office. (From a staff correspondent of *The Daily News,* "Roosevelt Takes Oath," September 14, 1901, p. 1)

Here the reporter (under a generic byline) performed like a novelist, although refraining from attributing states of mind to the various witnesses (named exhaustively in a fairly typical catalog). The emphasis was on a combination of solemnity and confidence. The deep silence indicated the gravity of the occasion, and the coolness of the new president reassured all that the crisis was over as soon as it began. (Teddy Roosevelt, famous for his energy, was a good subject for reporters. Not so the previous successor, Chester Arthur, described as almost "womanish" in his grief at Garfield's death.)

The Coolidge succession was similarly dramatic and more fully illustrated. Harding's unexpected death found Coolidge visiting his family in New England, where his father, a notary public, administered the oath himself. The homeliness of the event rooted the stable succession in the molecular American family. The *Times* used two retrospective pictures of Harding, as background for Coolidge's oath as an event: one of Harding on his way to his own inauguration, and the other of Harding with his wife as they returned from the oath-taking and entered the Executive Mansion (August 3, 1923, pp.

2–3). The *Times* on August 4 (p. 2) and the *Chicago Daily News* on August 6 (p. 5) illustrated Coolidge's oath-taking by running a picture of the new president with his father outside the Vermont farmhouse, posing after the event.

When FDR died, a picture ran in both papers showing Truman taking the oath (*Daily News,* April 12, 1945; *New York Times,* April 13, p. 3). The wide shot set the canonical form, with the First Lady, the Chief Justice, and all the witnessing leaders assembled. The *Times* the same day ran a file photo of FDR's oath-taking, again with the First Lady, various leaders, and the Chief Justice, before a prominently positioned flag (p. 6). The pictures had a posed, iconic quality, like a historical frieze.

Kennedy's oath, shown in a retrospective montage at the time of his assassination, followed the Truman model almost exactly, except that the First Lady stood not immediately next to her husband but instead at the far left, framing the picture on one side. The image ran on the first day of coverage in the *Times* (November 23, 1963, p. 15), but the more pressing event, Lyndon B. Johnson's oath of office, ran on the front page (Figure 5.12). Unlike Kennedy's formal event, this one occurred aboard the airplane in Dallas. Shot in close quarters, the picture shows only Johnson flanked by his wife and a few witnessing leaders on one side. Jackie Kennedy, prominently on his right, was closest to the camera. The picture, from the AP, appeared in both newspapers.

This image marks the completion of a shift from posed icons of a ritual event to the active dramatic moments preferred by photojournalism. In another sense, the use of oath imagery also followed a transformation of the act, from a private or hidden, unseen ceremony (in the pictorial dimension), into a public event seen at close range (the LBJ picture is a medium shot) designed to legitimize the succession. The repetition of images from wire services reinforced the moment as a shared public memory.

THE NEWS OF THE NEWS

In all the reportage of all the deaths, newsfolk were everywhere. They turned up as crowds, in a deathwatch with Garfield in Long Branch, with McKinley in Buffalo, and with Harding in San Francisco. They filled the tightly packed cars in the Kennedy motorcade in Dallas and followed the funeral processions in swarms. They also turned up as intimates, chatting with doctors, relatives, and heads of state, and, more and more often, with each other. At first they recounted what they saw. Later they recounted what they felt.

FIGURE 5.12. Lyndon Johnson takes the oath of office, as shown in the canonical shot by Cecil Stoughton, courtesy of the LBJ Presidential Library.

The reporters retreated as observers to the extent that photographers and then television cameras moved in. Reporters abandoned much of their descriptive function, even more so than this study indicates. Our sample features the powerful events that inspire reporters to haul out and dust off old tricks. Even the Kennedy assassination coverage included some walking description, extensive fine detail, and a good deal of dramaturgy.

More and more the reporter's tense had shifted from the present primarily to the past but also to the future. In the Kennedy coverage, reporters supplied whole volumes of retrospective and prospective material. If any type of story were signaled as the reporter's most important work, it would be the expert analysis, fully sourced, of the implications the change in administration might have for this or that issue. That reporters were on holiday when doing dramaturgy, for instance, is indicated by the fact that they dramatized themselves, something they never would have done in analysis. That a reporter could admit grief while covering grief meant that grief was no longer the best beat, that mourning was not a weighty or momentous subject. A reporter would never, in contrast, admit to being Republican while covering Republicans.

As reporters took to the future, they left the present to photographers and even more so to television. By the time of Kennedy's death, one of the most compelling stories concerned television. The coverage in both the *Times* and the *Daily News* turned repeatedly to what was happening on television. The shooting existed as a shared newsreel, the primary text, upon which print journalists could comment and expound. Television news took over for four consecutive days of broadcasting on all three networks. All entertainment programming was canceled. No commercial spots ran. Newspapers reported these acts as primary events in the chronicle of the president's death. Both newspapers told the story of the public witnessing the shooting, the death, the swearing in, and the burial as the story of the public watching television. Reports spoke in glowing praise of broadcast news, fulfilling at last its promise — and tacitly eclipsing print.

THE VISUAL REPORTS

At the beginning of the period, pictures were treated as the exception, interrupting the normal textual flow of news. Over the period we studied, pictures moved closer to the center of news. They became increasingly journalistic, emotive, and episodic. The changes are most clearly illustrated in the portraits or "mug shots" of the deceased presidents. The two newspapers followed a similar pattern, with the *Times* lagging behind (usually by one president) the changes at the *Daily News*. For simplicity's sake, this section describes only the *Daily News* portraits of presidents.

Pictures took their place at the center of news early in the twentieth century. At the time of Garfield's death, his portrait appeared paired with the picture of his successor. No other images of any sort ran in the subsequent coverage. In contrast, McKinley appeared in the same stock picture three times. Harding's portrait ran first, followed by continued coverage that included various shots from his life. Coverage of each president thereafter expanded on the pattern established with Harding. As pictures became more central to news, they took up more space in the newspapers. The scale of the images grew over time in relation to the page size and columns. The number of images grew dramatically as well. Garfield appeared only once, in a picture smaller than two square columns. By the end of the period, Kennedy appeared in five portraits, the largest running across four columns.

While expanding their territory on the page, pictures came under the control of modernist news values such as timeliness and prominence. Garfield's portrait appeared several days after his death, but such portraits were much more timely. By the time Harding died, his picture ran on the first day of coverage. Not only did the delay to publication shorten, but the images themselves became more recent. The newspaper began to emphasize the freshness or exclusiveness of its coverage. This first appeared after the death of Harding, when the *Daily News* announced that its portrait of the president in his youth was "previously unpublished." With Roosevelt's death, the paper ran the "Last Picture of F.D.R." and did the same again with Kennedy's death. In both cases the newspaper advertised on page 1 that its interior included full pages of pictures.

Pictures also fell into line with other canons of modern journalistic practice. With the growth of caption conventions, from Harding on, portraits moved firmly into the present tense of breaking news. The rise of photographer and agency credits marked the increasing professionalization of picture reporting, certifying that each photograph contained an eyewitness account. As pictures became a more prominent physical presence on the page, they also fell under the complex rules governing other news deemed prominent. Coverage of Harding set the pattern for newsworthiness: his portrait on the first day the story broke took the primary position, higher, larger, or closer to page 1, but with the passage of news days his picture lost importance relative to images of the new president.

The early portraits were stock pictures of the same sort used routinely as campaign icons, much like the souvenir engraved portraits that street hawkers sold of the dead president. A timeless portrait and label bear more resemblance to a painting in a museum or art gallery than to modern news. As the portraits moved from art to news, both the image and its context changed. For a time, the decoration around the pictures increased, isolating the icon as if for veneration. Photographic artists also signed their work within the picture, just as painters did. Then the fancy, sometimes oval, frames vanished altogether as other contextual cues emerged. Captions and credits focused on the picture's worthiness as news, rejecting the previous labels' emphasis on authorship.

Beginning with Harding, pictures no longer resembled treasured cameos. Instead, severe, undecorated rectangles left no border between photographs and other news. The new context emphasized the photograph as content. Rather than projecting a citizen looking at the image of a personage, the new form projected a bystander looking through the image (ignoring authorship) and into the events depicted there as if seeing them in person. Over the period, portrait shots shifted gradually toward the close-up, a form that highlights the expressiveness of the face and its mood. By the time of FDR's death the pictures had taken on a different quality, appearing more as personality studies. By then the shift from the honorific to the emotive mode was complete.

That shift was matched by the emergence of episodic relations between pictures. With the numbers of pictures increasing, the relations among photographs became more complex. The *Daily News* portraits began with side-by-side portraits of Garfield on the left and his successor on the right, suggesting the passage from time before to time after. McKinley appeared on page 1 whereas his successor, Theodore Roosevelt, followed on page 5. The Harding coverage began a pattern of showing portraits of the president as a young man. This trend reached its apotheosis in the *Daily News* in 1944 with a series of eight mug shots illustrating how Roosevelt had aged. By showing the president in various settings and poses typifying his life, framed by shots in youth and before death, the *Daily News* invited the viewer to examine the before and after in light of the president's life record — an elaborate narrative task. The full pages of pictures used in the Roosevelt and Kennedy coverage surrounded the portrait (usually quite large) with even more images from specific stories relating the events of the death, the funeral, or the earlier career.

Photography, then, implied a narrative task quite unlike the reading of earlier sketch art. Composite illustrations of events presented a panorama based on temporal sequence, inviting the citizen into a narrative of grand events (or events involving grand personages). The new episodic mode presented a series of unrelated visual statements, all documenting a present tense filled with fleeting emotion. Groupings or entire pages of images seem to invite the reader to examine a variety of events in much the way older forms of written journalism left the reader free to choose and make sense of news. Images thus took up a task dropped by the textual report. However, the form of presentation left occult the many operations of framing and selection — any evidence of journalistic authorship — and instead invited the viewer to experience nostalgia and loss as particular rather than public.

In this new form of narrative, the role of the journalist becomes paramount (although occult). The Kennedy coverage included a remarkable photograph of schoolchildren gathered before a teacher and a page of the *Daily News* bearing a portrait of Kennedy. The teacher is teaching the young to mourn, as if she were the mediator between them and the events of Kennedy's assassination. The page she holds up has all the characteristics of modern photojournalism: the images play prominently on the page, representing active, candid events, whose context on the page suggests direct observation. The photo implies an interpretation — newspaper as useful to a teacher as mediator — through juxtaposing images. What is not evident is the mediation of the journalists. Older portraits, although small, posed and static, with their artsy-decorative borders, implied simpler narratives with manifest, unshrouded roles for newspapers and citizens.

AUTHORITY
AND THE REGISTER OF NEWS

The development of news illustration worked dialectically with the history of reporting. Illustrators and reporters struggled to define and refine each other's tasks and create each other's claims to authority. After a long period of interaction, the reporter's task shifted from description to analysis, and the illustrator-turned-photographer took over the task of giving the news its immediacy and emotional force. As an analyst, the reporter explains to readers why things happened and what things are about to happen; the reporter's tenses are past and future. The photographer's tense is purely the present. The emergence of caption conventions, by the end of the period studied, imposed the strict use of the present tense.

Reportage has come to base its claim to authority on expertise, explaining a chain of events according to processes hidden from the casual observer. Photography bases its claim to authority on immediacy, on the conviction that nothing intervenes between a reader and a scene. In both cases the authority of the news presentation entails the effacement of the observer. Reportage — even in the most heavy-handed punditry — asserts that anyone expert enough (or "in the know") would give the same account. Photojournalism implies that the shot took itself, or at the very least that anyone present with a camera would have made the same picture. In neither case is the newsperson represented.

That the effacement of the observer accompanied the rise of the byline adds irony to this story. Bylines simultaneously assert authorship and guarantee that authorship does not matter. Reporters use them to take responsibility, but by signing articles they are certifying that they did not invent their report. It is news that other professional reporters would also report. When a shooter puts his or her name to a news photo, the act does not mean "This is my vision." It means "I was there when it happened." Were it the photographer's vision, it would not be news. It would revert to art.

Finally, the shift to photography heightened the emotional register of news. The early stories were moving at times but so thoroughly filtered as to render them safe, that is, unlikely to cause direct emotional distress. Even McKinley's decomposing corpse remained an icon of his office and history and therefore not a gross description. Kennedy, however, died in each citizen's living room (or in whatever intimate location). Citizens saw the spatters of blood on Jacqueline Kennedy's leg, watched the restless three-year-old salute in his tiny jacket, and, more than any other image, saw the moment of death as if witnessing the murder of an acquaintance. Photography, in allowing individuals to see history in intimate settings, intertwines that history with personal memory and shifts the telling firmly into the realm of raw emotion, with the filter hidden. The photographic report becomes a prosthetic memory (Lury, 1998). This process, accelerated by television, displaces the civic function of journalists as privileged witnesses to events and personages who would provide a patently filtered and vicarious presence for readers.

The Kennedy assassination and funeral therefore jump out from the rest. One reason why this moment remains a key element in the shared memory of professional journalists (Zelizer, 1992) is that it marks the inauguration of a new division of labor between word and picture. One reason why it remains so compelling for us personally, as people who lived through the events in childhood, is that the pictures themselves are our memory of the event.

PART III

THE RISE OF MODERNISM

Jack Delano, "Men reading headlines in street-corner window of *Brockton Enterprise* office, Brockton, Mass.," black-and-white photograph, Farm Security Administration, Office of War Information Collection (Library of Congress, Prints and Photographs Division LC-USF35-23), December 1940.

Conveyor of Facts

During the key years in the rise of modernism, between the 1890s and the 1940s, pictures of newspaper readers took an objective turn. They represented readers as if engaged in the rational process of seeking information. Imagery of reading aligned itself with the Progressive ideal of a democratic citizenry. Newspapers appeared in the hands of ordinary folks, suggesting the spread of information from authoritative experts to the mass of readers. The representations imagined news publication as a process of information diffusion.

The use of newspapers as sources of information has a long ancestry. An 1848 painting by Richard Caton Woodville, *War News from Mexico,* showed a single newspaper as the source for information shared aloud with an audience of eleven on a hotel front porch (see Brown, 1989, p. 259). William Sidney Mount's 1850 painting, *California News,* likewise shows diffusion, with a single newspaper and (at least potentially) an audience of nine (see Leonard, 1995, p. 16). Images from the nineteenth century clearly illustrate the hierarchy of readers, with white men holding, reading from, and standing closest to the newspaper and with women, African Americans, and children on the periphery.

As the turn of the century approached, the hierarchy began to break down. In an 1897 *Scribner's,* for instance, an engraving of "Wagons Distributing Evening Papers at Union Square, New York" shows a crowd of fifty-odd receiving copies (at least a dozen are shown in people's hands and many more are piled in stacks) from white men, who stand (perhaps on boxes) head and shoulders above the audience (*Scribner's 22:* 455; see Leonard, 1995, p. 156). The distributors, however, look down or away, while the most prominent readers, a white woman and a black man, occupy the foreground, dominating the image above the mass of newspaper pages in their hands, and they look out at the viewer of the engraving. The gaze of subjects in painting has special significance in the case of women. The downcast eyes of the nude made her body the object of male desire, and an odalisque (as such reclining figures are sometimes called) could be considered shocking for looking directly toward the viewer, challenging male dominance (an effect found in Eduard Manet's painting *Olympia,* from the realist movement of the nineteenth century). In the case of the *Scribner's* illustration, the white men demurely attend to their holy office of distributing newspapers. In the new industrial hierarchy, men became subaltern.

Jack Delano's photograph of the reading of headlines posted in the front windows of the newspaper office in Brockton shows a practice that had existed at least since the use of the telegraph for news transmission. The readers, five men and a woman, are anonymous and faceless, all looking away from the camera in long coats, their heads covered with hats. Every individual is reduced to a reading role, although the color of their skin is visible, and their gender can be surmised from their dress (trousers for men, exposed calves for the woman). The newspaper is giving away news but attracting readers who may want to know more. The newspaper office also houses a commercial printer whose sign, visible in the top of the frame, proffers office supplies. Reading happens en masse but not in a community. Each reader acts alone, suggesting an audience as a particulate substance composed of individuals who seek information and make separate decisions.

The audience as mass also emerged in the nineteenth century as a component of the market. The publisher's newspaper was involved in the news business, and publishers used any means, including gimmicks and stunts with or without newsprint, to get attention, spread news, and sell more copies. To reach the largest audience, according to *Chicago Times* editor Wilbur Storey's famous dictum, publishers had two duties: to print news and raise hell. Alden Blethen, renegade publisher of *The Penny Paper* in Minneapolis, projected election returns in the early 1890s on the side of a building (see Boswell & McConaghy, 1996, p. 85). By beating the competition he participated in the culture of the scoop, which is widely misunderstood as a product of pure journalism, and not only that but also as one of its defining characteristics. In fact, the scoop mentality provided a natural-seeming ideological justification for bending men's activities to the purposes of commerce.

The audience standing in rapt attention provides the other side of that equation. News as an industrial product could hold the faceless masses captive. Its power was never shown more eloquently than on the street, where it arrested people from the flow of their private pursuits. In the picture they align their gaze, forming a cohesive visual unit: the reading public. The image, however, contains a contradiction, because a handful of persons attending to a message board with-out interacting is no public. In Arthur Rothstein's (1938) photograph of street reading at a newsstand, the steelworkers likewise look down, wearing hats. One man looks over the shoulder of another, but all three are engrossed in private reading. They too are faceless subjects — the self presented in industrial attire melded into an audience. In other words, industrial processes define and control them not only in work (steelmaking) but even in a moment of leisure (news reading).

Although actual moments of public reading would largely vanish in the modern period of news form, the image of the audience facing the authoritative source of information and entertainment flowed through and covertly defined the relationship of news to audiences through much of the twentieth century. Movie viewers became a ubiquitous icon in the overt representations of audiences. The most memorable images come from the 1960s and show moviegoers wear-ing cardboard spectacles fitted with cellophane which were supposed to make the film look three-dimensional and by accident made the in-dividuals look identical. The audience represented in this manner typifies the ways that form imposes its vision of the world and also re-duces the supposed autonomous citizen into the atomized viewer.

CHAPTER 6

THE FRONT PAGE

Measuring Modernism and Its Phases, 1885–1985

The United States celebrated its centennial with a great Exposition in Philadelphia in 1876. The nations of the world were invited to set their accomplishments up next to those of the Americans, and a host of citizens — eight million paid admissions — thronged the exhibits. The crowd of 186,672 at the opening ceremonies, said to be the largest ever to gather in the Americas (Brown, 1966, pp. 116, 134), came to see the future while they celebrated the past.

Power, the unifying theme of the Centennial Exposition, had displays extolling all its guises: the physical energy that drove the machines in Machinery Hall, the mechanical force emanating from the Corliss Engine (the most talked about item at the fair), and the military and political might that had overcome regional differences and opposing civilizations to unite the central swath of the North American continent under one dominion. A steady flow of bearded dignitaries also represented power. A decade after the Civil War and in the midst of continuing hostilities with the Plains Indians — Custer's Last Stand took place halfway through the exposition run — the fair offered a willful, almost religious endorsement of U.S. power.

Henry Adams (1906), one of the great commentators on fin de siècle culture, in his famous commentary contrasted the display of modern mechanical power of the Paris Exposition of 1900 with the solidity and seeming permanence of medieval Christianity embodied in the great cathedrals at Mont Saint Michel and Chartres. He drew a line between these two points and projected it outward, predicting the decline of civilization in accordance with the second law of thermodynamics. Civilization must head toward entropy, he concluded, as chaos replaced organization. In keeping with his sketch of human history, he called his chapter on the 1870s "Chaos," and he had nothing to say about the Philadelphia Exposition.

Many years later, at yet another climax in the career of the U.S. imperium, we find it difficult to accept Adams' sense of decline. The forces of cultural cohesion, no matter how one judges their ultimate worth, proved stronger than he believed, having withstood wave after wave of disruption and distention. Race war, class struggle, Industrial Revolution, two World Wars, sexual rebellion, religious enthusiasm, generational strife, and all the elemental forces unleashed by the individualism of the marketplace have only redeployed the basic framework of power displayed in 1876. The dynamo *is* our virgin.

One network of cultural cohesion, the newspaper, featured prominently at the Philadelphia Exposition. A newspaperman chaired the organizing committee: Frank Leslie, the pioneer of illustrated journalism, whose weekly we have already discussed in some detail. Another titan of the press, George P. Rowell, who ran the nation's premier advertising agency, put together a Newspaper Pavilion that offered a copy of every one of the nation's 8,129 newspapers: "a monster reading room and an exchange for newspaper men" (Rowell, 1876, pp. iii–iv). He viewed the correspondence between the press, commerce, and power in simple terms, with the press as "the voltaic pile, where is contained the vitalizing power of a universe," and compared the Newspaper Pavilion to a mine he had visited in Nevada's Virginia City, where, "in the dark and dismal rocks, is pouring out constantly a stream of molten silver to enrich man" (p. viii). Rowell's fatuity aside, newspaperfolk found themselves drawn to the exposition. More than a thousand reporters received accreditation, and the nation's press carried news every day of the goings-on at the fair.

The Newspaper Pavilion showed the human face of the press. There visitors read their hometown papers and mingled with reporters, who used the pavilion as an informal news bureau. Rowell supplied free paper and ink at a gallery of writing desks for the convenience of the correspondents who adorned his exhibit. Here one could observe the press maintaining ties of conviviality across physical and social space.

The mechanical face of the press glowered in Machinery Hall, in the shadow of the Corliss Engine, where working installations of Hoe and Bullock web presses performed virtually worker-free for an awed public. Ironically positioned next to Benjamin Franklin's own hand press, the Hoe web press, one of only twenty three in the world, printed on a "continuous sheet 4½ miles long, and running through the machine at the rate of 750 feet per minute" (*Leslie's*, 1876, p. 274). The presence of these state-of-the-art machines allowed some of the New York dailies to send their stereotype plates by an early train to the exposition and print their daily edition on the spot (Bailey, 1877, p. 60).

The commentaries on the press equipment in Machinery Hall conveyed the sheer numerical delight of observers. They seemed to view the development of the newspaper quantitatively, as a history of the continual movement of the decimal point to the right, the continual adding of more zeroes. The ceaseless march to the northeast corner of the chart demonstrated the superiority of the industrial United States to the rest of the world unambiguously, in the unsurpassed output of its printing presses — 1,250,024,590 copies of newspapers in 1876, Rowell figured (1876, p. xii). A similar one-dimensional progression pervaded comments on the other communications technologies displayed at the exposition: the telegraph, the photograph, new systems of engraving, even typewriters. (Oddly, observers took little notice of Alexander Graham Bell's telephone.) Each of these technologies also became a point of national pride. For the United States, the world leader in communication innovation by 1876, the press was a source of the peculiar energy of the newly imperial republic.

As the overwhelmingly quantitative character of the commentaries suggests, the press in 1876 exercised its civilization-building power very much as a matter of form, through the sheer accumulation of content. The industrial newspaper — our term for the finished version of the publisher's newspaper — combined top-down control on the part of an owner with the rationalized production of the Industrial Revolution. As a mature type, the industrial newspaper provided a routinized framework for capturing the news of the day. Standard four-page dailies had collected information actively but often randomly. Unlike the printer's newspaper of the colonial era and Federal period or the editor's newspaper of the Partisan period, newspapers of the industrial era had no single functionary assembling the content. Instead, they compressed several different modes of composition together: clipped news and telegraphic digests and editorials and correspondence and reportage and official documents and records, all shoved up against each other. The industrial newspapers were multivocal. They carried incommensurable content, with editorial paragraphs contradicting telegraphic news and telegraphic reports out of temporal synchrony with correspondence.

The newspaper had the power to make everything fit, not intellectually but physically. The 1,001 happenings of the day all went on display. Newsworkers shoveled every available glimpse into print, making no attempt to control its meaning, leaving that task to the reader. The industrial newspaper retained Victorian design style, even as it adopted production routines that we might call modern. The resulting newspaper we understand according to the master metaphor of the department store, a copious market made somewhat less chaotic under one roof of industry, representing an abundant social world for the selective appropriation of self-directed reader-consumers.

The driving force of the social, industrial, and scientific logics of the modern would eventually transform the newspaper. The social logic required a more manageable form of apprehending the social world; the industrial logic drove in the direction of more control over supply and demand on the levels of both content and material production, with monopoly as the ultimate horizon; and the scientific logic demanded the sort of intelligibility provided by value-free experts rather than authors or scavengers or editorialists. The result was the appearance of the professional newspaper, a news establishment with elements of monopoly at several levels: at the level of content, with the wire services and other monopoly providers; at the level of the marketplace, with the appearance of conditions of natural monopoly in local markets; and at the level of the profession (so-called) of reporting itself, with a unified standard of verifiability and a code of appropriate comportment prescribed for journalism.

The rise of the professional newspaper occurred simultaneously with the development of an aesthetic of modernism. In the fine arts of the early twentieth century, modernism represented a response to conflict, to world war and the social disorder and economic dislocations occasioned in part by industrial capitalism. Emphasizing simplicity, clarity, and mastery, abstract art movements continued a long tradition of classicism, which admired those qualities in art from the ancient past, coupled with the urge to lay bare the underlying structures of aesthetic experience. Modernism ironically made revolution the norm in the visual arts, as each generation repudiated the past and laid claim to the future. As it spread from the fine arts and informed the styles adopted by newspapers, modernism retained the warring attributes of mastery and revolution.

Modern style, so appropriate to the professional newspaper, suggested a new master metaphor for the press: the social map. A map boils the complexity of the geographical world down to the minimum of lines and labels needed for political and commercial tasks, such as traveling, shipping, setting boundaries, and recording claims. From the churning and abundant mass that Victorian newspapers displayed, the modern style distilled an ordered view of the social world, one serving a similar list of political and commercial activities but meant to excite the enthusiasm of citizens and consumers.

At its height, the moment of modernism proved unstable on all fronts. The arts could not sustain the contradictory conditions of ordered calm and perpetual revolution. In newspapers, the social map could never be complete enough or consensual enough to match an increasingly multicultural society. The modern aesthetic resulted in design styles too austere for the abundance of an affluent society. The professional ideals of journalists proved unrealistic and deprived journalism of much of its power and allure. And the self-contained monopolistic newspaper enterprise became ripe for plucking.

In our lifetime the professional newspaper has yielded to the corporate newspaper. The corporate newspaper encompasses older professional ideals within an overriding concern for economic growth fueled by the increasing convergence of news with every other sort of enterprise. To journalists, always a frowning crew, corporatization has meant that the sacred public affairs mission of newspapers must make common cause with Disney World — a new form of Babylonian captivity. To designers, however, the rise of the corporate newspaper brought a new artistic freedom. Style became a language of its own, allowing the newspaper to now put on and now take off forms with the same freedom as a restless teenager adding or subtracting clothes, piercings, or hairstyles. In the late modern newspaper, the metaphor of the map no longer makes sense. Instead, the master metaphor has become the index, a comparison even more apt as the newspaper moves from paper to cyberspace.

This chapter lays out the shift in the formations from industrial to professional to corporate newspapers, in the periods from Victorian to modern to late modern styles, by studying in broad strokes the front pages of newspapers over a century.

THE DISPLAY WINDOW

Previously we proposed a variety of dominant metaphors for newspaper formations: a coffeehouse, a town meeting hall, a courtroom, and a marketplace. In the industrial era, the newspaper became like a department store (now a major source of its advertising revenue). Both offered a range of goods and services to a range of consumers. Both displayed their goods: the front page had become a crowded store window. Both gave the consumer a chance to live for a moment in a kind of dream world, a represented land of desire (Leach, 1993). The newspaper depicted the realm of prominence and conflict, a world peopled by leaders and criminals, artists and celebrities. Its display window portrayed the grand events of history and the timeless dramas of the everyday. Like a department store, the newspaper staked a claim to the real, positioning itself as this-worldly in a society ever more publicly secular even as it continued to wrestle with the deliriums of religion.

The face of the newspaper was now the front page. The design of the front page became the crucial feature in the form of the newspaper. There a newspaper announced its identity with a distinctive nameplate and showcased its content. During the ensuing century, which would witness the invention of the modern form of journalism, the front page would represent the serious intentions of the newspaper. Innovations would occur first elsewhere, of course. Advertising matter still held the leading edge, and the so-called soft news sections would be more experimental, but the front page was thought to signal the real function of the paper.

This chapter sketches out the pattern of front-page design development in the years from the height of Victorian design to the maturation of the wave of redesigns epitomized by *USA Today* in the 1980s (Stone, Schweitzer, & Weaver, 1978). We chose that time frame initially as a way of assessing the belief in what designers, journalism professors, and trade publications such as *Editor & Publisher* called a design revolution occurring in the 1970s and 1980s (see, e.g., "Front Pages," 1985). Conventional wisdom held that newspapers revolutionized their design as a result of a shift to new layout and printing technologies employing photographic and digital processes, and that the motivating urgency behind design changes came from a fear that newspapers had lost the competition with other news technologies, especially television (Hutt, 1973; Garcia, 1987). We wanted to test the notion that newspapers of the time changed form because technology allowed them to look like television. Had in fact a design revolution occurred? Did technology drive the so-called revolution? Or were we witnessing longer patterns playing out as the newspaper form developed?

The common sense of the period identified a coherent set of values behind the design changes of the 1970s and 1980s. The redesigns pursued a goal, according to Ben Bradlee of the *Washington Post,* to provide "readability, clarity, organization, order" (quoted in Anthony & Anthony, 1985, p. 31). These qualities were closely associated with what designers then called the modern style, which in newspapers referred to certain specific forms: the modern front page of the 1970s and 1980s had fewer columns, a horizontal layout, simplified headlines, many visual elements, and clear organization (Weaver, Mullins, & McCombs, 1973; Barnhurst, 1994). The animating notions behind 1970s modern style in newspapers derived from a classicist strain of modernism.

When intellectuals identified the modern and modernism as a distinctive cultural moment at the end of the nineteenth century, they observed new forms of both change and fixity. The world changed and people changed in more dynamic ways than ever before, and the apprehension of change on such a fundamental level disrupted older notions of fixity: the rigid identities of medieval Christianity, the changeless species of classical biology, the entrenched sovereignties of monarchical regimes, the stable cosmology of the ancient astronomers, the perpetual earth of ancient geology. The dynamism and boundlessness of a changing universe, epitomized by the new industrial order and the forms of capitalism that produced its productive regime, burst asunder all the sense-making apparatus of the feudal era. "All that is solid melts into air," Marx and Engels intoned in the *Communist Manifesto* (Berman, 1982). The changing universe became thinkable and understandable, however, through reason operating by fixed laws. Just as reason could apprehend the world, so too did reason both apprehend and constitute the new modern individual. The modern era would thus be full of confidence in Science.

Newspaper modernism thus fit into the longer emergence of the modern aesthetic that began at the end of the medieval world. The humanists of the Renaissance seemed to suggest that all beauty grew out of measurement, and the art and science of linear perspective proposed to harness the natural world in the webbing and buckles of geometry. Neoclassicism in art during the nineteenth century had rejected the decorative excesses of the Baroque period and renewed admiration for the ancient ideal (filtered through the early modern era). As it spread into the plebeian world of commerce and industry, modernism in the early twentieth century used the same logic. Modern designers admired the classic form of books from the incunabula and the clear geometry of humanist letterforms, based on the square and the circle (forms also reflected in the architecture of the Italian Renaissance). They looked forward by looking back, drawing on their reconstructions of the ancient world, and their designs proposed a reduction of ornament to fit a classical ideal of simplicity of line and purity of proportion (ignoring the fact that ancient ruins, with the passage of time, had lost their original chromatic ornamentation).

As a visual cognate of the modern in Western culture, modernist design logic seemed capable of providing stability amid changing external realities.

To that end, newspaper modernists embraced science, and so we find Ben Sherbow in the offices of the *New York Tribune* with a stopwatch, timing his assistants as they read headlines set in various typefaces and layouts (all uppercase versus sentence-style, longer versus shorter lines of type, flush left versus centered or indented by steps). Sherbow's experiments, although an extension of Taylorism, also expressed a faith in measurement that drew on mechanical notions, just as the early modern era drew on the accumulated mechanical inventions of the High Middle Ages.

The long trajectory of the modern into the mainstream of newspapers thus gave birth to a peculiar and powerful hybrid modernism. It drew on early modern ideas about geometry, on the neoclassical rejection of decoration, and on late modern faith in science, but brought those notions into the mainstream. Newspapers became a prime site where visual art and popular forces met and made their peace, and news contributed to the fullness of modernism as it arrived in the twentieth century.

News acted as an intersection where private and public versions of reason met and reckoned with each other. Elsewhere we discussed the particular notion of reason that came into existence with the bourgeois notion of the public sphere at the end of the eighteenth century (see Chapter 2). Such public reason came about through pragmatics. The reasonableness of an argument consisted of its framing as "anyone talking to everyone." Any argument that could be so framed was ipso facto reasonable, and any public deliberation honoring such framing was ipso facto rational. This form of public reason seemed obviously incorrect to moderns. One of the earliest discoveries of social science was the unreasonableness of the average individual, especially when individuals were agglomerated into crowds or masses. It followed that all democratic political processes must be finally governed by thinly veiled irrational impulses: greed, tribal loyalty, religious or racial prejudice, sexual passion.

The moderns therefore relocated reason from the public to the private. True reason became the province of the dispassionate expert, for whom long and arduous training had removed all the passions and idiocies of normal folk, at least in regard to one area of expertise. Economists might feel greedy, for example, but greed would not inflect their economic analyses and forecasts. Doctors may feel horny, but their professional identity will provide a shield; they won't get hot over their patients.

Politics presents a special problem for modern notions of reason. Reason, after all, discovered the rights out of which democracy was invented. Mustn't reason therefore bow to the rule of the masses? The solution to the dilemma was to privatize government. In response to the many dislocations of the Industrial Revolution and the many corruptions, real and imagined, of politics on both the local and the national levels, modernizing reformers took the government apart piece by piece, removed it from politics and placed it in the hands of experts. Public reason — the old politics — became in the modern era a form of acclamation, a periodic endorsement of the various bureaucracies that comprised the privatized government.

Journalism located itself at the nexus between public and private reason, that is, between the reason of politics and the reason of experts. Journalists were not themselves experts, but neither were they exactly the public either. Instead, their task became to translate the experts to the public. Modern journalism evolved from the dialectic of expert and public reason.

Likewise a dialectic of newspaper forms emerged from the combination of fundamental change and rational intelligibility that characterized the modern moment. To simplify, the explosive rate of change in the world coupled with the new technologies of production and exchange encouraged the development of Victorian design — a first moment of newspaper modernism — and then the concern with science and intelligibility prompted the rise of modern newspaper design, which took the complex world, expertly digested it, and represented it for rational readers. Such a narrative suggests that changes in front-page design will be culturally rather than technologically driven. If so, modern design should have resulted in rationalized and therefore relatively featureless and undistinguished front pages — something akin to the functionalist phase of modern architecture.

Designers of the 1970s who joined in the modernist movement disagreed over whether the imputed design revolution made newspapers look more alike or more distinctive. Some news designers argued that redesigns produced what they called cookie-cutter front pages in U.S. newspapers, while others countered that front pages had actually become more diverse as newspapers added to the range of available design elements (García, 1981; Rehe, 1981; Nesbitt, 1988). We suspected, however, that the variations among newspapers of the period contained a common modernist vocabulary, and so devised a study to weigh the various arguments.

We selected three newspapers for study: the San Francisco *Chronicle,* to represent metropolitan dailies; the Springfield, Illinois, *State Journal-Register,* to represent smaller urban dailies; and the *Peterborough* (formerly *Contoocook*) *Transcript*, of New Hampshire, to represent small-town weeklies. To get a long-term perspective, we collected data at ten-year intervals from 1885 to

1985.[1] The random sample gave us a focused look at front pages for three types of newspapers reaching across the geographic and cultural breadth of the United States.

MEASURES OF CHANGE

During the century, the newspapers in the study shifted from the abundant complexity of the Victorian era to the fixed simplicity of modernism. They adopted all the specific forms commentators identified with the modern style: fewer columns, prominent illustrations, horizontal layout, and simplified headline typography. The front pages clearly became less dense and more orderly, as indicated by several measures. The average number of items (such as images, heads, and blocks of text) on the front page declined from a high of 58 for the *Transcript* of 1885 to a low of 7.29 for the *Chronicle* of 1985 (Figure 6.1). The average number of stories (groups of items related to the same event) on front pages declined from a high of 32.3 for the *Register* in 1895 to a low of 5.25 for the *Transcript* in 1985. Interestingly, for both these measures, we found wide disparity among newspapers studied until the 1920s. Beginning with the 1925 data, increasing uniformity among newspapers accompanied the declining density of their front pages, apparent in the declining standard deviations among newspapers within each year.

The highly ordered front page appeared as a rather recent phenomenon. We take the number of stories on the front page to be an especially significant measure (Figure 6.2). The modern newspaper, by the mere act of selecting only a half-dozen stories for front-page treatment, radically simplified the news of the day and offered an insistent commentary on what mattered most. Although newspapers had been reducing the number of front-page items from the 1920s on, the process proceeded rather gradually through the middle of the century. The average number of stories dipped below ten only between 1965 and 1975, although the decline had been clearly linear for forty years by then.

The declining population of front-page items accompanied declining density in other measures, as the modernist penchant for clarity and order required. The number of columns decreased gradually from a high of nine

---

[1]For each year, we sampled a reconstructed week of the dailies and a reconstructed month of the weekly, balanced among seasons. The random sample for each year included the following: seven issues for each daily newspaper, and four issues, one for each season, for the weekly. In all, 198 front pages containing roughly 5,000 individual items were coded.

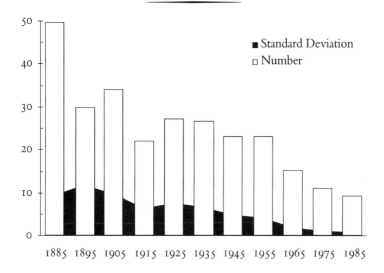

FIGURE 6.1. Front-page items. The mean number of items by year for the sample newspapers. Standard deviations are shown in absolute value (all are negative integers). One-way analysis of variance (10 df), $p < .000$, $F = 14.6$.

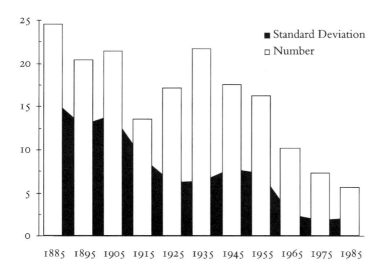

FIGURE 6.2. Front-page stories. The mean number of stories by year for the sample newspapers. Standard deviations are shown in absolute value (all are negative integers). One-way analysis of variance (10 df), $p < .000$, $F = 27.9$.

to a low of five or six, while the number of lines per column also fell — two measures of the shrinking physical format of newspapers. Besides publishing on smaller sheets of paper, newspapers enlarged their text typography. As a result, the number of words that the average front page could accommodate shrank from more than 10,000 in 1885 to less than 4,500 in 1985, with a sharp drop again coming in the last years studied (Figure 6.3). The variation also went down, as newspapers uniformly became less dense.

If we consider design as a continuum ranging between two poles from books to newspapers, with the former referring to single-column formats with larger type and continual, coherent subject matter, and the latter to the opposite, then front pages over the century moved back from newspaper to book forms. Of course, magazine forms had already staked out the interme-diate position between the two, and newspapers in effect came more and more to imitate magazines in design through the twentieth century (a point we take up again in Chapter 7).

Headlines also changed in accordance with the tenets of modern design (Figure 6.4). Modernists replaced the multiple decks of Victorian headlines, in the form of a list, with the streamlined heading that summarized the story in one truncated sentence. Measurements of form only hint at the change,

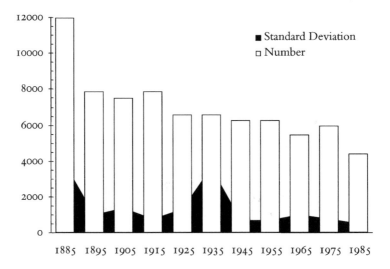

FIGURE 6.3. Capacity in words. The mean number of words per front page by year for the sample newspapers. Standard deviations are shown in absolute value (all are negative integers). One-way analysis of variance (10 *df*), $p < .000$, $F = 20.7$.

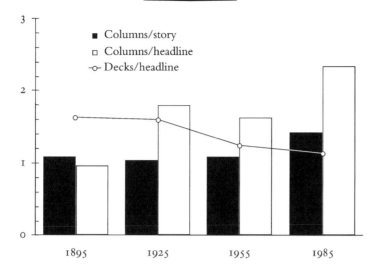

FIGURE 6.4. Story layout. The mean of sample front pages for several indicators of headline and story shape. (The data for 1895 show slightly less than one column because a few stories were not headlined.)

first, because only a few articles received deck headlines on any Victorian front pages, with most article titles instead occupying a single line; and second, because streamlined headlines on modern front pages occasionally carried a subtitle. On average, then, the number of decks went down by half a line, a small amount despite a pronounced change in visual form.

Other aspects of headline design contributed to the change. As the number of decks in headlines declined, the width of the average headline more than doubled. The wider headline dominated and gathered related items, including photographs and captions, under its umbrella. The change yielded a simpler hierarchy of emphasis for content. Along with the width of headlines, the width in columns for text running in the average story also increased somewhat. The removal of decks, the arraying of text across (rather than down) columns, and the creation of headlines spanning text and pictures together marked not only the visible form but changed the function of headlines.

In the earliest newspapers we examined (see Chapters 2 and 3), headlines appeared more or less as titles or as labels. That function followed the traditions of the book, where chapters had titles. It also followed the function (and subsequently the form) of advertisements. The heading European Intelligence, for example, looked and acted like the label New and Imported: For Sale. The uniform style remained typical of the printerly era, including the editors' newspapers of the Partisan period. In the Victorian period, the function and form of the headline shifted, again in line with advertising practices but also in response to the rise of telegraphic news, to produce multiple tiers, typographically differentiated, within a single stacked headline. These headlines still acted as titles, but also were more descriptive of the content of the news item (or items) that followed. One might think of them as a table of contents.

Modernism changed the headine's function from a table of contents to a statement of the meaning of an event. No longer an outline, the headline instead gave a pointed summary of the news. We use *pointed* in the sense that it denoted and captured (the point of) the story and also in the sense that it compressed and (pointedly) connoted the story: "Headless Body in Topless Bar." The modern headline carried deeply embedded codes of news values and cultural values, in this example ranging from the unusual and the timely to the powerful and the moral.

Modern headlines called for horizontal layout. Written usually as declarative sentences, they asked to be read across the page, proportional to their size, just like any other sentence. The layout of the stories followed this same practice on the whole, becoming more horizontal as measured in the width of the average story in columns. Although the number of columns each story occupied grew over time from a nearly universal single column in 1895 to a more expansive column and a half (with fairly high variance) in 1985, the pronounced expansion of headlines across columns led the way. Of all the design aspects of the newspaper, headlines spoke most directly to the audience and stood out on the page as sense-making devices. The headlines gave meaning in much the same way that the enlarged names of countries and major cities signal what matters on a map.

Although the trends toward horizontal forms continued throughout the years sampled, a real quickening occurred in the last few decades of the twentieth century. Not every measure followed the same pattern (Figure 6.5). In other headline characteristics, the changes largely fell into place before the so-called design revolution. Sans serif typefaces, a marker of modernism, increased in the first half of the twentieth century. Headlines in all uppercase letters, a marker of Victorianism, began declining after the 1920s. Then the Victorian effect of condensed type dropped off later, after midcentury.

The aspects of headlines reflect three values of modernism: simplicity, efficiency, and tranquillity. A sans serif typeface exposes the structure of let-

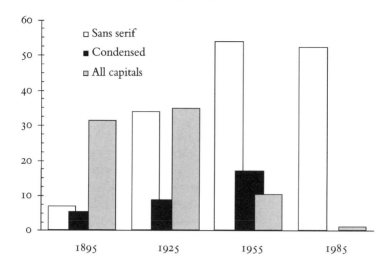

FIGURE 6.5. Headline typography. The percentage of headlines from the sample front pages for selected years. Each typographic characteristic is a discrete measurement, unrelated to other characteristics (and thus not adding to 100 percent).

ters by leaving off the customary decorative flourishes at the ends of the strokes. Serifs connote the handicraft of calligraphy and stone inscriptions, and modernism continued to use such classically derived forms, but sans serifs connote a desirable simplicity of geometry and logic. By midcentury serifs had become secondary to plain sans serif typefaces in headlines as an expression of the professional bent of newspapers.

Type in all capital letters fell victim to the modernist inclination for seeking efficiency. Studies of legibility and readability, employing the methods of social science, showed uppercase letters less easy to distinguish from each other, compared to the lowercase letters. When used in quantity, capital letters slowed down the process of reading. Those results accumulated into an irresistible force for modernists working after the 1930s, and all-capital-letter headlines dropped off in the second half of the century.

The serenity favored by modernism could not enter a landscape dominated by conflict so readily as did the modernist values of simplicity or efficiency, which matched the journalistic preference for quick and clear reporting. Condensed typography provided a form of emphasis, a way for newspapers to call out to readers in the printed parallel to a street vendor. All-uppercase headlines did the same, and that declamatory capacity helped delay their decline. Such modes of selling events eventually decreased under the modern conception of news. Condensed types followed an up-and-down course (and reemerged in newspapers at the end of the century).

The use of bylines provides another measure of the rise of modern design. Bylines of all sorts became much more frequent by the 1920s (Table 6.1). Shifts in bylining indicate a series of changes in news production that also involved the continuing impact of modern notions. Although bylines became a familiar element in newspapers, not until the 1960s were front-page stories routinely bylined, and only then did the individual reporter's byline become prevalent. At the same time, the array of different agencies cited in bylines contracted.

We can summarize the process of change in bylining as the simultaneous institutionalization and personalization of reporting. Bylines that attributed news to wire services had become general by the 1920s, and Associated Press (AP) attributions remained commonplace thereafter. In fact, the data understate the importance of the wire services as named sources of content, because our study focused on the front page, where newspapers in the second half of the century tended to showcase material their own reporters produced. Institutional sources of news became regularized and received routine credit in bylines to an extent even greater than the

TABLE 6.1. FRONT PAGE BYLINES

The number of bylines from all three newspapers at 30-year intervals (percentages for the year in parentheses)

KIND OF BYLINE	1895	1925	1955	1985
NONE	260 (88)	195 (63)	180 (61)	23 (27)
REPORTER	36 (12)	21 (7)	11 (4)	39 (45)
NEWSPAPER		4 (1)		
ASSOCIATED PRESS	1 (*)	37 (12)	58 (20)	23 (27)
UNITED PRESS		7 (2)	31 (11)	
INTERNATIONAL NEWS SERVICE		43 (14)	15 (5)	
COPLEY				1 (1)
MULTIPLE		5 (2)		

*Less than 1 percent.

data suggest. At the same time, individual reporters became more likely to be named on front pages.

A complicated story lies behind the rise of the modern news byline, a story we discuss in more detail later (see Chapter 7). Suffice it here to note that the byline to a significant degree recognizes the reporter's subjectivity (Schudson, 1978). The discovery of the subjectivity of the perceiving individual is one of the prominent features of the modernist moment. The novel science of psychology grew out of the challenging of fixed notions of human nature that modernism encouraged. In conventional memory, Sigmund Freud's so-called discovery of the unconscious mind was the founding event in this history; in the United States, the more prosaic psychology of William James (1890) also drew attention to the crucial role of a subject's intentionality in constructing the world.

Another design feature, illustration, also indicates an awareness of subjectivity. We previously discussed some of the philosophy behind illustrated news (see Chapter 5), particularly its aims to provide vicarious experience for readers, to convey series of events, and to depict important personages. The mere existence of illustration in the news indicates an initial engagement with modernism. Not surprisingly, we found that the prominence of illustrations on the front pages of newspapers increased.

The change reflected the hegemony of modern design ideas, which included the demand for a larger range in the scale and a clear dominance of some images (or one image) on the page. Not only that, but the change also marked the acceptance of photographers as partners in journalism instead of merely as hired artists. At the same time that the number of photographs on the front page grew, the total number of items declined (see Figure 6.1, on page 195). Photojournalists thus took a greater share of the shrinking front page, and their centrality to the task of reporting top-priority news increased.

Under modernism, the relationship of illustrations to the verbal content of the front page grew more complex. A rather striking upswing took place in the number of illustrations included with stories, from 5.7 percent in 1895 to 21.5 percent in 1985 — an increase accounted for by charts, maps, drawings, and other forms of what news editors called infographics. The change, of course, related to the role of headlines already discussed, but also marked the integration of visual forms of information into the older verbal center of news. Meanwhile, the percentage of photographs directly related to accompanying stories declined from 90.5 percent in 1895 to 66.7 percent in 1985. Pictures came commonly to stand on their own on the front page, although stand-alone photographs remained in the minority. By every measure, the rise of modernism enhanced the status of the image and along with it the status of the photographer.

PHASES OF MODERNISM

Our findings support the notion of conspicuous design change in the 1970s and 1980s, although clearly the term *revolution* overstated a shift underway for a long time. The pattern of change might be summarized thus: Sometime in the World War I era, the newspaper front page became more open to new design ideas; sometime between 1955 and 1965, these new design ideas began to dominate the front page. Newspapers adopted all the specific forms that commentators have associated with the rise of modern design: fewer columns, fewer items, more prominent illustrations, horizontal layout, and simplified headline typography. The shift occurred gradually, but an acceleration in the final ten-year period of our study contributed to the widespread conception of a revolution.

Our survey of front-page design change suggested the need for a closer analysis of the phases in the course of modern newspaper design. Clearly, modernism in newspapers reached an apex in the twentieth century, not only in circulation and influence, but also in the visual landscape. The collages of Cubism incorporated everyday articles on a ground of newsprint, thus not only associating the newspaper with modern art but also identifying the press as the substrate of contemporary life. Although the newspaper in novels, television, and film became fixed as an icon, with the modern look of a 1930s daily, newspapers people read every day changed incrementally over the century.

Our analysis of the twentieth century identified several phases in the emergence of the modern movement in newspaper design. The earliest modifications began to align newspapers with the changing styles in the fine and applied arts. Shifts in industrial organization based on notions of efficiency and a redefinition of citizens as consumers contributed further design expressions. The organization of news pages also responded to an increase in the cultural value placed on clarity and order.

Protomodern Phase, 1910s–Present

In the larger cultural history of the United States, the First World War produced a climactic shift in expectations. A generation of Progressive reform had encouraged thinkers to embrace the hopeful belief that continued (quantitative) development of production would lead to (qualitative) moral and political improvements, that democracy would be realized as systems of manufacture freed people from drudgery and systems of education freed people from ignorance. But World War I showed that increases in *productive* capacity could translate directly into increased *destructive* capacity. The war proved not just bloody but also stupid. To this day historians can give no reasonable explanation for its origins, beyond the platitudinous: Shit happens in the Balkans.

The stupidity of the war did not, however, emanate merely out of passivity. All the major players were also complicit in actively producing stupidity. The United States first experienced one barrage of propaganda from European countries and then another produced domestically, as the Wilson administration's Committee on Public Information cranked up its panmedia artillery. Critics could only conclude, with Walter Lippmann (1922), that the industrialized media had inverted the relationship between knowledge and power: instead of empowering the people with knowledge, they enmeshed the people in an increasingly overwrought pseudoenvironment.

The press responded to the ensuing crisis in confidence by instituting modernist reforms. In law, the news media came to support increased First Amendment protections on both the federal and state level, asserting for themselves an institutional claim to a privileged status in public communication. In journalism, reporters and editors began framing codes of ethics, underscoring the special responsibilities of the media in a modern age. The professional newspaper replaced the industrial newspaper. In news design, the parallel development was the first, or Protomodern, phase of the modern movement.

Protomodernism had its origins around the time of the First World War, when Ben Sherbow began a redesign of the *New York Tribune* (Hutt, 1973). He imposed a single typeface for headlines, combining upper- and lower-case letters, with the goal of typographic simplicity. Then, in a move called streamlining, John Allen (1947) pushed in the 1920s and 1930s for flush-left, asymmetrical headlines using type produced by his employer, the Mergenthaler-Linotype Co. (Barnhurst, 1994). Streamlining aimed for efficiency, the outcome Allen promised would follow from his innovations. Through such small steps modernism gained initial entry into the production of newspapers.

The larger contribution of Protomodernism affected how journalism conceived of newspaper pages, especially the front page. Modernist designers proposed a new way of viewing that took the entire page as a single canvas. Except on the occasional illustration page, traditional newspapering had ordered its physical existence on the column, measured by the square or the inch. Pages, as receptacles for columns, had little significance, and newspaper conductors would fill the columns out of other motivations, such as chronology or the flow of typesetting (see Chapter 3). The page as canvas (drawing a metaphor from art) or as display window (drawing from commerce) imposed on journalism the logic of the social map. Within the newly conceived front page, professional newsworkers provided an orderly array — a functional map — of the day's news from top to bottom. Like a map, the front page also supplied a legend, that is, an index (an invention arriving very late in newspapers) that catalogued news in priority. Certain breaking events also received front-page notice in the form of summary boxes that pointed into the newspaper's interior. The elements of journalistic mapping guided readers through the news and, by analogy, into the world itself.

The Protomodern newspaper looks hopelessly old-fashioned today. Its gray palette, limited illustration, and small scale for items seem closer to Victorian antecedents than to newspapers at the end of the century (Figure 6.6). Nevertheless, it challenged fundamental notions of journalism that had reigned from the mid-nineteenth century. In place of the declining metaphor of the market cornucopia, the top-down order of Protomodern news asserted clearly for the first time the sense-making power journalists wielded.

Classicist Phase, 1930s–Present

As a cultural movement, modernism had many faces. One turned toward the people and expressed itself in a demotic reaching out toward crowds and masses of atomized individuals. The popular and tabloid press followed its own course (see Chapter 8). Another face of modernism turned backward and advanced by recovering from the archive of the distant past the forms that could replace the despised and flawed designs of the immediate past. The Classicist phase of modernism looked back.

A concern with authority drove much of the culture of the 1930s. In the United States, the massive federal projects of the New Deal consciously borrowed from Neoclassical forms of the Federalist era that had in turn recovered earlier English borrowings from ancient Greece and Rome, simplifying and popularizing them. In Germany, of course, the same stylistic drive inflated misappropriations from the mythologized past into the imperial forms of Nazi public culture, in a grotesque version of classicism. Be-

FIGURE 6.6. Perhaps the best known example of Protomodern design is the front page from the *New York Herald Tribune*, shown on February 16, 1943.

hind the classicist movement lurked a real crisis in political authority. Woodrow Wilson had proclaimed that the Great War would make the world safe for democracy, but authoritarian movements seemed to flow naturally, even inevitably, from it. Economic crisis deepened political troubles, prompted fears of disorder and class warfare, and called for top-down management of more and more of civil society. Democracies generated massive and intrusive bureaucracies, while other countries produced dictatorships.

Newspapers felt these developments keenly. In the United States, the precipitous decline of advertising revenue and the loss of readers newly impoverished in the Great Depression required newspapers to shorten themselves and wrung many weaker papers out of competitive markets. By the end of the Great Depression, no real question remained about whether the local daily newspaper formed a natural monopoly. Politically, the news media became increasingly conservative on the whole, protecting themselves from the New Deal and from various allied reform movements. The high point for Classicist concern about the crisis of democracy came with the 1947 report of the Hutchins Commission, *A Free and Responsible Press*. Here scholars and citizens fantasized a socially responsible press, one that would abjure profit in favor of civic leadership and evenhanded representations of the diverse public.

In the visual arts, modern abstractionists (unlike expressionists; see Chapter 8) sought classical clarity in pure form. In newspapers, the most authoritative design movement took on a classical mien. Stanley Morison, who directed the redesign of the *Times* of London beginning in 1929, most influenced the development of Classicist modern style, elements of which newspapers adopted later (Figure 6.7). Like colonial printers, classicists admired the printed book, and their designs aspired to a similar intellectual status. Although they employed many of the tools of modern design, including indexes, hierarchical order, and some asymmetrical layout, they did so with a gray reserve suitable for the voice of authority, sometimes unpunctuated by pictures.

The step from the Protomodern to the Classicist modern newspaper showed most clearly in spatial organization. Individual articles of news adopted from advertising the conception of unity within clear borders. For news, the most desirable form became the rectangle (although other shapes continued; see Barnhurst, 1991). Rectangles also, of course, reflected geometric notions greatly admired by abstract modern artists. The *Washington Post* provides the most consistent example of Classicist design (illustrated in

FIGURE 6.7. The Classicist Modern design pioneered by *The Times*, London, in the 1930s, is exemplified in its mature form in this front page of October 2, 1970.

Hutt, 1973, p. 214). Horizontal forms came to the fore as central in the organizing scheme, a further expression of the ordering and taming power of journalism over runaway events.

These two phases, the Protomodern and the Classicist modern, coexisted through midcentury. After the initial explosion of modernist energy, newspapers continued to elaborate the visual and content vocabulary of modernism. More newspapers moved from their older designs into modern ones. The redesign of the *Los Angeles Times* in 1936, which the following year won the Ayer Cup as the best designed U.S. newspaper, used streamlined headings that anticipated designs still in use in the 1960s (illustrated in Hutt, 1973, p. 128). The look of modernism over the period became more pronounced. Space entered more firmly into daily use. Pictures took their place as (almost) full partners in the journalistic enterprise. Newspapers took advantage of technological changes, especially the development of offset printing and phototypesetting, to enlarge space and pictures and to refine the levels of emphasis available in headlines. The new methods provided a full range of type sizes (subject only to the telescoping of phototypographic lenses), unlike the limited sizes usually available in metal type.

High Modern Phase, 1970s–Present

The cold war demanded a firm consensus on U.S. values: the precise meanings of American institutions and their unique superiority to other national traditions, the precise genius of the American character and its unique invulnerability to fascism, the precise classlessness of the American economy and its unique ability to provide luxury for ordinary folk, and other classic elements of the American self-image. These found wide acceptance. Supporters included not only anti-communist liberal and conservative elites but also the newly affluent middle class, now buying homes and cars, phones and refrigerators in ever greater numbers and going into debt at an unprecedented rate. The social revolution experienced by the middle class underpinned the apparent consensus. As the automobile, subsidized by massive federal highway programs, helped move the home out to the suburbs, appliances brought bread and circuses — the refrigerator full of farm produce, the television full of amusements — into the home (Nasaw, 1993; Jackson, 1985). Home became an ideal self-enclosed world (Spigel, 1992), and the ironic endorsement of the hydrogen bomb gave a new meaning to the term nuclear family.

The powerful consensus achieved full expression in U.S. newspapers when it had already begun to unravel. The dislocations of the Vietnam era made only slow inroads into the world of the newspaper, which ironically continued to pretend to be reporting World War II until quite late in the affair — noble exceptions to the contrary notwithstanding. Even as things fell apart in the short decade from Tet to Watergate, the news media continued to hover above the disarray, secure that they represented a moral consensus that was, to say the least, no longer fully believable.

When it reached its height in the 1970s, modernism had reduced the complexity of the news page to a series of rectangles (sometimes erroneously called modules). Publishers hired artistic consultants from outside the U.S. newspaper industry, such as the British artist Frank Aris and the Italian graphic designer Massimo Vignelli, to accomplish redesigns based on Swiss-style grids (see the 1971 Vignelli design of *The Herald,* in Barnhurst, 1994, p. 186). The horizontal form dominated layouts, although not without some strong vertical elements. Indexes and summary boxes grew in importance along with promotional items, called sky boxes, meant to entice the reader to look inside, in a direct borrowing from advertising and marketing. Larger display type and dominant images, often in color, imposed a simple order on the few remaining stories on page 1.

In short, the High Modern phase brought all the tendencies of modernism to their culmination. The entire page worked together as a conceptual canvas, or, in the case of front pages, as an architectural facade, in the phrase preferred by design consultants. One element provided a center of visual attention, signaling the most important content judged according not to news events but to the entertainment value of the image (Figure 6.8). In High Modernism, graphic-design professionals ruled supreme or close to it (despite their many demurrers).

Late Modern Phase, 1980s–Present

Cultural moments often exhaust themselves in bursts of nostalgia. Reaganism surely marked the exhaustion of modernism. Nostalgia for simpler times and their simpler virtues punctuated a triumph in the cold war that ironically produced a further wave of nostalgia for cold-war-era certainties. If the emperor's new clothes were all traditional costumes, however, any little boy can see that they really aren't clothes at all. That is, what seemed backward-looking was actually quite revolutionary. Although Reaganism dedicated itself to dismantling big government, it really did no such thing. Instead, it re-orchestrated big government into a closer harmony with global capital,

FIGURE 6.8. The High Modern style first appeared in the Aris design for the front page of the *Minneapolis Tribune,* in 1971 (see Hutt, 1973, p. 213).

removing (under the guise of the new economic mandarins) limits on capital flows and market forces both domestically and globally and encouraging the rise of truly transnational champion corporations with U.S. bases. This economic revolution — already begun under previous administrations — coincided with a similarly disingenuous cultural revolution, in which traditional values simultaneously concealed and called attention to a continual drift toward rearranging domestic life according to market imperatives.

The exhaustion of modernism was felt too in newspaper design. When the Society of Newspaper Design (SND) organized in 1979, newspapers had begun to enter a new phase. Many of the modernist urges continued: from advertising, more promotional strategies, boxed items meant to sell the stories inside; from journalism, more mapping techniques, indexing and ranking the news content; and from design, more visual structures, seeking control-by-rectangle within a grand (and more or less fixed) architectural page design (Figure 6.9).

The Late Modern newspaper became a designer's newspaper. Editors and journalists began to define their own tasks as taking part in the design of news, planning stories with visual packaging in mind. Observers and practitioners alike assumed that newspapers exerted their power on a meta-discursive level — not through what a story said but through how it was framed, which narrative strategies reporters used to deploy information, and where designers positioned it in a flow of reading. The assumption translated into a quantitative rule of thumb: the more the media cover something, the more the public talk about it, or, in the common phrasing, The media don't tell the public what to think but what to think about. The so-called agenda-setting function assumes a notion of news as a functionalist map of public affairs.

Scholarship and newspaper practice both worked from a self-consciousness about the artificiality of newspaper design in the corporate era. No longer did the look of the news seem to flow naturally from the world, we suggest, because it no longer extruded socially or physically from the routines of the newspaper enterprise. It came from designers, who could make it look industrial or partisan or printerly or whatever else they liked.

Late Modern designers borrowed freely from older newspaper styles, especially those elaborated under high Victorianism: an increased typographic contrast, a higher story count, more maps and informational graphics, and a smaller scale overall for pictures and other elements. USA Today, probably the best known example, did not originate but imitated a style that preceded (and flourished since) the newspaper's founding in 1982. The artificiality of Late Modern style becomes readily apparent in the global context

FIGURE 6.9. A Late Modern front page that had lasting impact was the *Morning Call,* Allentown, Pennsylvania, shown here from May 23, 1980 (see Lockwood, 1992, p. 47).

(see Chapter 8), where U.S. newspapers remained relatively tranquil in design even while their influence in the world, on both visual and corporate models, grew. Elsewhere, however, the Late Modern has assumed many forms.

THE DESIGN REVOLUTION

Our results confirm the triumph of modern design elements but show a gradual and accelerating, rather than an abrupt, change. Although modernists would like to trumpet a sudden revolution, newspapers reflected a much longer cultural shift. The longitudinal study of design history as well as our measurement of modernist elements revealed a slow transition from the Victorian and then a continuing evolution in the modern (see Chapter 1, Table 1.2).

Modernists chose to call the mature Victorian style by the name Traditional, a term filled with the opprobrium they usually assigned anything considered old-fashioned, out of date, or behind the times. As design became a self-defined profession and the visual appearance of newspapers increasingly lost any necessary connection to productive processes, the visual history of the press lost its periodic quality. The phases in modern evolution nevertheless did produce a new formation, in which the modernist index (originally a product of early modern Europe) began to act as the controlling metaphor.

Journalists and designers did observe correctly that newspapers by the 1970s were becoming more uniform. By the end of the century newspapers came to share certain design features: six columns, modular layout, a small story count, two or three front-page illustrations, sans serif and upper- and lowercase headlines, and so forth. In order to present a uniformly crisp, modernist facade, newspapers had become less diverse, not unlike the glass boxes of modern architecture. Small variations from newspaper to newspaper masked the uniformity, as did the relative isolation of the press, which published under conditions of local monopoly.

Our results challenge the view of technology as the motive force for change. No discontinuities turned up that might have resulted from the introduction of new newspaper technology. The trends we observed predated the introduction of new technology, and most of the specific changes we tracked did not depend on technology. Certainly technology does not account for the decline in the density of the front page. Typography has always had the capacity to vary the number of columns and the number of lines per column of type per page. Newspapers did not need new technology to reduce the number of words on the page or to simplify headlines. Nor did the prominence of illustrations depend on technical change.

Although the publisher's newspaper of the nineteenth century seemed to push forward the techniques of printing and papermaking, twentieth-century newspapers adopted new technologies with a notorious *lento*. They resisted the 35-mm camera, they remained the last holdout for letterpress printing, and they did not rush into computer pagination. Nevertheless, the pace of change may have accelerated late in the century. Newspapers showed real alacrity in moving onto the Internet (see Chapter 8). The picture journalists and designers painted to justify Late Modern variations takes on significance because it shows the cultural values of the modern era.

Much of the resistance to change in newspapers resulted from the characteristic divisions of labor in the news workplace. Historically, newspapers followed a pattern of gradually adjusting to the push by some (often younger) staffers for new techniques. New techniques, extrasocial and disembodied, did not simply invade and transform the newspaper. The introduction of technology occurred adventitiously. Newspaper publishers resisted the risks and costs of change, but by invoking technology editors and designers made change seem inevitable. Technology took the blame, removing the onus from those urging change and pressing those who resisted. The rationale itself was an artifact of the internal politics of newspaper publishing. Technology supplied an important element in the background, but was not the cause of newspaper design change.

Another background element was competition. Beginning in the 1940s, editors and artists became aware that their audience was increasingly attracted to radio, news magazines, and later, television. The new visual media presented a clear challenge, illustrated dramatically when radio quickly lost its dominance to television. Competitors either differentiate themselves, as radio did by shifting to music, or imitate the opponent ("go head to head" in business parlance). Newspapers responded by moving to imitate, opening themselves to changes in their visual form. Although competition encouraged newspapers to experiment with new visual elements, it did not dictate either which elements to adopt or how to integrate them into the overall pattern of the front page.

An example of this influence is so-called modular layout. In the received history, newspapers adopted the modular style of layout used by magazines in order to compete with them. Modular layout in a magazine, however, differed from what newspapers came to call modular. In magazine design, the modular concept employed the same unit of measurement (a square or rectangle) to determine the scale and placement of every object in the layout. Newspapers developed no such module, and, in fact, the term only incorrectly described what newspapers did. So-called modular layout, as it developed in the 1970s, did no more than square off the doglegs that characterized layout earlier in the century. Newspaper modules were arbitrary rectangles, a far cry from modular design in other fields. Magazine design probably encouraged newspaper editors to innovate, but the editors themselves invented the new layout pattern.

Technology and competition provided convenient rationales for change, which, because editors and designers used them freely, inevitably found their way into scholarship. In the foreground stood the editors, acting under certain urgings and constraints, making a series of decisions about the form of newspaper front pages. In place of the standard explanation, we propose that two motive forces led to the specific changes they made.

First, newspaper editors and artists participated in the broader cultural drift from Victorian style to modernism. Twentieth-century design in general lagged behind the triumph of modern style in the fine arts, and newspaper design lagged behind even further. That tardiness makes our history of news form a history of mainstream U.S. culture. In the print media, modernism made its impact felt first in magazines and advertisements and then diffused slowly into the news media. The design ideas behind the creation of modernist front pages, traced in articulate form to the work of Allen (1947), Sutton (1969), and Arnold (1956), borrowed partly from news magazines and predated the major newspaper redesigns by several decades. By invoking the challenges of technology and competition, these writers managed to rationalize stylistic decisions. They attacked the so-called Traditional style and prescribed the specific forms of modernism — simplicity, order, and authority — without regard for the ideological underpinnings of those forms.

A second motive force, the emergence of an increased attentiveness to issues of journalistic practice, we can sum up in the term *professionalism*. The decline in variation in design signaled the appearance by the 1920s of a shared notion for the function of the front page. Front pages of 1885 presented a dense jungle of news items and (quite often) advertisements, giving an impression of diversity, randomness, and complexity that left the reader to make sense of, to draw a map of, the world. Gradually, newspapers lost the habit of placing dozens of stories on the front page. As modern front pages became more structured and less populated, their form bore frequent witness to the newspaper's efforts to map the world for its readers. Among the examples our study documented, the most powerful came from headlines: the primitive headline, with its multiple decks stacked vertically above a single column, offering an outline of the story, verses the modern headline, telling readers the point — the import — of the story. The changes suggest a wholesale shift in the meaning of headlines.

Bylines tied this pattern of change to both institutional and ideological developments in the media. The more frequent bylines of the 1920s reflected the growth of wire services and syndication and an increased attention to journalistic professionalism. Bylines, meant to give credit to authors, in the process lent gravity to their stories. Authorship, as a form of authority, found typographic expression in bylines, the frequency of which provided a good indicator of the newspaper's endeavor to map the world for its readers.

Mapping is also a visual activity, and newspaper front pages became defined in the professional lore as primarily visual, a shop window that gave a glimpse of the world (and encouraged sales). The number of illustrations increased, and more of them stood alone; especially as the century wore on, information became packaged in graphic form. The development of the concept of the newspaper as a visible map making sense of events opened the press to the stylistic phases dictated by the general cultural embrace of modernism. The visual (as well as the textual) presentation of news demanded order, hierarchy, and usability. Once a stylistic vocabulary colonized newsroom discussions, journalists could embrace changes more easily and with greater speed.

The transformation of the newspaper into a map became more important as newspapers grew in another dimension. The declining quantity and enhanced orderliness on front pages helped organize and frame the expanding information that went inside. The newspaper itself grew fatter. Total page count for the average daily edition gradually increased, a trend pushed by the growth in advertising and the decline in competition from other newspapers. As newspapers became longer, they added sections with fronts of their own, permitting them to reduce even further the density of the front page. They also began *jumping*, or continuing, stories to inside pages, which in part explains why the word count declined faster than the story count.

THE MANAGERIAL NEWSPAPER

In the course of the twentieth century, U.S. front pages became more orderly. They abandoned the dense, random appearance of the nineteenth century in favor of a more spacious, more overtly patterned appearance. Modern front pages sought to map reality for their readers. The shift in appearance was rooted in changes in journalistic and design ideas. Designers, beginning in earnest in the 1940s, sought to rationalize the front page, to make it more readable and structured, in line with the modern approach to visual arts. Journalists, sensitive to the responsibilities of their increasingly professionalized vocation, sought to do a more thorough job of digesting and organizing the news for their readers. These stylistic and professional concerns played out on a background of technical change and competition. Newspapers adapted slowly to new technologies; competition with other, more visual media also encouraged adoption of design innovations. They acted in ways consonant with the cultural context.

As newspapers became more structured, their appearance also became more homogenous. Virtually all newspapers came to share the design features of modernism: format, layout, illustrations, headlines, and so forth. The similarities might be called *structural*. Every newspaper would carry a front-page photograph of a president's inauguration, for instance, but each might use a strikingly different photo, or the same photo in strikingly different sizes. The differences in pictures selected was only superficial. On a deeper level the structural similarities betokened a shared sense of the purpose and meaning of front pages, headlines, bylines, and stories: they proposed to present an authoritative map of the day's events. Moreover, the maps presented by different newspapers became strikingly similar.

In the Late Modern phase, the professional newspaper (with all the dogged resistance to changes that might reduce the power of reporters over the social map), gave way to the manager's newspaper. Designers entered newspapers under the patronage of the corporate side (at the *Boston Globe,* for example, their offices started in the company headquarters and infiltrated the news bays only slowly). The course of modern design became, at least at the end of the century, a barometer of corporate managers overruling reporters' interests.

Corporations' aspirations to survive (their greatest advantage over natural persons) require a certain bland external face and a resistance to clear and easy identification. The larger and more intricate and multifarious the entity, the greater its interest in anonymity or invisibility (in something akin to a J. D. Salinger effect) — traits also valued the closer the entity moves to the sacred zone of public affairs. Thus News Corporation, by having no identity, can work effectively across national boundaries. Corporations also seek profit, of course, and try to reduce loose ends and nail down anything that could make profit seeking less manageable. The cookie-cutter effect we measured resulted in part from the growth of newspaper chains and the centralizing of design control at corporate headquarters.

The Gannett newspapers developed the longest history of manager controls and the most elaborate mechanisms, in line with the company philosophy of maximizing profits and minimizing risk. Corporate design managers made their papers follow detailed design specifications that constrained local journalists to create what analysts call a monolithic identity for Gannett newspapers. News Corporation holds many such properties through generic entities — The News Limited, News America, News Finance, News Group Newspapers — a system of holding that allows for branded identity but doesn't allow for any corporate accountability (Mirsky, 1995).

The corporate formation for newspapers deals not in coffee talk or the sale of goods in the marketplace or the expert analysis of the sociopolitical sphere, but in the manufacture of product. Late Modern newspapers provide containerized receptacles for units of product, with each container highly standardized and differentiated. Newspapers then train their staffs to manufacture a truly modular product in uniform doses at regular intervals. Product has uses beyond the initial appearance as a newspaper story, and corporations can recycle product among other branded entities, making it into a television news story, or a plot element in a sitcom, or a movie, or a mass-market paperback. Such product, as advertising managers say, has legs.

Understanding the later phases of modernism requires a more thorough understanding of its origins. In our quantitative study, we found measure after measure shifted toward modernism in the decades of the 1920s and 1930s. We have pointed to the pivotal role of the First World War, and next we turn to the interwar years, when modernism took root in the U.S. press.

CHAPTER 7

VISUAL MAPPING

Modern Design and Cultural Authority, 1920–1940

Conventional wisdom holds that new technologies and competition from television drove U.S. newspapers into a redesign revolution in the 1970s. The previous chapter showed that news design did not change suddenly in that decade, although it did accelerate. In fact, the direction of change had been established much earlier, in the 1920s and 1930s, when newspapers began to develop modern designs with fewer items and stories under simplified headlines running across more columns. What motivated the transformation of the newspaper in the period between the wars? At a time of turbulent social and cultural change, why did newspapers adopt a calm, rational face? What course or courses did newspapers follow as they set the new direction for change?

This chapter seeks to answer those questions by examining design change during the 1920s and 1930s in five newspapers: the *Denver Post*, the *Chicago Daily News*, the *Boston Evening Transcript*, the *Chicago Herald and Examiner*, and the *Syracuse Bugle*. We chose these newspapers to reflect the varieties of newspaper design and patterns of design change during the period. The *Denver Post* was a notoriously sensational paper in a booming western city; the *Chicago Daily News* was a bastion of popular journalism in an established midwestern metropolis; its competitor, the *Herald and Examiner*, was a Hearst paper that evolved into a tabloid; the *Boston Evening Transcript* was a relatively staid paper that first adopted a more emphatic style and then dramatically streamlined; and the *Syracuse Bugle* was a short-lived weekly tabloid in a small eastern city. Although no selection of newspapers would yield a representative sample of the era's design, this group allows us to discuss a broad range of patterns and shifts beyond those exemplified in the era's elite papers, which tend not to lead in design innovation.

NOT A MIRROR BUT A MAP

The timing of the initial shift to modern design is important. It indicates that the change was not a side effect of recent technical advances but a response to social and cultural trends and conditions. Specifically, modern newspaper design seemed to address two features of industrializing society: the reallocation of cultural authority to new professional groups and transformations in the configuration of space and time.

The rise of the professions as locations of authority in the Progressive era is a familiar theme in U.S. history. In the realm of journalism, the professionalizing impulse is apparent in the appearance of journalism degree programs at universities nationwide; in muckraking indictments of the newspapers of the industrial era, like Upton Sinclair's (1919) *The Brass Check* and Will Irwin's (1916/1969) *The American Newspaper*; and in Walter Lippmann's (1922) call for "intelligence bureaus" to supplement newspaper reportage in his *Public Opinion*. Michael Schudson (1978) has usefully summarized the development of a stance of professionalism and the concomitant rise of an ethos of objectivity in *Discovering the News*.

Although the textual aspects of the shift to professional reporting have been debated, the discussion has generally gone on without reference to the visual history of the media (Epstein, 1974; Gans, 1979; Tuchman, 1978; Leonard, 1986). Yet a connection between journalistic professionalism and modern design is evident. Individual accounts by professional journalists — the content of the newspaper — were embedded into the larger visual form, the newspaper's physical format and design. Also, clearly, readers read newspapers and not reporters.

Modern design was not simply a side effect of the professionalization of journalism, however. Ironically, changes in visual form affected not just the elite press but were perhaps more strongly felt in the demotic (and deprofessionalized) world of the tabloids, still novel in the 1920s. What, then, connected professionalization with modern design? The simple answer is that they were parallel responses to massive changes produced by the industrializing process, abstractly grasped as reconfigurations of space and time.

Cultural historians have noted that modernism generally emerged in conjunction with changes in the organization of space and time (Kern,

1983). Such shifts, associated with new communication and transportation technologies, have long interested communications scholars (Carey, 1988; Innis, 1951; McLuhan, 1964). Not only did modernism and industrialization alter physical space in ways that social theory should note, but social transformations connected first to modernization and then to postmodernism challenged existing configurations of cultural space (Jameson, 1991; Soja, 1989). Commentators on the postmodern condition have argued that postmodern folk, for a variety of reasons, are unable to construct adequate maps of their social worlds. The modernist newspaper style that came into existence in the 1920s and 1930s presented itself as just such a social map, one redrawn on a daily basis, that is, with a spatial rather than a temporal bias, to borrow from Innis. (A medium with a *temporal bias* allows for its preservation through time — clay tablets, for example — whereas one with a *spatial bias* allows for its broad dissemination through space — network television, for example. These biases Innis and others considered to have consequences for social and cultural coherence and for the creation and erosion of centers of control.)

Mapping the social, however, required authority of the sort claimed by professionals — that is, authority supposedly derived from superior expertise. Professional expertise in turn justifies the erection of barriers to entry. Professions considered legitimate can erect barriers, such as licensing exams for doctors and lawyers. Other groups may mimic the professions by erecting barriers of other sorts, but must then justify those barriers by a claim to expertise and a professed commitment to public service. In the United States, constitutional guarantees of free expression prevent the licensing of journalists. Such factors as economies of scale for attracting advertising and investing in printing plants, however, created conditions of natural monopoly, bottlenecks that in turn allowed for the creation of pockets of professional control. Statistics suggest that conditions of local monopoly existed for most daily newspapers by the 1920s.

The particular set of bottlenecks that allowed for the creation of professionalism in journalism came into existence at roughly the time that the visual shape of the newspaper changed, that is, the period between the world wars. Achieving industrial stability and local monopoly allowed newspaper professionals to act as gatekeepers and consequently required them to profess an ethic of public service. The American Society of Newspaper Editors (ASNE) first adopted a code of ethics in 1923. In the words of the Hutchins Commission (1947), modern newspapers had acquired a responsibility to present the news of the day in a fashion that citizens could understand and use as a basis for action. This is a pretty fair description of the social mapping undertaken in modern newspaper design. The statement of responsibility emerged just when a series of design elements used sporadically for decades — typography, headlines, pictures, bylines, indexes, and sectioning — all congealed into a particular form.

The design shift inaugurated around 1920 amounted to the visual analog of professionalism. The modern newspaper replaced the so-called primitive (or Victorian) newspaper in the same fashion as the medical doctor replaced the itinerant snake-oil hawker. The Victorian front page had consisted of a cascade of items, organized in thin columns on a very broad sheet, with headlines in multiple tiers stacked like an outline on top of a story (Figure 7.1). Victorian pages often had an obvious symmetry but little hierarchy, exemplified by the alternating heads sometimes found at the top of columns (Figure 7.2). One exemplar of this type of design in English-speaking countries was the *Times* of London (Figure 7.3); in the United States, imitating the *Times* signaled a newspaper's seriousness (although no U.S. newspaper could quite match the *Times* in overall monochromatic reserve). A second quite different exemplar was the *San Francisco Examiner*, which used a variety of headline typographies to present a loud, insistent presence (Figure 7.4). These two exemplars may stand for two schools of Victorian papers: the *Examiner* school was emphatic, the *Times* school was reserved.

The newspaper in modern style was quite the opposite. Fewer items occupied more space; there was a clear hierarchy, so that the front page constituted a map of the day's events; headlines told the point of an item rather than outlining its content. Again, we can divide modern style into two schools. In this case, the reserved school was exemplified by the prestige broadsheets — the *New York Times,* the *Wall Street Journal,* the *Washington Post* — whereas the emphatic school was represented best by the tabloids. (*USA Today* is sometimes said to represent a next style — the postmodern newspaper. In fact, one might as readily understand it, in terms of design, as a throwback to *Examiner* style — an emphatic Victorianism.)

The designations for styles (Victorian or modern) and schools (reserved or emphatic) apply not only to front pages but to the whole form of the newspaper. Inside pages were designed like front pages, although with subtle differences. Moreover, the overall shape of the newspaper, including its size and its division into pages and sections (that is, its internal division of labor), was also a matter of design. Modern newspaper formats (broadsheet or tabloid) developed a clearer internal division of labor to go with their more streamlined external face; the spaciousness of the modern front page was matched by the increasing thickness of the whole newspaper overall as well

FIGURE 7.1. Note multiple-tiered headlines and alternating-column symmetry in the *Boston Evening Transcript* front page, from November 14, 1921.

as by the expansion of busy *pages*, such as the sports page, into roomier, less frantic *sections*. The entire newspaper came to express the heightened professional status of journalism.

A DESIGNER REVOLUTION

Design change involved more than newspeople; it was also a designer's movement. As such it reflected artistic and design trends evident throughout the industrialized world. Commercial design in the 1920s and 1930s re-

FIGURE 7.2. The *Chicago Daily News* achieves front-page symmetry by alternating headline type on neighboring columns and centering a cartoon, from January 3, 1920.

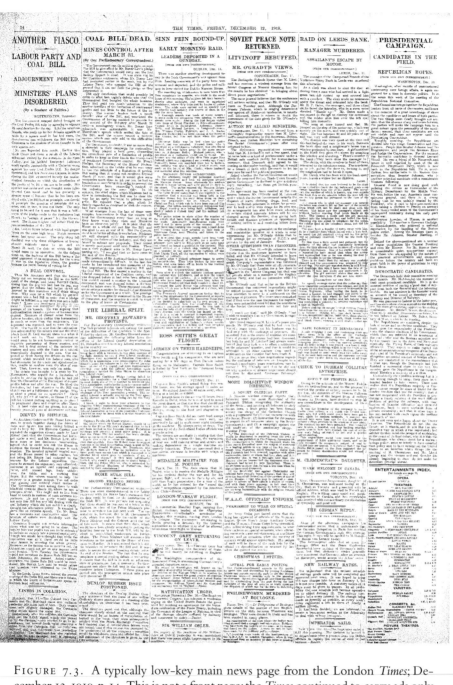

FIGURE 7.3. A typically low-key main news page from the London *Times*; December 12, 1919, p. 14. This is not a front page; the *Times* continued to carry ads only on the front page through the 1930s.

225

FIGURE 7.4. An emphatic Victorian front page typified the *San Francisco Examiner*, from November 11, 1918.

sponded in general to the avant-garde art movements collectively identified as modernism (Meggs, 1993). Modern art's arrival in the United States dates from the Armory Show of 1913, which showcased the design ideas of Europe. Later, European refugees from the Great War, trained in fine arts, brought visual ideas with them. Some landed jobs as commercial artists, principally designers and illustrators for fashion magazines such as *Vogue* and *Harper's Bazaar,* where their work gained a wide audience.

The burst of creative energy these artists carried with them had begun early in the new century and had at its root the broad changes in industrial machinery, transport, weaponry, communication media, political order, and intellectual life. These changes and, more importantly, their very speed invited two contradictory responses, giving birth to the artistic movements that gave modernism two distinct faces, the functional and the expressive (Ferebee, 1970). The urge to order, clarify, and make functional all that was new — and to disregard the old — found an outlet in art movements such as cubism, constructivism, de Stijl, and suprematism. The principal tool of these movements was geometry, at least as they spread functionalism into commercial arts, where they took typographic form in the geometrically pure (unadorned) sans serif. The opposing urge led toward the expressive extreme, found in movements such as fauvism, dadaism, and surrealism. The principal tool of expressionism (besides color) was the image, enlarged to become dominant in any context, with dramatic emphasis on emotional appeal, the subconscious, and the supralogical.

The new visual ideas invaded slowly. Modernism, a harbinger of cataclysmic change in Europe (Haskell, 1993), found the capitalist United States hostile ground at first. The ordering impulse lagged especially, because it arrived tainted by leftist and socialist political agendas in several European countries. Instead modernist forms entered by a circuitous route that bled them of their political associations and turned them, ultimately, into tools of corporatism and consumerism. In the case of newspapers, modernist ideas from the fine arts found entry through two vectors. Type workers at newspapers provided the first. In the 1920s, typographers, who admired the new asymmetrical type design as well as the revival of classic typefaces demonstrated in the private presses, attempted to transfer their ideas into newspaper work (Barnhurst, 1994). Later, avant-garde artists who found employment in the advertising business applied their ideas to ads, which began to appear in newspapers during the 1930s.

General observations from cultural history suggest a linear narrative of design change for the period, moving the Victorian newspaper toward a vessel of modern design, from a mirror of the disordered world to an authoritative social map. Testing that narrative requires a detailed examination of newspapers from the period, with particular attention to three topics: typography, imagery, and layout.

TYPOGRAPHY

Typography, although subtle and easily overlooked, provides the clearest evidence of how the newspapers evolved. Typographic changes were not random or highly individualistic, but conformed to larger constructs about how a newspaper ought to look. We encountered two general models in the initial years under study: the reserved *Times* school derived from the Victorian era and the emphatic *Examiner* school of the turn of the century. Newspapers differentiated themselves by selecting and deploying typography to match their self-definitions.

The *Boston Evening Transcript* of the 1920s, as a serious newspaper of record, wore headlines in several decks, stacked above a single column of text. Heads were middling to small in a mixture of three typefaces. Although it strayed quite far from its roots in the reserved Victorianism of the London *Times*, all of its subsequent design changes, mentioned in what follows, conform to expectations that the *Transcript* took important matters seriously.

The *Chicago Daily News* sought a middle road in the 1920s. Its main front page and news pages relied on three fairly gray typefaces, adhering to the *Times* school. Its street wrapper and some interior pages, however, added a few typographic signs of the emphatic school, including banner headlines and bold secondary headlines. In its changes over the two decades, the *Daily News* continued to invoke both declarative and exclamatory modes, even as it shifted toward modern styles of type.

In contrast, the *Chicago Herald and Examiner* began the period with type that leaned strongly toward the emphatic school. Banner headlines topped the pages, and subordinate headlines were made of moderately sized contrasting typefaces. This exclamatory and energetic quality makes intelligible some later design decisions that would otherwise be surprising.

Finally, the *Denver Post* and the *Syracuse Bugle* stayed firmly in the emphatic camp. The *Post* typography had a wild energy produced by extreme contrasts, not only of typefaces but also of fonts: bold and light, capital and small, condensed and expanded, and italic and regular letters. The *Bugle*, in its pursuit of ribaldry and farce, provided constant surprises with its type, sometimes importing a completely new headline face for a single story. Despite some variations, both these newspapers remained quite stable in their display typography; for all their energy, the type did not go through the great changes found in other newspapers.

Most of the changes in typography occurred in wave-like patterns, that is, variations that came and went with short-term daily practice or longer term with changing fashion. For example, the popular typeface Cheltenham with its blocky serifs first appeared on feature pages of the *Transcript* in the 1920s, disappeared in 1928, reappeared in 1930, grew in importance to become the principal headline face in 1935, dwindled in 1937, and reappeared in 1940 in banner headlines only. Such changes at times produced a ratchet effect, imparting each time some element that permanently redefined the newspaper and made its typographic image more modern. In the *Transcript* example, another typeface, Bodoni (a high-contrast modern roman with hairline serifs), became the standard head dress in 1928. Its use also waxed and waned, until it was superseded by Cheltenham in the 1930s. But the short period of Bodoni use left a residual effect. Its specific features required heads in upper- and lowercase to run larger and use more space to be legible. Headlines thereafter remained larger in scale and continued to use upper- and lowercase letters, two signs of modernism.

The vector of innovation ran consistent through all the papers, guided by the canons of serious journalism. Front pages, news pages, and sports pages (in that order) remained more or less sacrosanct, ruled by conservatism and resistant to typographic change. Feature pages, such as radio, books, entertainment, and women (in roughly that order) were more open to typographic variation, available for experimentation. A typical example occurred in the *Chicago Daily News*. Bodoni first appeared in 1929 on feature pages, then moved to news pages, and made the front page by 1931. By 1932 it would be chosen for one of the three or so largest headlines on a given front page. As it traveled from women's stories, through local news, to page 1, Bodoni appeared in increasingly strident fonts: bold, condensed, italic, and all capitals for emphasis.

Change itself was a constant, revealing the ongoing struggle to redefine journalism through its visible form. Despite day-to-day wobbles in the trajectory, two general processes were clear. Most changes were evolutionary, gradually shifting the mix of types used. The *Herald and Examiner* headline dress began in quite pure state in the early 1920s and wove tenaciously in and out of all subsequent type variations. The back page of the paper, which started out in typical news dress, slowly came to accommodate many tabloid stories of crime and emotional distress. From about 1935, the page began to acquire distinctive typefaces in larger sizes — a particularly tabloid look. The paper then, predictably, became a tabloid in 1938, applying generally many of the typographic effects developed on the back page.

The second process involved abrupt typographic change. The precipitous redesigns in some cases left only the nameplate intact. For example, in 1928 the *Boston Evening Transcript* suddenly abandoned its Victorian-inspired head dress in favor of streamlined Bodoni, a new, purist typography that lasted only until 1930. After a period of tinkering, the newspaper underwent another complete facelift in 1940 and then ceased publishing in 1941, right after its dramatic redesign. Although giving the impression of decisive action, quick makeovers indicated a newspaper had lost its way, whereas evolutionary, sometimes random-seeming change moved a newspaper more resolutely toward modernism.

The forces driving typographic changes we could only surmise from the printed record. Two are most salient: the influence of artistic styles, contemporaneous and antecedent, and the influence of the underlying political economy. In the more serious press, hard news pages seemed influenced only by design styles derived from newspaper fashions (rather than from the arts proper). The typeface Bodoni in streamlined (upper- and lowercase) headlines became established as the height of newspaper fashion in 1931, when the Ayer and Sons advertising agency gave its first newspaper design award to the *New York Herald Tribune* designed by Ben Sherbow (Hutt, 1973). The *Boston Evening Transcript* had made the shift to Bodoni in 1928, and the *Chicago Daily News* moved the face from feature pages onto the front page in 1931.

The soft news or feature pages proved more directly amenable to design styles found in the fine as well as the commercial arts. This is especially true at the emphatic papers. The *Herald and Examiner* played with art deco-inspired types. The *Post* tried on unusual fonts (such as outline versions and a cursive based on Roman lettering) for full-page features. Other newspapers were less likely to venture into the art realm. In the *Chicago Daily News*, art deco-inspired nameplates for feature sections appeared in 1932 but lasted only a year before being replaced with something more classical. The reserved *Transcript* was the least experimental, using such conservative devices as a blackletter (or Old English) label for its genealogical column. Feature typography also felt the influence of European émigré artists in the United States, whose work as magazine art directors had a secondhand effect as newspapers redesigned the special sections. When the *Daily News* Midweek Features section separated from the broadsheet paper and became tabloid-size, it acquired a magazine-style logotype. The book review section of the

Transcript came out in 1937 with a typeface entirely unrelated to anything in the newspaper: an odd, sinewy echo of art nouveau designs.

Within the twenty years studied, the rate of design change generally increased to match the pace of political and economic change. The relative stability visible in the early 1920s designs crumbled around the time of the stock market crash. Typographic changes began to accelerate in 1928 and 1929 and reached a quick tempo in the early 1930s. Like other industries faced with a sudden collapse in demand, newspapers began to encourage consumption by using planned obsolescence, a strategy of regular redesigns to make products fulfill the social urge to keep up with the latest style (Arens & Sheldon, 1932). The *Chicago Daily News,* for example, began periodic redesigns for section headings in 1932. The heads were altered in 1933 and completely replaced in 1934 (with a type similar to the old *Saturday Evening Post* logotype), and these in turn were supplanted in 1936 only to return in several versions from 1937 through 1939.

Changes in the 1930s also opened the door to forms of modernist order originally inspired by the leftist European thought mentioned previously. When redesigning its section headings in 1932, the *Chicago Daily News* introduced standardization. In place of the vernacular newspaper notion that type for each section should match the news content, the redesign imposed a modern notion of consistency and uniformity of design throughout. The balance of power between news and art at the newspaper had shifted, but the new design control served marketing rather than socialist purposes. Related changes occurred throughout the decade, as newspapers saw continuous experimentation, with a surge of change from 1938 to 1940. The most dramatic of these (setting aside the *Herald and Examiner* conversion to tabloid) was the *Transcript*'s move in 1940 to a front page containing only news summaries, set in authoritative modernist typefaces (such as Futura). This change followed a proposal by Herbert Brucker of Columbia University, who experimented with the format by converting a sample front page of the *New York Herald Tribune* into a summary front page he called *Gist* (Brucker, 1937).

The modernist system of design control also advanced as the newspapers moved toward greater emphasis and hierarchy. Contrasts grew between typefaces used together, between fonts (such as bold or light, condensed or expanded, italic or roman versions) of the same typeface, and between headline sizes. The newspapers used such contrasts to assign emphasis and to rank stories. Greater hierarchy resulted by the end of the period in the *Transcript*, the *Daily News*, and the *Herald and Examiner*.

Hierarchy also grew as the news sections followed a typographic pecking order, not only defining an inner sanctum where typefaces slowly gained entry but also establishing a standard presence beneath the veneer of typographic flourishes on feature pages. Clear hierarchy required that the newspapers adopt a grander scale. Typography, on the whole, got larger, and big headlines occupied more space on the page. This tendency held for all the newspapers, but especially for the *Herald and Examiner* and the *Bugle*.

Typographic trends clearly marked the newspapers' shift from Victorian to modern design and from vernacular (journalistic) to professional (artistic) design. At the end of the score of years under study, two new, modern schools had emerged in the typography. One for serious newspapers included streamlined large-scale headlines typically in Bodoni, with standardized nameplates for section headings, and, in some cases, for the logotypes and sigs (the individual designs combining type, lines, and sometimes imagery) used to mark regular columns. The other, for popular broadsheets and tabloids, included the brash circus of high-contrast typefaces descended from the turn-of-the-century emphatic Victorian style.

PHOTOGRAPHS AND OTHER IMAGERY

Pictures of all sorts moved erratically toward modernism and its two schools. The growth in the number and scale of images expanded the expressionism of the emphatic newspapers and the hierarchy of the reserved newspapers. Traces of handiwork that characterized vernacular design went into decline. Nonphotographic imagery, such as illustrations, logos, editorial cartoons, and comics, followed the general pattern, with exceptions that reflected internal power struggles and paid growing attention to the marketing and entertainment aims of the newspapers.

In 1920 a fair amount of hand-drawn imagery ran in the newspapers. The reserved front pages of the 1920s often carried a political cartoon, a practice that had been common in newspapers through the Victorian era, but front-page cartoons died out in the 1930s. The front was also the least active page for logo design over the period. Elsewhere the *Herald and Examiner* ran many hand-lettered logos for regular columnists until 1934. Fancy, illustrated logos appeared most commonly above columns dealing with movies, sports, and society. In all the newspapers, cartoons, small line cuts, and drawings decorated pages for women (and, later, for children), appeared as diagrams on the radio page, and also popped up on the sports page. A few maps, tables, and diagrams, and even some reproduced documents, sprinkled the pages carrying the softer news and features. By 1940, the hierarchy of news had hardened, making the front page sacrosanct and leaving other sections open in varying degrees to homemade-looking items.

The transition from vernacular to professional design, evident at most of the newspapers, at times met resistance from journalists. In the 1930s especially, artists regularized and streamlined the imagery for all the newspapers. At the *Daily News*, despite the fairly complete design overhaul in 1933, when all section heads acquired similar illustrated nameplates, other standing heads survived or reappeared. One sports columnist managed to retain his 1929 sig after the redesign. In such cases the celebrity or authority of a columnist overruled the designer's effort to control and unify the appearance of all standing elements. Vernacular designs at reserved newspapers more often lost their power struggles with the professional designs of modernism.

Sparked by an enthusiasm for marketing and brand identity, logos proliferated dramatically during the 1930s. The most common form for section or column headers employed distinctive typography flanked by two line-drawn open boxes called ears (for their shape and position). The most active page for such designs was sports. In the *Daily News*, at least six distinct designs for the sports nameplate appeared from 1930 to 1938. Some *Daily News* sports columnists had their own column heads in singular type as early as 1920. Financial columns did the same in 1929, at a time when the newspaper sought to market their expertise. The sports columns then outdid them, acquiring pictorial sigs. The reserved *Herald and Examiner* preferred simple boxed typography but likewise publicized its regular columnists.

Hand-drawn imagery also prospered wherever it helped make the newspapers more entertaining. Over the period, papers adopted more comic strips, single panels, editorial cartoons, and cartoonish flourishes in sigs and as ears next to section headings. A page of comics in Sunday editions in 1920 (in every paper except the *Transcript*) expanded to a full section by the 1930s, apparently with color added in the process. Daily editions picked up a comic strip or two in the mid-1920s and then added more, until by the 1930s they ran a full page. The *Transcript* didn't acquire a comic strip until the 1930s, although its comics had grown to fill a page by 1936. Editorial cartoons moved to the editorial pages of the *Daily News*, *Herald and Examiner*, and *Post*. Even the *Transcript* ran a daily cartoon in the 1930s.

Photography at the newspapers progressed to modernism from typography-centered (so-called literary) journalism through a period of decoration (as described in Chapter 5). The reserved school of Victorian design resisted pictures and used less adornment. The *Boston Evening Transcript* ran fewer news pictures and, for example, separated wedding pictures from type by demure embellishments. The emphatic school used pictures more freely to ornament the page and employed elaborate frames: hand-drawn borders, bric-a-brac, and space (left by showing the figure in vignette, with the background removed). In the *Daily News*, the *Herald and Examiner*, and especially the *Post*, these artistic frames flourished around pictures of women and feature subjects.

At first the newspapers crafted narratives from art concepts of picture making, especially portraiture and landscape genre painting. The two genres sometimes joined together in montage: cut-out close shots of the principal faces, mounted on a static landscape taken after the fact, at the scene of the events. The *Denver Post* and the *Daily News* used montage more extensively than did the other newspapers, but the technique died out completely, along with borders and silhouettes, in the early 1930s, once photographers could compose shots at the scene using small-format, easy-to-operate cameras. The new photojournalism, according to Hicks (1952), encouraged sequences of pictures and gave rise to the picture essay. Sequences first appeared, however, in the 1920s. The *Denver Post* ran a series of close-ups from a motion picture camera in 1922. Action sequences like the pictures of a bombing raid in the *Daily News* of 1937 (Figure 7.5) then became more common in the 1930s.

Pictures did not move directly from the static montages of illustrated news to the action shots of modern photojournalism. The *Daily News* picture of two divers on a 1929 sports page illustrates the transition between the two: the divers hover midair, frozen in modern action, but the picture was obviously staged, evidence of Victorian visual habits (Figure 7.6). The vast majority of photos throughout the period were posed: wedding portraits, sports-hero poses, group portraits, and a few scenes of historic significance. Although modernists disparage the clichés ("the handshake," "chalk-talk," "me and my prop"), posing continued unabated. Action shots quietly entered the *Herald and Examiner* in 1931 and the *Daily News* in 1935, after the wire services were operating, and generally gained ground by the end of the decade.

The modernist notion of photographs as another form of news content was not entirely clear in the 1920s and 1930s. The trend toward stand-alone pictures, for example, appeared muddled during the key decades of change. *Transcript* editors showed no clear preference for running photographs with or without an accompanying story. The *Daily News* meandered between the two options. Only the *Herald and Examiner* moved smartly toward modern-

The U. S. gunboat Panay rides to Davy Jones' locker under the devastating force of Japanese bombs. From the moment the first bombs fell on the ship, which prominently displayed the American flag, it required two hours and twenty-five minutes to sink the Panay.

FIGURE 7.5. An action sequence ran in the *Chicago Daily News*, December 30, 1937, p. 1, using motion picture technology.

GEORGE LE BRET (above) straightens out in a swan dive in the Chicago Athletic association pool, while Frank Snary completes a jackknife. Both boys were snapped during a workout for the meet tonight between their club, the C. A. A., and Northwestern university at the Cherry Circle tank.

FIGURE 7.6. What at first glance might look like a live action photo is on closer examination obviously a shot the photographer set up for the *Chicago Daily News,* December 15, 1920, p. 27.

ism: stand-alones accompanied features exclusively in the 1920s, invaded news pages by the mid-1930s, and arrived on the front page in 1938.

Other changes enhanced the expressionist tendencies of photographs: they got larger on the page and began portraying greater detail. In all the newspapers, the scale of pictures increased over the period. Although large photos appeared in the 1920s, the contrast of scale between small shots and large increased, making large pictures look even more dominant by contrast. At first the photos presented mostly long- and medium-range shots. Closer shots (or cropping) became more common in the late 1920s, and longer shots declined after 1936. As a consequence of more close-ups and tighter cropping, the pictures had a heightened emotional impact. These shifts were consonant with the emergence of modernism, which valued dominant imagery and emotive detail.

The conversion of the *Herald and Examiner* to tabloid format intensified the use of photography and other imagery. The tabloid ran many more pictures than in previous years, often several to a much smaller page. Unlike the modern broadsheet, which moved to unadorned rectangles for pictures, emphatic newspapers gave play to vernacular journalistic design, cutting pictures into irregular shapes, for example, by retouching a photograph of a teacher to show her shaking hands with a cartoon-style John Q. Public (Figure 7.7). In emphatic journalism, the subjective power of these photographs supplied an additional measure of moral authority (Szarkowski, 1973).

A similar tendency to emphasize imagery reigned at the *Bugle*. Although it began with few pictures, fairly quickly the *Bugle* was running a wide variety of doctored photos, engravings, and gag shots, along with reproductions of documents and suppressed images. The tabloid reached a fevered pitch right away and kept up until the last a constant and ever more shrill concern with what they called fairies and perverts, along with the usual mass of tabloid murder, corruption, and sexual naughtiness.

Modernists tend to ignore the expressionist side of the movement, but some newspapers gave full play to emphatic imagery. Although the record revealed many reversals and contradictions, the imagery on the whole moved in the direction of modernism. The resulting action, emotion, and detail, although usually invoked as serving the public need for information, also served other goals of the newspapers: to engage audiences in consumption and private diversion. Images also contributed to the other side of modernism, its hierarchy and organization.

LAYOUT AND ORGANIZATION

Several generalizations apply to the organization of all the newspapers: All experimented with their design order as the decades passed. All used more horizontal layouts that made their stories wider rather than taller. All began to package stories that shared a topical similarity, compartmentalizing them first into pages and then into sections. Finally, all used more bylining. These changes confirmed our expectations that newspapers became more modern in design.

Yet the pages remained dense and crowded. Newspapers did not become more spacious, contrary to our expectations, although the number of items on front pages declined over the two decades by about a third, from

FIGURE 7.7. Another photographic trick typical of vernacular journalistic design appears on the front page of the *Chicago Daily News*, December 16, 1937.

roughly thirty to twenty items. New space came from streamlined type and upper- and lowercase headlines. An increased orderliness on the front page also generated the appearance of spaciousness. Contrast, for example, the whirlpool effect of an early *Denver Post* front page (Figure 7.8) with a later front page, organized in a more top-down fashion (Figure 7.9).

Simple visual ordering became less of an overriding concern at most papers. The early years, especially on front pages, saw an attempt to achieve some kind of balance — either with stable diagonals (Figure 7.10) or with formal symmetry (Figure 7.11). Such layouts typified vernacular, rather than professional, design. Holding obvious layout in low regard, as a sign of the amateur, professional designers and photographers tended to frame things off-center. For their part, professional journalists did not fetishize a forced

FIGURE 7.8. The whirlpool of headlines surrounding the nameplate of the *Denver Post* confuses the hierarchy of stories — each headline seems to proclaim its preeminence, July 8, 1922.

FIGURE 7.9. A calmer *Post* front page, organized in a more top-down fashion, maps the news for its readers on January 7, 1935.

FIGURE 7.10. The *Boston Evening Transcript* achieves front-page symmetry by running boxed items in a diagonal line from lower left to upper right, July 1, 1925.

FIGURE 7.11. A top tier of headlines on the symmetrical *Boston Evening Transcript* front page, featuring left-to-right balance, also includes a diagonal line of headlines through the middle of the page, January 12, 1934.

visual symmetry for clearly asymmetrical content. Where naïve layouts might impose obvious balance arbitrarily, the ministrations of the professional would assign places according to some rationale. The diminishing concern with such ordering, then, reflected the mentality of the professional reporter as well as the aesthetic values of design professionals.

As obvious forms of balance declined, hierarchy generally advanced. At the beginning of the period under study, most papers distinguished top stories by using either a banner headline or a dizzying stack of subheads (see Figure 7.1, page 223). Beyond that, at least in visual terms, papers did not clearly signal the importance of individual items. Throughout the period, newspapers experimented with hierarchy, deploying and discarding a variety of different patterns. Some were confusing — the *Post*'s whirlpool, for example (Figure 7.9), or the stacked banner heads on the *Herald and Examiner*. By the end of the 1930s, however, most papers had come to a modern sense of hierarchy: they ran a banner head for the top story and placed the text in a right-hand column, often accompanied by illustrations or related stories. They also respected a hard-versus-soft distinction by placing stories above and below the fold.

All the newspapers grew more concerned with topical packaging and segmentation through the course of the two decades, without following a unilinear process. Some papers regressed. The *Boston Evening Transcript* began the decade with a system of topical banner heads for inside pages, so that a page with a couple of stories on politics was headlined Politics. The heads were ad hoc, changing from day to day and from page to page, but told the domain of the news, not its substance (Figure 7.12). Such heads yielded first to a more random grouping, a regression probably prompted by the need to crowd content into the shrinking size of the paper in the Depression years, and then to permanent, consistent topical heads such as International, clearly differentiated typographically on the page (Figure 7.13). The *Transcript* thus achieved topical regularity, but only by shifting to a very gross level of labeling. Beyond that level, the paper, like the news, was more of a mess in 1940 than it had been in 1925. The *Herald and Examiner* also moved backward in terms of topical packaging, losing all topical cohesion in its full tabloid incarnation.

Compartmentalization into sections proceeded in a more linear manner. All the newspapers developed sections early in the 1920s, and some apparently had them earlier in their Sunday editions, which generally advanced ahead of the weekday editions in design. Typically, a section began its evolution as a page, then grew into several pages; the number of pages in most of the papers increased through the 1920s, but the number of

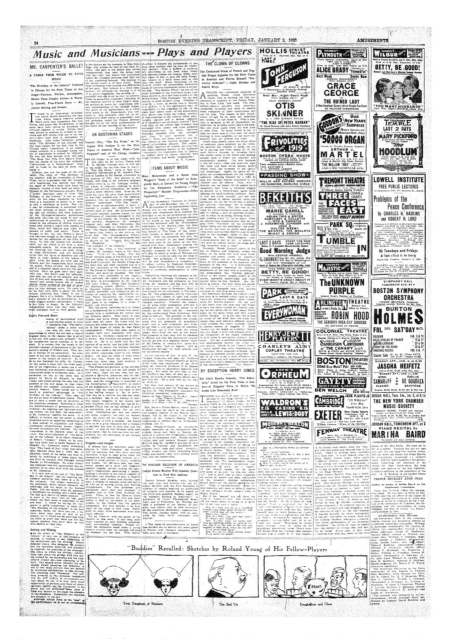

FIGURE 7.12. The banner heads on the inside sections of the *Boston Evening Transcript* describe the domain of news, not the substance of any particular story. This entertainment page doesn't distinguish between live and filmed entertainment, January 2, 1920, p. 8.

FIGURE 7.13. The *Boston Evening Transcript* later changed to standard topical heads that were typographically differentiated from the rest of the page, as shown on July 17, 1939, p. 2.

pages in sections increased far more rapidly, revealing overall a process of colonization. The newspapers each had a sports section and a business section in their weekday papers; various kinds of entertainment pages that did not always cohere into a section (although they seemed to move in that direction over the period); a women's page; and a Sunday magazine of some sort (and the *Denver Post* had a daily magazine). Most featured occasional travel, real estate, automobile, and book sections.

The sections topically shared two features. First, they all dealt with civil society as opposed to the state or the public sphere (Habermas, 1963/1989). That is, they centered on the private sphere — intimate, cultural, or financial matters — and they covered soft, not hard, news (although the business section might be called hard news). Second, each had some kind of advertising infrastructure. Newspapers developed automobile sections when auto manufacturers and retailers began to advertise, and likewise radio and movie pages, travel sections, and the rest. The only exception was sports, but clearly the evolving sports sections themselves acted as de facto advertisements for professional leagues.

The sports section merits further discussion. At the beginning of the period, newspapers carried sports pages, usually untitled, often including nonsports items. Sport was not confined to that page, and could even be the top story of the day. More commonly, sports news associated with schools and colleges might mix in with other educational news. By the mid-1920s, however, sports had become clearly segregated into sections of at least two pages. At the same time, the content of the section had come to emphasize professional rather than amateur sport. One loser in the transition was women's sport. Shown frequently (by sports standards) as amateur athletes, photos of women in assertive poses stood in vivid contrast to the demure portraits on the society or women's pages. As sports sections modernized, however, the female speed skater disappeared, replaced by the male baseball team.

A similar but contrasting story describes women's sections. In 1920, newspapers all carried a Society or Personals page filled with the doings of upscale women. The pages kept matriarchs of the local first families in the public eye, not least by regularly running photo essays about individual women. The photos, invariably done in highly stylized poses and conventional dress, had the effect of minimizing each woman's distinctiveness until they all blurred into one unending Mrs. Claypool (Figure 7.14). Such pages were not a good carrier for the practical concerns of women, however — at least as conceived by advertisers. One would not associate these matrons with pricing pork cutlets or buying dress patterns; such mundane concerns required a different sort of women's page.

The practical women's page first appeared in newspapers that appealed to the working class, but became a feature of every daily by the end of the 1920s. Sometimes it merged with the society women's page, but often it stood apart or instead melded with the entertainment page. It grew through the Depression, as newspapers made themselves useful to homemakers trying to make ends meet. Like the sports page, it was a fertile field for sigs, bylines, and graphic experimentation.

Other sections such as entertainment pages also responded to the marketing concerns of the newspaper and to broader social changes. In 1920, the dailies usually ran one page that included ads for live theater and movies, plus a (usually bylined) review or two, and occasionally a photograph (see Figure 7.12). Several features of these pages seem dated. Neither the editorial matter nor the ads distinguished between live and filmed theater, and the

FIGURE 7.14. Society matrons appear in highly stylized poses and conventional dress in the *Boston Evening Transcript,* December 10, 1921, part 3, p. 5.

printed word dominated the page. In the course of time, the entertainment section changed, but not in any clear direction. In 1922 all the dailies added a radio page built around a nationally syndicated column about equipment for the enthusiast, along with ads for radio sets. Within a few years, the page focused on programming for the general public, with extensive schedules, previews of shows, and articles on radio celebrities. In some papers the radio page merged with other entertainments; in some it remained distinct. Other papers combined book reviews, comics, crossword and other puzzles, and serialized fiction, items usually present elsewhere in the paper, to form a larger amusements section.

The clear direction through all these changes went from text to visuals. In entertainment sections photos proliferated, mostly shots of stars — taken from a movie, for instance — following the conventions not from journalism, in the sense of capturing developments, but from publicity. In short, the entertainment pages came to feature a cult of celebrity.

The journalist's ideology of the public mission of the newspaper partitioned the sections into ghettoes filled with the concerns of specific subgroups (like women and children) or special interest groups (like businessmen and baseball fans), stuff that didn't pretend to general importance for the common public. As serious journalism came to shun the sections, they became centers for design innovation. This was a logical development. Sections first developed fully in the Sunday editions and dealt with matters readily divorced from a local context. Many items were nationally syndicated, including bylined columns. The sections thus ran weekly, with the same time frame as a magazine, and allowed more time for design. They pioneered design innovation by imitating national magazines.

A final organizational tool, bylines, also became more modern. Schudson (1978) identified bylines as one of the devices instituted in the 1920s and 1930s that facilitated objectivity, understood as the rigorous attempt to separate personal values from reporting. Bylining reassured readers that an individual with a particular reputation and values wrote a news story. According to Schudson, bylines tacitly acknowledged the irreducible element of subjectivity that distinguishes objectivity from *naïve empiricism,* the notion that the facts can speak for themselves. A byline indicated a commitment to explain rather than simply to relate facts. It also signaled the rise of professionalism in journalism, because explaining the facts required expertise. Moreover, the fact that some journalists could command bylines indicated their elevated prestige, above the status of general reporters, whose pay (by the line or the inch) was vulnerable to the copy editor's scalpel (Solomon, 1995). Bylines, as a by-product of rising objectivity, would of course appear first in the parts of the newspaper where objectivity mattered most — on the front page, especially.

In the newspapers, however, bylines appeared earlier and more often in the sections than on the front page. Front-page bylines remained the exception through the early part of the period under study, while they teemed in the sections. Why? The byline appeared as a signature not of an expert, as expected, but of an author. Bylines indicated that what followed would be a performance by a literary celebrity, that it would be inimitable. Experts' work was expert only because any other qualified expert could replicate it. (For the same reason doctors' signatures blur into one ur-signature for the whole profession.) Writers in the sections acquired stardom because they flaunted what front-page journalism prohibited: idiomatic self-expression, strong opinions, and so forth. Serious journalists wanted stardom but had ideological and practical reservations about acquiring it by, for example, covering the statehouse as if it were the ballpark.

Hence the delay between the use of bylines in the sections and their adoption on the front page. Serious journalists needed a more fully developed and ideologically secure justification for appropriating this artifact of literary stardom (which later analyses of objectivity provide). Accordingly, bylines appeared first on the front pages of papers that were the least concerned with professionalism and objectivity, and apparently migrated to the elite press somewhat later. Along the way, bylines became associated with modernism and professionalism, so that today elite papers are more likely than others to byline a front-page story.

WHAT DESIGN CHANGE WAS NOT

We began this chapter by suggesting a narrative of linear design change. A messy form was reconstructed into a tidier, more didactic form through the agency of professionals newly empowered by conditions of monopoly and a cult of expertise. The modern newspaper, then, was a visual tool of social control. As we examined more closely developments of the 1920s and 1930s, we found the actual transition from Victorian to modern styles extremely complicated, with considerable meandering and much doubling back on a course full of conflict and contradictions.

Change, as it turned out, was neither sudden nor linear. It came about only through experimentation — the wilder the better. One of the crueler ironies is that usually after a period of experimental playfulness, its memory is condensed into a notion of heroic revolution or suppressed as a kind of juvenile rebellion against historical inevitability. Our history shows that such truncated memories miss the broad range of outcomes possible.

Outcomes were not determined by technology. Sometimes a technology facilitated a particular design feature, but every feature we identified here was in play before the so-called breakthrough technologies were introduced (Crary, 1990). Going back a century, news digests were a common feature before the telegraph became the preeminent tool for constructing columns labeled The Latest News. Likewise, photos turned up all over the newspaper before the wire services started distributing them, and, as we discovered, sequence shots ran before the advent of the small-format Leica supposedly made them easier to record. Technology did not lead but followed after journalistic agency.

Nor was design change unopposed in the newspaper world. We found most interesting the existence of friction between journalists and designers (here we use the term *journalist* to include all editorial personnel). Journalists and designers conflicted on two levels. On the level of the material interests of the different occupations, journalists did not want to take orders from designers. On the level of representing events, the clarity of design contradicted the jumble of news. Journalists had an investment in traditional and vernacular design, which seemed to express a newsperson's world, full of eventful fury: they resisted unfamiliar forms that would change the meaning of the newspaper and threaten its familiar relationship with its steady readers.

Journalists' best technique for resisting design innovation was to shuffle it off to the emerging soft-news ghetto. They protected the seriousness of their domain and buttressed their command over it by keeping a regressive control over design. Even in jazzed-up newspapers, the editorial page remained gray, and every significant design innovation became common in the inside sections before journalists allowed it to infect the front page. This finding seemed counterintuitive. Because journalists tend to think of the front page before anything else, we expected it to be the leading edge of change. We were thinking of design change as the shared endeavor of an occupational group rather than the negotiated result of battles among several such groups.

Instead, design overcame editorial reluctance by appealing to perceived threats to profitability. Twentieth-century newspapers repeatedly encountered potential agents of their demise or transfiguration; in the 1920s and 1930s the chief bogeymen — radio, film, and news magazines — each in turn seemed to strike at the circulation or advertising base. The climate of crisis was apparent in the practitioner manuals and college journalism textbooks that argued for the adoption of modernism as a response to the threats presented by new communication technology (Allen, 1947, originally published serially in the 1930s). What was true generally we found even more acute in specific cases. Newspapers in extreme financial difficulties turned to designers to adjust to changes. The complete makeover of a newspaper became common just before its demise. Modern designers in that case performed the role of undertaker, painting an untroubled face to hide the signs of imminent death.

THE SOCIAL MAP

We have phrased the friction between journalism and design broadly in order to capture the conflict not only between the material interests of reporters and those of designers but also between the messiness of news and the tidiness of visual design. These two conflicts are expressions of the same landscape, with the typography providing the cover vegetation for the underlying topography of social relations.

It seems to us that news by definition is messy. The very category, as socially constructed, emphasizes novelty, conflict, and timeliness, among other things. The news is weird, new, and dramatic; it is, in short, a jumble. The primitive Victorian newspaper, rather than constructing the world for its readers, subjected them to a bombardment of undigested stuff; copious and busy, it used design elements inconsistently and in ways ordinary readers might not expect to decode.

Modern design, by definition rational, functional, and premeditated, instead tamed the mess through artifice. The streamlining of the front page helped readers navigate their world with more confidence and efficiency. The appearance of new clusters of interests (sports pages, women's pages, entertainment pages) indicated a liberation of popular energy in all its contradictions — the leisure of news consumerism, the radicalism of the Great Depression, the conflicting energy of the jazz age.

On the modern front page the absence of disorder may have signaled the triumph of design over journalism, or the triumph of designers over journalists, but that would tell too simple a tale. In fact, the modern front page was also a reporter's front page, but for a different kind of reporter. The modern reporter — the professional journalist — was an expert. The expert explained the news, where the old reporter retold it. The virtues of the professional journalist, expertise and discernment, found the timeless moral or the historical significance behind a rush of events. The virtues of the old reporter came from showing that rush and revealing its urgency, compelling in and of itself. One found sense and historical drama where the other showed profusion and amazement. We have explored an inexact measure of these differing journalisms, the use of bylines and signatures, in some detail. Bylines illustrated in microcosm the flow of authority from reporters to experts. So-called sigs exposed the workings of celebrity and consumerism. Through such elements, social control mapped onto the physical form of newspapers.

During the interwar years, newspapers constructed two fairly definite forms. One form, the reserved broadsheet, the *New York Times* still exemplifies today. Here news items build up a clear hierarchy from a grammar of design elements like front-page story placement and headline size. Beyond the front page, the newspaper became segregated into sections (local, sports, features, classifieds) where news acquired further hierarchy. A separate opinion section employed distinct typographic styles for the newspaper's editorials, letters to the editor, and op-ed pieces. Crudely put, this newspaper form carved the social world up into separate domains and assigned affairs differential import within those domains. To a habitual reader of a paper like the *New York Times*, this form seemed self-evident: it corresponded to the manifest world, with the newspaper's latent function in mapping the world taken for granted.

An emphatic newspaper form also congealed in the interwar years, exemplified in its extreme version by the tabloid. Although reserved tabloids differed from broadsheets only superficially (*Newsday*, the *Sun-Times*), the emphatic tabloid embodied a strikingly different form. Its front page flaunted a single story with a huge headline; the interior left content unsegregated into sections; photographs and other illustrations throughout dominated the pages. The tabloid's map of the social, although perhaps less nuanced and intelligible than the broadsheet's, was more morally charged, full of heroes and villains. Put another way, where the reserved broadsheet form told readers what was important, the emphatic tabloid told readers what was evil.

The emphatic tabloid was the dialectical twin of the broadsheet. To our knowledge, tabloids existed only in markets already served by a conventional broadsheet daily; they presupposed their broadsheet rival and more or less yielded to it the role of prime mapper. This left the tabloid free to pursue fun, blood, and moralism. In this, the modern broadsheet and tabloid reflected the contrasting modernist movements within fine art. The garish colors and emotional imagery of the expressionists found journalistic embodiment in the emphatic tabloid; the cerebral purity and geometric order of the abstractionists entered the reserved broadsheet. In the spirit of the Bauhaus, both forms infused modern art into a commercial and industrial product.

Clearly these alternate newspaper forms incorporated different relationships between news producers and news consumers. The broadsheet was the professional form par excellence; its reporter was an apparently value-free discriminator and explainer; and its reader was a pupil. Tabloids deemphasized professional in favor of moral authority; its reporters served up hot prose while its columnists and photographers delivered pointed sermons; its readers crowded the pews before these moral censors. Yet the same industrial society spawned both the broadsheet and the tabloid. Both fed on a marketplace of industrial consumers, and both saw their missions as providing a center of gravity, either informational or moral, for the mass of citizens.

Although the reserved broadsheet appeared superficially the more modern of the two, both forms were creatures of the same historical moment — the tabloid involved a different but equally modern kind of visual, and therefore social, mapping. They shared their didacticism with other modernist forms of the interwar period, years that marked the creation of a "culture for democracy" broadly shared across regions and social classes, even while established patterns underwent severe strain (LeMahieu, 1988).

By the end of the interwar period, modernism had clearly established itself in U.S. newspapers, at least in its Protomodern form. In London, Stanley Morison had already redesigned the *Times* and the Classicist modern phase had dawned, but the United States became amenable to its severe simplicity only in the 1950s, when at least a veneer of U.S. culture aligned with the serene and uniform typography of that phase. The High Modern phase that followed required the clear institutionalization of U.S. journalism, with print as the mother of serious journalism setting the standard not only for its sister journalisms in the broadcast (and later cable) industries but also for journalisms in other countries.

A new type, the professional newspaper, reached its apex somewhere in the transition from the Classicist and High Modern phases. The anointment of reporters as the soul of journalism followed various moves in the interwar period to create standards of professionalism and ethics and reached a fullness before the meteoric rise of celebrity journalists beginning in the late 1960s. Ironically, a lesser breed, the television journalist and especially television news anchors, led the way into the fame and the high incomes that followed. Newspaper journalists would eventually follow suit, often using television and radio talk shows as avenues to the speaker and book-tour circuit (Fallows, 1996).

The seeds of later phases of newspaper modernism all sprouted in the 1920s and 1930s. Elements of classicism, such as the uniformity of type, and of the High Modern, such as the emphasis on hierarchy, all had their incipient forms in place by the outset of World War II. An emphasis on technical rationality also began then, only to flourish in the Late Modern phase. By the 1970s the pendulum had again swung, from the Classicist's public-mindedness (reminiscent of the printer's newspaper of the Federal period) to the commercial and advertising aims that had firmly asserted themselves with the editor's newspaper and reached an apotheosis with the industrial newspaper. In the next fin de siècle incarnation, press commercialization not only expanded the emphasis on journalists and journalism as controller of the social map but turned dramatically to the techniques of promotion and marketing (Barnhurst & Steele, 1997). The Late Modern phase had arrived. We next turn to the spread of newspaper modernism beyond the United States and into the Internet.

PART IV

AFTER MODERNISM

Hilda Kassell, East 53rd Street, New York City. "Father reading newspaper, two children viewing television," black-and-white photograph, Gottscho–Schleisner Collection (Library of Congress, Prints & Photographs Division LC-G613-57609), July 12, 1950.

Icon of Isolation

Images of the mass audience represent one dimension of the media as an environment. In everyday life, the news represents aspects of experience that are far away or largely out of reach: the invisible regulations of federal and state government, the inaccessible power of corporations, the unapproachable behavior of the nonconformist *other,* and the distant events in foreign countries. The form of news not only conveys a diorama of such things, it also contains the rules for representing them and for responding to them. The environment of news about distant affairs could be called a *macrosystem,* to borrow a term from social psychology (Bronfenbrenner, 1993).

The media environment simultaneously operates in another dimension, as what social psychologists call a *microsystem,* in which the individual reader encounters and makes reply to a host of other voices and images that seem to exist nearby: columnists, reporters, sports figures, politicians, and cartoon characters. Unlike face-to-face microsystems, where people confront the complexity and unpredictability of, say, coworkers, the media environment provides simpler personalities acting in repetitive and predictable ways. The fact that they arrive on paper or on screen does not make them seem less real or proximate to the viewer. Imaginary friends and enemies in the press fully engage the emotions, for example, sparking fear and anger as well as love and joy. Readers encounter them in the home (or in some other familiar place), and not in the indeterminate locations where their words originated.

The photograph from the Gottscho–Schleisner Collection depicts two such microsystems, the long-familiar newspaper and the then-novel television. Since television spread through the consumer market in the 1950s, domestic architecture has reconfigured living space to enhance the experience of viewing. A separate tee-vee-room (later rechristened a family room) provided the ideal conditions for entering into television space, a microsystem that best radiated its blue-grey shadows away from the light of day. Television allowed a surprising degree of social interaction among viewers — certainly more than movie theatres permitted. Here the two children watch together, and in anticipation of domestic rearrangements, a folding screen cuts them off from their father and shields the television from sunlight. Of course, the picture has the children staring absurdly at the test pattern and the father holding a much too neat and rigid newspaper in impossibly cramped quarters. The family acts out the separation of the generations and their media with all the stiffness of amateur thespians.

In fact, newspapers allow and even encourage interaction — for example, reading aloud, recounting, or expressing shock at events — but their representation has moved away from that role. Images of newspapers as an isolating environment emerged in the nineteenth century. Besides the cartoons with a father sitting behind the paper while children play, others dating from the Civil War point to the ways that newspapers sequester the reader. In one example from a children's book (*Universal*, 1863, n.p.), a soldier reclines in a rocker, reading news of the battle of Gettysburg from the *New York Herald*. Copies of newspapers lie strewn about: the *New York Ledger, Harper's Weekly, New York Daily News,* and others. Through the window soldiers can be seen training (a joke that might have escaped young readers of the *Universal Picture Book*). The newspaper blocks off the reading soldier's view of the real world outside, insulating him in the secluded microsystem of newspaper experiences. Similar images typically show a white man, slouching in a chair and surrounded by newspapers, completely engulfed in the news environment (and balancing precariously on a chair; see Leonard, 1995, pp. 10–11).

The form of news defines a topological region, one that provides both a panoramic view of the events of the day (the macrosystem) and a big easy chair (the microsystem) where a reader can spend time in the company of witnesses to and purveyors of those events. The two systems fit neatly together, like nested Russian dolls, along with other microsystems (such as the family) and mesosystems (the institutional environment). Newspapers array content and form to create tension between the shock of new, foreign, bizarre events in the macroenvironment and the friendly comfort of the microenvironment. Through its extended history, the representation of newspaper reading has moved decidedly away from the macrosystem to emphasize the microsystem. Newspaper reading is now a private affair, and although the change does not necessarily point to the demise of the medium, it does coincide with its abandonment of much of the public-spirited mission that animated newspapers earlier in U.S. history.

Computers have contributed to the move from public to private reading. Not only does each reader read alone; with an electronic newspaper each reads a different medium in a different environment. Electronic forms of news alter both macrosystem and microsystem, changing the possibilities for interacting, despite the fact that Web news does not necessarily provide new vistas on the world or allow different voices to report on it.

CHAPTER 8

BEYOND MODERNISM

Americanization and Its Consequences, 1910–2000

At the height of modern newspaper design, the rules of form were widely understood and rigidly enforced in the United States. The debates of the period occurred over details only, not over fundamentals. Protomodern old-timers clung to Bodoni headlines despite withering attacks from the young High Modernist bucks who pushed for Helvetica. Everyone, however, was in broad agreement about making reading more efficient and attracting the eye — the basic modernist tenets. Another argument raged over whether the lead story belonged on the left or the right side of the front page, but both sides assumed the same functionalist logic, that the form was a tool for professionals to guide readers through the day's events. Modernism permeated thinking about news, extending as far as civics teachers, who explained the rules for newspaper reading in their classes: the hierarchy of large-to-small headlines, top-to-bottom layout, and news arrangement, from stories leading on the front page or appearing on a section front to those buried inside. That's just the way things were done.

In the long history of journalistic form, the look of news always corresponded rather tightly to the reigning newspaper type at any given time. Despite some variations, the printer's newspaper had a look that we call the Federal style, and the editor's newspaper had a look we call the Partisan style. Victorian design came into existence with the industrial newspaper, and Modern style with the professional newspaper. The productive mode influenced style in many ways, some practical, such as the printers' limited design resources; some political, such as partisan appeals to citizen-voters through republican simplicity; some economic, such as industrial newspapers' increasing reliance on advertising revenue from mass retailers, especially department stores; and some cultural, such as the modern professionals' need to clarify their authority. In every case, the networks of relationships that constituted the newspaper connected clearly to the imagined network of relationships that the newspaper form represented.

At least in retrospect, the connections seem clear. In the case of Modern style, it is difficult to convey how rigid the rules were, especially looking back from the perspective of the twenty-first century. Today the type of newspaper production no longer marches in lockstep with a characteristic style. The corporate newspaper — our designation for the current type — breaks apart that connection and treats design history as a grabbag, employing elements from every other period and using them to signify wildly different things. The look of news has become relatively autonomous from its system of production. At the same time, the newspaper organization itself has become more complex, as the previously direct lines between the departments and the functions of the medium have blurred and as marketing has become (again) more urgent.

In other words, the modernist culture of newspapers has reached the brink of exhaustion. The sources of exhaustion lie deep in the internal structure of newspapers and in their external social, cultural, and political environment: fear of competition from other media, the rise of news design as a fully institutionalized profession, the widespread challenge to modernist apparatuses of objectivity and expertise, the growing awareness of cultural heterogeneity, and the predictions of newspapers' demise in the face of the unlimited possibilities new technologies seem to provide. These factors have a long history, coextensive with the career of modernism and not appearing only at its end. Together they have destabilized modernism, bringing another formation to a close.

The history of U.S. news form therefore stands at a moment of epochal change — perhaps. In the last decades of the twentieth century, the modern impulse seems to have run its course not only in news form and practice but also in art, design, and culture generally. At the same time, national distinctions and boundaries have become less monolithic and more permeable. Two dynamic repertoires of design innovation flank the U.S. newspaper: first, the practices of the press elsewhere in the world and, second, the spread of news onto computer networks. U.S. newspaper designers have moved swiftly into both those regions, spreading U.S. styles but not emerging untouched themselves. In other countries and in the foreign territory of computer publishing, the modern rules of news form must bend or even break. The future of news design will spring from those conditions, as newspapers encounter both frontiers.

To understand U.S. news form and its authority on the new frontier, we explored international newspapers and electronic newspapers, first surveying broadly and then looking at a selected area in depth. In general we found intriguing sources of design innovation in places removed from mainstream Western news, but computer news sites, surprisingly, have largely abandoned the form of newspapers. The new media versions gobble up the contents of print versions and stand ready to dispense them in a different environment with different visions of the public and its uses for news.

INTERNATIONAL STYLE

In our examination of the international setting, we studied several hundred newspapers from around the world (Barnhurst, 1995). We focused on authoritative forms by gathering elite and powerful publications from embassies and libraries in New York and Washington, D.C., which tend to subscribe only to newspapers considered serious (or at least those too widely circulated to safely ignore). Working inductively to group similar papers together, we found three clear dimensions in the form of news. Our history of U.S. news form has already presented the dimensions in some detail: first, the existence of vernacular forms indigenous among journalists before the arrival of modern style; second, the phases of modern design from the Protomodern to the Late Modern; and third, the vocabulary of visual expression ranging from the most reserved to the most emphatic.

Vernacular design, the first dimension, springs from journalistic processes before modern design intervenes. Vernacular form has always existed in the United States and is evident throughout the world. A broadsheet such as *New Era* of Addis Ababa, Ethiopia (Figure 8.1), can serve to illustrate the crowded space, irregular layout, mixed typography, and inconsistent decoration characteristic of the vernacular today. Each trait expresses some aspect of the marriage between the reporting of public affairs and the business of making news profitable. Space, for example, is at a premium. After selling space to advertisers, newspapers never have enough left over to accommodate editorial contents, and that pressure gets expressed in visual form. What little space that remains must be rationed, leaving a minimum separation between lines of type, columns, and headlines. Layout is done on the fly. The speed of production leaves little time for rearranging items, and so the layouts tend to be haphazard, with one article wrapping cheek-by-jowl around another. Typography follows local traditions. The habits and preferences of editors, columnists, and others involved in daily production yield a mix of

FIGURE 8.1. Vernacular front pages in the international survey characterized the economic margins, such as the broadsheet *New Era,* of Addis Ababa, Ethiopia, from September 6, 1981 (see Barnhurst, 1995, p. 23).

264

typefaces and type sizes. Other visual decoration serves the needs of the moment. The daily demands to emphasize or set apart certain items yield a miscellany of borders and ruled lines that decorate each page.

In vernacular design, publishers, editors, and production personnel since the nineteenth century have wielded control over news form, without much cognizance of or self-consciousness about trends and movements in visual design, and without the intervention of design professionals. Editorial and production personnel today continue to leave the traces of their work in the visual form of news without regard to the niceties of typography or the fashions of art. The resulting form does, however, share in the broad culture of its time and place. For that reason, we found vernacular designs among the most interesting. They tend to employ visual signs in ways that connote production processes and cultural values. At the same time, they always manage to look vestigial. Change has never come easily for newspapers, and publishers continue to resist abandoning traditions that seem to embody in visual form the authority of the journalistic craft.

In our international survey, vernacular newspapers existed at the margins of the international political and economic system. Some, such as the *Manila Bulletin* in the Philippines, looked like throwbacks to an earlier time, frozen in their visual form perhaps by work routines and equipment unchanged for many decades. Others had a thrown-together appearance, such as the *Ghanaian Times* of Accra. Although they often held a place as leading newspapers, they also expressed the status of their countries' economies, as in the case of the *Daily Ittefaq*, in Dhaka, Bangladesh. The most distinct cluster of vernacular broadsheet newspapers turned up in Africa. The *Times of Zambia* in Lusaka and the *Egyptian Gazette* in Cairo are typical examples. Others published in isolated pockets within powerful economic blocs. In Europe, the *Nationalist* of Clonmel, Ireland, adopted vernacular design similar to that found in the United States among some small-town and weekly newspapers.

The second dimension we identified in our survey ranged across the phases of modernism. Once newspaper conductors begin to see vernacular designs as stodgy and conservative and then allow modern design ideas to enter the daily production of news, a process of stylistic change follows. Modern design brings with it the notion of design obsolescence, which aims to encourage consumer interest (and greater market penetration) by periodically giving the news a different look. Newspapers begin by making simple changes to unify their appearance, the first step toward Protomodern style, and that process seems to lead in many cases to increasing design control. The result is the clear organization of social mapping and typographic purity of modern style. A Classicist Modern newspaper, such as the broadsheet *Frankfurter Allgemeine* of Frankfurt, Germany (Figure 8.2), can illustrate the outcome. In contrast to the vernacular example, the Frankfurt newspaper is fully modern. The space, although only slightly more generous, is consciously arranged. The layout relies on regular patterns, usually simple rectangles, which can be produced through the rationalization of design and production. The typography is extremely uniform and arrayed in a fixed set of sizes, with any contrasting type carefully matched to the main typeface. All the decoration has a consistent weight and texture. In every trait, modern design stands in opposition to the vernacular form of news.

The varieties of modernism we found in newspapers worldwide do not obey the chronology of phases of modernism that marked developments in the United States. In line with Fredric Jameson's (1994) argument that what is called postmodernism is really incomplete modernization under conditions of global capitalism, various modern styles have moved from other countries and other industries to colonize the world's newspapers. As a result, what was sequential in the United States is synchronic in the world. All phases of modern design are happening simultaneously as stylistic influences invade newspapers from outside. Modernists themselves customarily invoke the invasion of market forces when arguing for greater design control: To attract readers, newspapers need to look up-to-date. To wield influence, they need to adopt the latest effects found in authoritative newspapers elsewhere. To attract advertisers, they need to conform to the standards of modern production used by leading advertising agencies. These arguments disguise their professionalizing and corporatizing motives. Shifting to modern design justifies large and regular investments of capital and labor: newer presses, computer front-end control systems, and highly skilled design professionals. It is evident that in some places the finances of newspapers constrain the advance of modernism. In our survey, many authoritative newspapers in national capitals continued to publish in the Protomodern form of broadsheets, like 1930s U.S. newspapers, with designs that minimized space as if to suggest economic limits and a closed public discourse.

Newspapers in our survey also seemed to follow national or regional schools of design. Many from the Indian subcontinent, for example, as well as from the Middle East, shared a preference for Protomodern design, down to the use of Bodoni-inspired headlines. Some German newspapers favored Classicist Modern design for authoritative broadsheets. High Modern designs clustered in England, Canada, and a few national capitals, and Late Modern in centers of design innovation, such as Japan, Italy, and Brazil, and in centers of economic development, such as the countries of northern Eu-

FIGURE 8.2. Classicist Modern front pages appear at the centers of international power, as does the broadsheet *Frankfurter Allgemeine,* December 17, 1994, of Frankfurt, Germany (see Barnhurst, 1995, p. 23).

267

rope as well as Japan. By comparison, most broadsheets in the United States fit into the High Modern category, a tendency that accounts for the much maligned cookie-cutter uniformity of broadsheets in larger U.S. cities (see Chapter 6). The newspapers most admired for their visual appearance, such as the *San Jose Mercury News* in California, follow Late Modern design, a tendency that many other U.S. newspapers verge on while still retaining mostly High Modern elements.

The third dimension in our survey was the range of visual expression from the most reserved to the most emphatic. The quiet constraint of the Classicist Modern phase in the *Frankfurter Allgemeine* (see Figure 8.2) plots one end of the continuum. Dominant newspapers maintain the most reserved designs to encode their established authority, and competitors often move to the other end of the continuum, adopting a range of visual effects that provide emphasis. A Late Modern newspaper, such as the tabloid *La Prensa* of Buenos Aires, Argentina (Figure 8.3), illustrates the emphatic mode. Compared to the Classicist phase, Late Modern design is a study of contrasts. The typography includes the most exaggerated differences in typefaces, weights, and sizes. The layout contrasts extremely tall with extremely wide shapes. Decorative lines are also either heavy or light, and the use of color provides an additional tool for emphasis. The contrasts, however, all fit within modern constraints. The shapes are rectangular, not irregular, and the variation in type and decoration is not random or haphazard but follows a set pattern. Ruled lines, for instance, are limited to two or perhaps three specified weights.

The previous example also introduces a fourth dimension, format, which distinguishes tabloids such as *La Prensa* from broadsheets. The broadsheet format (roughly 13 by 23 inches) has a long history as an establishment symbol. Its authority derives in part from the nineteenth-century Imperial period of style (reflecting the huge investments required for large presses and mechanized papermaking) and in part from the older tradition dating to the large format of great folio books held at European universities. Broadsheets have flourished under modernism because their grand format accommodated the modern notion that news should appear in visual priority from large stories to small, from the top of the page to the bottom, and so forth.

However, the meanings of format appear to be in flux. In our survey we found a complex give-and-take between the reserved-to-emphatic dimension and the format of newspapers, which turned out to be the principal source of design innovation internationally. To simplify our presentation of that interplay, we will first describe the categories of tabloid newspapers and

FIGURE 8.3. Late Modern front pages, such as this one from the tabloid *La Prensa,* January 30, 1995, of Buenos Aires, Argentina, form an international mainstream (Barnhurst, 1995, p. 23).

then return to the broadsheet, where we found the most intriguing examples of how news form is being reconceived.

THE TABLOID ZONE

Small-format newspapers have existed since the earliest news sheets appeared in Germany in the seventeenth century. As mainstream newspapers grew ever larger, reaching blanket size in the nineteenth century, smaller formats became a region of change and experimentation. Illustrated newspapers, for instance, adopted a small format and helped establish its special visual role. The irreverent, screaming tabloid is a twentieth-century invention, usually dated from 1903, when the *Daily Mirror* was founded in London. Within its small size, a tabloid offered a moral rather than an intellectual picture of the world. Instead of pretending to map the world for readers, tell them what mattered most, and predict their future, the tabloid attempted to move readers by activating fundamental values and replaying timeless narratives.

Through their gimmicks and stunts, tabloids became a popular alternative, surpassing the circulation of serious broadsheets. Both formats became fixtures in major cities through much of the twentieth century — London is the prime example. The tabloid format developed not only to fit emotion-laden contents but also to heighten their visual impact. One large headline or single image could fully dominate the small tabloid page. The small size of the page made the large item all the more dramatic by contrast. The drama of tabloid news was a modernist invention. In the arts, expressionism developed dialectically, as a response to the abstract and idealist tendencies within modernism. Abstractionists celebrated precision and purity of form and saw the potential of machine processes and industrial organization, where their opposites sought to express human suffering at the hand of modern industrial and war machinery and its vast destructive capacity. The counterpoint between tabloid and broadsheet reiterated the dialectics of artistic modernism.

Over the course of the century, however, the alignment of form and content eroded. Large newspapers were unwieldy to read and costly to produce, and broadsheets eventually shrank so much that the smallest of them became hardly much larger than the largest tabloids. For a time, the format distinction came to depend less on size and more on proportion and sectioning. The standard broadsheet remained slightly larger, but the ratio of page height to width became more telling. The taller, narrower proportions of the broadsheet page allowed the sort of subdividing required to build a visual hierarchy with several levels, from the most to the least important news. Also, the long page fairly insisted on being folded in half, and that quality allowed the format to hold together when assembled from separate sections, which in turn permitted further rationalizing and subdividing of content.

The modern penchant for organizing things, however, pushed the two forms closer. The tabloid's squat proportions couldn't accommodate sections as easily, and as all newspapers got fatter from more advertising, the tabloid resisted folding at all. But tabloids could organize content in other ways, by providing alternative entrances such as the back page and by developing upside-down and pull-out sections. The qualities of tabloid format also appealed to modernists. The slightly smaller size seemed more manageable, for example, and satisfied the modernist preference for forms convenient to use. By midcentury the linkage between a newspaper's format and its editorial approach became open to challenge. On Long Island, outside New York City, *Newsday* under the publishership of Bill Moyers, for example, gave new seriousness to the tabloid format in the 1960s (Hutt, 1973).

In our survey we found that tabloid newspapers reiterated and replayed the main forces behind the development of the format: the conflicting claims of traditional versus modern authority, the contradictory appeals to moralistic emotion versus abstract rationality, and the push of past successes versus the pull of innovation. At the end of the century, tabloids were no longer recent inventions but one more traditional form of news. The fate of the tabloid paralleled that of many modernist ideas: it joined the mainstream. The process was aided by the fact the modernism so closely aligned itself with corporate interests. Modernist abstractionism and expressionism reiterated themselves in the corporate world as the dialectic of production versus marketing. Production demands rational, repeatable processes, but marketing demands creative and original appeals to emotion.

The most traditional in their approach to the form of news were the vernacular tabloids in our survey. They stuck with long-existing nameplates and other marking devices, such as sigs for columns that appeared in every issue. They also gave pride of place to miscellaneous content. News items ran in widely varied levels of emphasis, drawing from a range of typefaces, decorative or ruled lines of various weights, tint or shadow boxes, and so forth. The miscellany of news seemed to imply a populist lack of uniformity, calling forth a reader capable of picking and choosing. Only the discipline of traditional, repeated forms intervened to hold off chaos. In diversity of visual items, vernacular tabloids were similar to broadsheets, but the reserved-to-emphatic dimension was more pronounced in tabloids. The range of visual mood went from the calm reserve of *Trybuna,* in Warsaw, Poland, for example, to the anguished emphasis of newspapers such as *Nova Bosna,* in Bosnia-Herzegovina. The emphatic side of the range was the more inventive. The most extreme examples, which weren't included in our survey because they weren't represented in the collections of libraries and embassies, are the U.S. supermarket tabloids, throwaway advertisers, and fringe weeklies — all in tabloid format. These provide a counterpoint to the power of mainstream newspapers and also act as a zone of innovation.

Modern tabloids in our survey used their different format to assert a different sort of authority. The main national newspapers (or those with ambitions to that status) in many countries adopted modern style as they allied themselves with central authority. Modernist tabloids confronted a contradictory task: to speak simultaneously with the voice of passion and with the voice of reason. As a result, they adopted many, but not all, of the ordering and mapping devices found in their broadsheet counterparts. The phases of modernism are less clearly demarcated than in broadsheets. Some shared many qualities from the Protomodern phase, but we found it impossible to divide our tabloid sample into Classicist and High Modern phases. Instead, these two categories merged into a phase we'll simply call Modern. We did find a preponderance of Late Modern tabloids, the most corporate of design styles, as well as an anti-establishment alternative, magazine style.

The Protomodern phase in tabloids seemed to aim for the tranquillity of serious broadsheets without entirely abandoning traditional authority. The *Baltic Independent* of Estonia, for example, adopted some but not all of the features of modernism: uppercase and lowercase headlines, fairly uniform typefaces, rectangular-shaped layouts, indexes, promotional items, and a larger scale for elements on the page. The authority of such newspapers as the *Guardian,* in Lagos, Nigeria, produced more fixity of design than we found in other tabloids. Publishers apparently resisted tampering with what had worked, and that success stymied any arguments for following the avant garde further into modernism.

The Modern phase in tabloids (which collapses together the Classicist and High Modern phases) struggled to balance the rational and expressive sides of the style. The *Weekly Mail & Guardian* in South Africa, for instance, countered the quieting effect of uniform typography with large-scale headlines and pictures to suggest passion. Other Modern tabloids lacked extensive indexing and devices such as promotion boxes to indicate the hierarchy of content. In *Clarín* of Buenos Aires, Argentina, the social map was less clear — especially compared to modernist broadsheet front pages — and the varieties of emphasis overshadowed rationalizing features such as uniform typefaces, enlarged spaces, and top-down organization. The Modern phase most clearly illustrates the divided soul of the tabloid.

Tabloid newspapers most often adopted Late Modern design, converging with the predominant phase for broadsheets internationally. *Libération,* in France, for example, employed charts and graphics, contrasting type, and many small items thoroughly indexed and well promoted, all squeezed into relatively small areas. The space used by all the organizing and publicizing devices further reduced the scale of everything else, making the tabloids into miniature versions of Late Modern broadsheets. We found that the tabloids spanned a range from somewhat emphatic, such as *Eleftherotypia,* of Athens, Greece, to somewhat reserved, such as *La Jornada* of Mexico City, just as in the broadsheets. The particular format, along with other aspects of the look of news, no longer has a necessary relationship with the mode of production. The Late Modern newspaper, whether tabloid or broadsheet, envisions the reader as a consumer moved by style to carry, use, dip into, and scan the many small items that comprise it, not as a reader but as a participant in the marketplace of appearances.

Our survey also identified an alternative to the mainstream tabloid press: tabloids that took on the look of an opinion or literary magazine. Their earliest antecedents were colonial newspapers that used the front page as a cover, emphasizing a single story in a form that became rare as newspapers grew into broadsheet format (where single-story front pages appeared only for coverage of events of historic import). The magazine tabloid descended more recently from the *Newsday* of the early 1970s. Magazine style appeared to follow the modern convention of treating the page as a canvas but often without many of the promotional and organizational devices of newspaper modernism. A defining trait was the use of long stretches of text, especially on the interior pages. More than any other news form, the tabloid magazine seemed to imagine an audience of readers prepared to respond not merely to events but to ideological (and countercultural) positions. Europe made a specialty of serious, intellectual tabloids — such as *l'Humanité* of Paris — that appear in magazine style, but some larger U.S. cities could boast one as well.

The organizing tendencies of modernism have not fared well in tabloids, where space is restricted or arrayed in a wider rectangle less open to subdivision. Otherwise, modernization has encouraged tabloids to reproduce the repetitive High Modern designs found in mainstream newspapers of all shapes and sizes. The more interesting tabloids occupy the margins, where they do ideological work in magazine style or push the expressive range of news to new limits, rebelling against the authority and rationality of modernism. Our survey of tabloid newspapers internationally suggested the possibility of a return to ideology and text, on the one hand, and to emotion and visual experimentation, on the other.

Emphatic Broadsheets

While modernist notions were spreading to the tabloids, emphatic modes of design had invaded the broadsheet format, bringing the chain of influence full circle. The region spanning central Europe, Asia minor, and central Asia led the way toward the new form. It was less a factor in Western countries, where format-defined content distinctions equated broadsheets with serious news and tabloids with popular news. The emphatic broadsheet nevertheless found a foothold in major Western cities. A Turkish-language newspaper, *Tercüman,* appeared in Frankfurt, Germany, for instance. In the United States the form had spread to the foreign language press, such as *Maariv Israeli Daily,* which a Tel Aviv newspaper published in New York City. The flow of innovation throughout the history of news form has moved from the periphery, and this instance is no different. The new broadsheet designs not only come from marginalized geographic regions but also draw inspiration from the fringe of tabloid format.

Of course, emphatic broadsheets are not entirely new. We found a similar experimentation in the 1930s, when the *Chicago Herald and Examiner* developed a tabloid-style outer cover (see Chapter 7). Like that earlier effort, the current examples can be classified as vernacular in style, an extrusion of the work of news. They mix type exuberantly and juxtapose all manner of decorative borders and boxes in irregular shapes. The large scale of the page makes these the most expressionist of all newspaper designs, with contents that combine high visual energy — extreme contrasts and variations — with miniature tidbits of news in a volatile mix. The form seems especially apt in its expression of social conditions in the unsettled regions where it emerged most recently, such as eastern Europe and the Balkans.

Rational corporate processes have nevertheless had an impact on emphatic broadsheets. Some we found were hybrids, employing the cool of modern rationalism along with the heat of the shrieking tabloid. In Sarajevo, Bosnia, for example, the designers of *Avaz* (Figure 8.4), combined unified type, neat rectangles, and the promotional and mapping strategies of modernism with the high-contrast emphatic modes of the tabloid, all on a broadsheet page. The result most closely resembled the Late Modern mainstream of news form. In the age of the corporate newspaper, the marginal zones propose creative recombinations. The mainstream can then adopt these innovations at least in their surface manifestations, stripped of their connections to social conditions, and use them to add new visual elements and effects to existing product. The corporate newspaper uses emphatic expressionism as a way to market to the young and to stimulate the jaded. In the process, corporate interests disconnect the processes of production from the form of news. The network of relationships that constitute the newspaper no longer coincides with relationships that the form of newspapers represents.

AMERICANIZING FORM

The world's newspapers draw stylistic inspiration from a whole chorus of influences. But the somber tenor of U.S. styles has a special resonance, accom-

FIGURE 8.4. Some emphatic broadsheets were influenced by modernism, as illustrated by this front page from *Avaz,* January 25, 1995, of Sarajevo, Bosnia (from Barnhurst, 1995, p. 23).

panied as it is by a symphony of economic and ideological winds and strings. The resulting strains in design trends defy transcription into a simple register of Americanization.

The notion of Americanization itself has changed over the course of the twentieth century. At first it was thought of as technological progress, in which U.S. inventiveness was exported and, it was assumed, brought democracy in its wake. Following the Second World War, the process became much more direct. The United States began to impose its ways by intervening with military force, applying economic pressure, and exporting a flood of cultural products. Because the form of news followed a different path internationally, the example of the press illustrates another mode of Americanization, one that is also consonant with the growth of global corporate culture.

U.S. newspaper designs in the first half of the twentieth century responded to movements in the arts which originated primarily in Europe. Early practitioners of self-conscious modern news design, such as John Allen (1947), operated primarily within the domestic industry. Allen's disciple Edmund Arnold (1956) continued to press for modern design, principally as a consultant with local newspapers. At the height of the movement, when modern principles largely ruled news production, the United States also became a key exporter of design ideas. The successors to Allen and Arnold carried the U.S. brand of newspaper modernism first to Latin America and then to Europe and Asia (Barnhurst, 1994).

The historical development of newspapers paralleled the rise of other U.S. media to a dominant position in the global communication setting. Output such as commercial film and television programming could be exported as integrated cultural products (after some tinkering with titling or dubbing), but there was no parallel market for newspapers, except among a limited number of U.S. expatriates and language students abroad. Although individual newspapers remained local or at best national products, their form could be exported. To succeed in other countries, the form of news had to invade the local products without seeming to invade at all. Modernism provided its own rationale as a servant to the instrumental aims of anyone employing it. U.S. consultants spread their design sensibility by touting modernist form as an efficient conveyor of local journalism and advertising. To bolster the argument, they could claim the ostensibly neutral support of legibility research and psychological principles.

The spread of news form accompanied a general understanding among modernists that form could be divorced from content. Design, in other words, could be sold as a soft technology, a set of procedures and standards that would rationalize news production and news reading, while local control continued over content. The argument was, of course, not quite accurate. Modern style favored a certain view of readers (or, one could say, brought certain kinds of readers into view while obscuring others) and invited them into a relationship with the polity and the culture. Modern readers, although not very well informed or well equipped to judge the complexity of public affairs, did appear capable of making consumer decisions based on the stylistic appeal of products. That capacity meant that the visual effects used in marketing could be applied to news of public affairs. Modernism played a little trick on people, calling them together as an audience of consumers but then turning them into a public. The modern formation conceived of the newspaper itself as primarily a commercial activity, centered in corporations where journalists and reporters held key roles. The network of relationships implied by the formation had to be suppressed in order to market news form as independent of content. In other words, the form of news acted like a Trojan horse, an apparently empty vessel that appealed to a monumental visual sense and implied a symbolic victory. With those rewards and the promise of greater efficiency and better control, publishers in other countries adopted U.S. design models without any cognizance of their ideological contents.

As Late Modern design spread internationally, it took root in ways peculiar to its new surroundings. Some aspects of the form appealed to particular cultures more than others. In order to understand the flow of design innovation, we selected a developed country in which modern design had a recent impact. Based on our initial overview of international newspapers, we identified Spain as such a site. The country's transition from the closed society of the Franco dictatorship meant that its newspapers revitalized in the last quarter of the twentieth century, at the same time that modernism reached its height. We conducted an in-depth study of the press in Spain after gathering a sample that included all of the national, most of the regional, and many local Spanish newspapers (Barnhurst et al., 1999).

Spain had been at the forefront of newspaper innovation almost a century earlier, when *ABC* began as one of the first picture newspapers. *ABC* stuck tenaciously with that initial innovation, continuing to publish drawings, cartoons, and other illustrations rather than turning to photography, and it proved stubborn as well in its support of monarchy, even during the long years of Franco, who called the newspaper the enemy. By the time of his death in 1975, *ABC* stood as a bastion of conservatism in its form as well as its content. Modern design entered Spain fully developed, in the form of a new tabloid newspaper, *El País,* founded as the country began its transition into democracy. The newspaper adopted a left-leaning socialist editorial line and a very reserved design, infused with aspects of the High Modern. Thereafter modernism spread rapidly through the regional and local press of Spain, accompanying general economic growth as the country entered the European Community. The Spanish press drew on U.S. newspaper designs and on modernist layout ideas filtered through Europe, principally Germany, an important center for the printing trades (Lallana, 1999).

Modernism in Spain favored the tabloid format. It may seem unusual that the reserved version of modernism in Spain wedded with the tabloid. There the press did not follow the historical pattern set by the United States and the United Kingdom, where tabloids pursued emphatic forms of journalism, developed out of the illustrated press, and moved into serious content much later. The history of *ABC* accounts in some degree for the lack of emphatic newspapers in Spain. One attempt to launch a newspaper on the model of the English popular press, the short-lived tabloid *Claro,* failed almost immediately despite backing from the German firm Bild Zeitung and the publisher of *ABC,* Prensa Española. During the transition to democracy, newspapers in Spain adopted a seriousness that modernism helped express and applied a reserved design palate to the tabloid format, which was considered serious because of the example of *ABC.* The High Modern form of *El País* emerged when publisher Juan Luís Cebrian directed the initial design team to create the look of a modern broadsheet in tabloid format. The result confirmed the alignment of reserved design and tabloid format. Ironically the longevity and success of *ABC* undermined its experiment in popular tabloid publishing. In any case, the argument that the tabloid format is more manageable for readers, that is, more in line with the modern aim to increase functionality and efficiency, carried the day in Spain.

In contrast to the English model, Spain's newspapers have limited circulation (reaching only one in ten of the adult population). They encourage a clash of ideology, rather than the bland uniformity needed for mass circulation in the mainstream, and the often-understated designs reflect the commitment to debate in the public sphere. Spain shares the European custom of publishing ideological newspapers, which we mentioned earlier, a custom largely missing from the U.S. press. Other nations' media take a combative stance in part because of conditions of centralization and competition. In most countries, such as, say, Mexico or the United Kingdom, a dominant capital city produces a range of truly national media, which then differentiate themselves topically, ideologically, and economically. In the United States the only truly national news media, the broadcast networks, developed under the influence of advertisers and under federal regulations that encouraged the most bland forms possible. Meanwhile, most U.S. newspapers, including the premier dailies, operated either as local monopolies or within comfortable market niches. The differences stand out in comparison to Spain.

Founded in the 1950s under Franco, Spanish television always played a political role. Televisión Española operated first one and then two television stations under a state monopoly that served the regime. After the death of Franco, national television aligned with the centrist transitional government, but also acted as a force encouraging citizens to compare and weigh the political ideas found in newspapers. In the 1980s the government revised its regulations for broadcasting, allowing commercial television stations onto the airwaves. Under conditions of market competition, the new stations quickly adopted (and the state channels slowly shifted toward) U.S.-style news coverage, with its informal talk among anchors, foregrounding of private tragedies, and dramatic visual effects. The process of Americanization had begun.

With television as a background, Spanish newspapers also began to Americanize. The press entered a period much like the ferment in the United States between the world wars, but without as much raw experimentation. Spanish journalists and academics attended newspaper industry institutes in the United States, then trained designers to reproduce U.S. layouts. Regional newspapers redesigned and reformatted themselves. Vernacular forms, such as *El Día de Cuenca* (Figure 8.5), *El Faro Astorgano, Área,* and *Soria 7 Días* persisted in marginalized areas, although not without some elements of modern design. The growth of newspaper chains led to the imposition of U.S.-style cookie-cutter designs. The largest of these was *El Periódico,* which required an identical nameplate for each of its holdings in various cities, such as Aragón (Figure 8.6).

U.S. influence of a different sort figured in the birth of *El Mundo,* inspired by the investigative reporting of Watergate. Its founder, Pedro J. Ramírez, was working as a young intern in the *Washington Post* newsroom the day Nixon resigned. Ramírez was an admirer of *USA Today, Newsday,* and U.S. magazines such as the *New Yorker* (Lallana, 1999). *El Mundo* adopted a Late Modern design and a more earthy and strident tone than *El País,* and it focused coverage on the scandals surrounding the socialist government of Felipe González.

U.S. styles provided preset patterns that happened to fit local needs in Spain. The High Modern design of *El País* expressed the initial moment of transition, when peaceful discourse was the most urgent necessity. The Late Modern design of *El Mundo* coincided with the completion of Spain's dem-

FIGURE 8.5. In the Spanish press vernacular front-page design appears in the tabloid *El Día de Cuenca,* October 27, 1996, from the central Castilla region near Madrid (see Barnhurst et al., 1999, n.p.).

ocratic transition, when the socialist government that *El Mundo* opposed gave up power peacefully.

But the influence of U.S. styles went beyond local needs. Modernist news forms encouraged and fostered elements of the U.S. news model, characterized by local newspaper monopolies, ideological neutrality within authoritative designs, and the conception of the audience as consumers of a product subject to design obsolescence. The professionalization of reporting and design in Spain followed the U.S. model. The institutional embodiment of the newspaper design profession went forward apace, with one of the

FIGURE 8.6. Look-alike newspaper designs emerged under consolidated news-paper ownership, such as the El Periódico chain, as seen in the tabloid *El Periódico de Aragón,* April 28, 1993, from eastern Spain (see Barnhurst et al., 1999, n.p.).

most active chapters of the U.S.-based Society of Newspaper Design. In Spain journalism schools had always been run by newspapers, but the U.S. model prevailed when the schools acquired the status of university depart-ments and encouraged the publication of professional manuals to standard-ize practices. Contests and awards emerged to recognize and encourage adherence to modernism. For example, the university program in Navarra, an industrial region in the north, became host to a world competition in the design of information graphics.

The newly arriving corporate newspaper, however, clashed with the long-standing political stance of the Spanish press. The model of news as an arena for ideological competitors had been a defining aspect of newspapers in Spain, but began to lose ground to modern, functionalist notions. Late Modern design, such as that found in *La Vanguardia* (Figure 8.7), of Barcelona, with its tightly structured pages created by U.S. designer Milton Glaser in 1989, became a mainstay in Spain, as it did internationally. The corporate newspaper packaged the news, molding real events to occupy spaces

FIGURE 8.7. Late Modern design was imported from the United States in the tabloid *La Vanguardia,* December 3, 1996, published in Barcelona and distributed nationally in Spain (see Barnhurst et al., 1999, n.p.).

predesigned to serve market demands. Instead of *ideological* competition, the modernist requirement to stay in vogue in the face of design obsolescence helped spread the U.S. notion of *market* competition between newspapers and other outlets, such as radio and television. By the 1990s, the Spanish press saw a growth in news focused on personality, celebrity, and on the attention-grabbing genre called *sucesos,* which highlights private tragedy rather than public debate over ideology. The influence of U.S. design reached so deeply that in 1999 Glaser returned to Spain, this time to redesign that bastion of national pride, *ABC.*

Adopting U.S. design had complex and contradictory consequences in Spain. Most dramatically, the Spanish press abandoned the broadsheet format entirely by the end of the century, reading a particular line of modernist reasoning to fit local history. Newspapers also became more visually active, updating their news presentation and engaging in frequent redesigns. Design obsolescence increased awareness of and interest in newspapers as objects in the market but also made them seem less powerful and serious.

It might seem that by imagining the audience as an aggregate of consumers, Spanish newspapers paradoxically enhanced the independence of readers, who when faced with a less serious press had to think for themselves, but that would be too optimistic an assessment. Among young adult readers, the new designs did make newspapers more appealing, but also fed a growing disaffection with politics (Barnhurst, 2000). Young readers in the United States, faced with news media that have subordinated public service to the search for market share, have been abandoning newspapers in accelerating numbers during the Late Modern phase. Although U.S. modernism entered Spain under the guise of pure form, intended to enlarge the market potential of newspapers, the corporate formation of news also carried an ideological cargo, which now seems to be infecting young Spanish citizens with the same malaise found in the United States.

INTERNET DESIGNS

Even as the modern news style conquered the world, newspaper publishers began to fear conquest at the hands of the World Wide Web. Soon after its development pundits and technophiles began to predict the demise of newspapers. In the best known pronouncement, writer Jon Katz (1994) predicted in the pages of *Wired* magazine that newspapers would vanish without a trace within ten years. His apocalyptic message found believers in the corporate offices of newspapers, which moved quickly into publishing their contents electronically, led by two design innovators, the Raleigh, North Carolina, *News & Observer* in 1994 and the *San Jose Mercury News* in 1995. Major newspapers such as the *New York Times* followed in 1996. Throughout history, change at newspapers has come deliberately and often with great reluctance (it took the *New York Times* decades of debate to remove the period from the end of its nameplate). In the history of news form, the leap onto the Web came precipitously. By the end of the century, almost all daily and most larger weekly newspapers had established electronic versions.

Newspapers outside the United States moved just as quickly into online publishing (Quadros, 1999). In Spain, several newspapers in the industrialized province of Catalunya (*Avui, El Periódico de Catalunya,* and *La Vanguardia*) began their Web versions in 1995, shortly after the first U.S. sites. On-line editions of the major national newspapers published from Madrid (*ABC, El Mundo,* and *El País*) ensued within the year. Newspapers in Latin America followed a similar, fast-paced course. In visual design as well as in content, innovation flowed from the United States. Take the example of the newspaper *O Estado de São Paulo,* published in Brazil's industrial heartland. It established the on-line NetEstado in 1995 and within two years turned to one of the better known U.S. newspaper designers to create a look for the site. Like other international publishing entities, the Estado corporation joined News of the Future, a project established at the Media Lab at Massachusetts Institute of Technology to send regular updates on form and technology to its subscribers. The flow of design innovation, although rapid, still went from the United States at the center to other countries as a periphery. Scholars in Latin America called the process anglophone, Westernized, white, and consumerist (Amaral & Rondelli, 1996).

The growing practice of publishing news on computer networks is the second dynamic repertoire of design innovation flanking the U.S. newspaper. Like previous technologies, the Internet's intrusion into newspaper operations has been both conservative and revolutionary, both progressive and retrogressive. Although often considered the antithesis of the press, the Internet in daily use has so far acted as a surrogate print medium. Users share Internet news in much the way that they used to clip and mail newspaper stories. The result is not homemade news but something very much like it. Users at home can print out items and post them like newspaper clippings on their refrigerators. They can effortlessly clip and instantaneously mail items to each other, much as family members used to read the newspaper over breakfast and pause to say, "Oh, wait, listen to this." In that sense, online newspaper users become narrowcast versions of the colonial printer, who clipped from many sources and selected from many letters to broadcast in each issue. The narrowcasting of electronic news allows users to scavenge similarly but share narrowly, clipping news on a particular topic and sending it to a select few.

One fin de siècle commonplace is that industrialized Western societies have become more oriented toward the visual. Memory has become photographic, imagination cinematic, and the everyday televisual. Interactive multimedia on home computers and over networks have provided the newest — and most visually varied — outlet for news. Understanding on-line news requires an examination of form in the context of the history of similar innovations, such as the rise of photography a century earlier and of the video cassette recorder in the 1980s. To examine the visual forms of newspaper on-line editions, we studied the sites of major American newspapers, including the *New York Times,* the *Washington Post,* the *Wall Street Journal,* the *Chicago Tribune,* the *Los Angeles Times,* and the *Atlanta Constitution.* We also scrutinized the newspaper sites that led the way in Web design, such as Mercury Center (*San Jose Mercury News*) and NandOTimes (*News & Observer*). This selection we supplemented by studying on-line newspapers from Europe and Latin America, to track the flow of design forms.

To get a bottom-up view, we probed all the sites associated with a particular geographic location, taking the Pioneer Valley of Western Massachusetts as our base. Besides the *New York Times* and the *Wall Street Journal,* a range of newspapers circulate print editions to local residents in the Pioneer Valley: the *Boston Globe,* the *Springfield Union-News,* the *Keene Sentinel,* the *Daily Hampshire Gazette,* the *UMass Daily Collegian,* and the weekly *Valley Advocate.* All these publish on-line versions as well, which are linked on active regional clearinghouses run by nonprofit (such as public radio station WFCR in Amherst) and commercial sites (such as InstantPioneerValley.com).

The most striking quality of on-line newspapers is the dominance of promotion. Ads include a banner across the top, many others forming a chimney down one side of the page, and several more across the bottom on most newspaper sites. The advertising, much of it self-promotional, commonly overwhelms the other content. The ads come up first, blink, move, run ticker-style text, and employ intense colors and dramatic images. The commonplace that advertising quickly flooded the World Wide Web takes on special importance for a medium such as newspapers, in which the bulk of design innovation grew out of advertisements.

On-line visual culture has trumped the cherished print-shop traditions of newspapers in their electronic editions. Print nameplates play only a minor role, upstaged by the site name in most cases. Nameplates appear usually grayed down from their solid-print versions, as a very small reminder in the background of the screen. Other accoutrements of newsprint culture hardly appear at all: columns, column rules, visual predominance of text, or variously sized headlines. Instead, the logic of the index takes control. All items lead elsewhere: small photographs to larger versions and associated text, headlines to text, blurbs to text. If the printed book, with its long line of text from beginning to end, is one-dimensional, and the printed newspaper, with its larger multicolumned page, is two-dimensional, a Web news site is three-dimensional: a two-dimensional index plus depth. The *Chicago Tribune* dramatizes its three-dimensionality by openly imitating the look of a file drawer on its home page, suggesting to the reader a similarity between clicking on the virtual tab (for access to a story) and opening a physical file folder.

The Internet began as a simplified print medium. Early users relished the simplicity and austerity of the new medium, and a conceit among e-mail and newsgroup users held that the real Internet guys never used capital letters. At that early point, the Internet offered a new location for reading and writing, a return from the immediacy of broadcasting to the calm of words in type. The original textuality of the Internet became submerged, however, as the World Wide Web appeared and then grew in size, approaching the scale of a mass medium. Especially as newspapers have exploited the medium, on-line news has on the whole removed any extensive text from the viewer's first encounter, giving only headlines, blurbs, and index listings as links instead. Every move then leads to more advertising and more links, sometimes associated with disappointingly tiny bits of text. To read a single news article generally requires several clicks of the mouse or scrolls through the promotional maze, with each few paragraphs of text involving yet another exposure to ads (which usually must download first). Complaints about connection delays aside, the promotional mission clearly dominates or makes its presence insistently known.

Within each screen, all elements follow the logic of Web design, with the interactive link intruding where the editorial judgment once prevailed. In print newspapers, reporters and editors basked in sublime ignorance of the actual readership of any particular item, assuming that their choice to display an item prominently on the front page translated directly into readers' attention and esteem. Web design flattens the steep hierarchy of the modern front page. Top stories don't look so top anymore. At the same time, Web technology allows publishers to count how many readers click on a particular story. For the benign dictatorship of the editor, Web technology substitutes the tyranny of the mouse.

Content gains its prominence in the on-line environment from the frequency of user activity, not from the priorities of public affairs reporting. The hit-counters on many sites clearly display how many browsers have visited a page. The prominence of sports in Internet news follows from its history of building audiences, as it did in the early years of radio. Other content marginal or unknown to newsprint plays a leading role. Besides the on-line archive of previous editions, a fixture on most sites, the instant-response poll figures prominently. Print editions limit archival matter to a few items From the Files, usually from This Date in History, and run days-old telephone-response polls. Internet news polls, however, have the capacity to tally and display results in real time.

Other on-line content originates in the multimedia environment. The NandOTimes consistently offers a daily animation, a QuickTime movie combining video with *USA Today*–style charts in motion. We found one item on women in the workforce that showed a briefcase opening and bar graphs popping out. The graphs would have conveyed the same information without any visual effects, but the information paled in comparison. Such effects offer pure entertainment value, conceiving of viewers as an audience seeking spectacle and novelty. The World Wide Web based its early success on the power of a few displays that users copied, bookmarked, talked about, posted to on-line discussion lists, linked to, or exchanged as URL addresses. The notorious dancing baby drew large numbers of obsessed viewers, who went on to create all sorts of iterations and embellishments of the original. Users could not resist the slightly repellent marvel: a cherub pirouetting on the pixels of a screen, vacant of substance but able to move traffic.

Although Internet technology would seem to diminish the stratifications of the print world, substantial differences turned up in our study between the major newspapers and local ones. The major sites have the most elaborate designs, predictably, as well as the most extensive links to other sites and options for viewer interactions. They require viewers to subscribe, often for a simple exchange of information (for the *New York Times*) if not a paid transaction (for the *Wall Street Journal*). Many sites set up mechanisms to charge users for access to archived news (almost two dollars for each article from the *Chicago Tribune*). They also publish multiple editions daily, with the time of last update displayed prominently, and include more content (longer articles or several versions of an article). Local newspapers do not provide as varied or as timely a service and also cannot make demands. They open up fewer opportunities for viewers to respond and give feedback. In short, they do not exploit the interactive capabilities of the medium. They look like pages on the Web, not newspapers, but they don't act like either medium.

At the longest running news sites, applications have completely abandoned the distinctiveness of the newspaper form. NandOTimes and Mercury Center bear the least resemblance to print newspapers. Like the thoroughly commercialized site of the *Wall Street Journal,* they provide an experience almost indistinguishable from that of any large search engine or Internet gateway, such as America Online (AOL), or Netscape NetCenter. The fully developed on-line news site has become a creature of computer networks and browser software, the offspring of commerce in all respects, and a product wholly distinct from the parent newspaper.

In these sites readers quickly find themselves shuffled off to other news providers. Even the most conservative sites, such as the *New York Times,* incorporate sidebars on many pages to link directly with the Associated Press and other news outlets. The portal function is most apparent on the most fully commercialized and most popular pages: the business page and the sports page, respectively. Business pages route readers to financial information providers in a fashion almost indistinguishable from the ads appearing on the same page. Electronic sports pages in metropolitan papers route readers to the sites of the local teams, the NFL, or Major League Baseball, or to any of a number of related commercial venues.

The one obvious exception to these observations was the site of the *New York Times.* Following its long tradition of design conservatism, the *Times* for several years maintained its site to invoke most of the particulars of the newspaper form. Upon entering the site, a reader first encountered the solid print nameplate, along with other elements of Victorian design, such as the so-called ears on either side of the nameplate and vestigial column rules that appeared first running the length of the blank page and then remained at the page top once the content was loaded. The black on white of the site contrasted starkly with other on-line newspapers. The screen presented a page-like vertical form (with roughly a one to four aspect ratio) requiring scrolling, and no advertising interrupted reading until further down. An extensive index along the left of the page visually resembled newspaper chimneys more than the usual Web-based indexes. The entire on-line edition clearly reflected the newspaper's position of authority as an institution, which gave the designers apparent freedom from the dictatorship of measurable clicks that has tended to drive other sites.

For a time, at least, the power of the *Times* allowed it to reproduce its printed authority on-line. But even the *Times* couldn't resist the tide of on-line design. In November 2000 it redesigned its Internet site. The new design retained the blackletter nameplate, but few other vestiges of printedness remained. The gray-on-white background is now a characteristically online deep royal blue. The new main page resembled any other portal, with a cluttered arrangement of links to different sections of the newspaper, as previously, but more links to other content providers, more displays of the paper's partnerships with other organizations, especially ABC, Inc., more options for nontextual material, and more opportunities to personalize what is supposedly your news. This apparent abundance has displaced the previous magisterial authority of the *Times*. The new Web design still allows users to view the print version's front page, but that link is buried in a low-profile stack of other options. The one exception-that-proves-the-rule has now complied with our argument. News organizations do not transfer the mapping function of their print versions to their on-line services. Instead, even the grayest of them embrace the logic of the index.

UNDERSTANDING WEB NEWS

The visual relationship of on-line operations to their sponsoring newspapers resembles that of advertising to journalism. Like printed advertisements, on-line sites provide another stream of revenue, their excesses tolerated because of their indirect support for newspapers. That relationship helps provide the key to understanding the impact of electronic forms on the newspaper. The process of change, as the new technology of computer networks becomes incorporated into the landscape of news, does not resemble a sudden revolution, although it may seem that way. Instead, the process probably had many antecedents and crept up on newspapers gradually, somewhat like earlier visual changes in newspapers, such as the introduction of photography and the spread of modern design.

The forms of the industrial newspaper emerged from the entanglement in a series of relationships. Elsewhere we discussed how the development of the newspaper in the nineteenth century resulted in the accumulation of different flows of content and audiences (see Chapter 3), so that by the end of the century the metropolitan daily had become the meeting ground for different readers with different agendas. Newspapers segmented those agendas into departments, but fixed all of the departments in the overall form. As a result, the sports fan, the entrepreneur, the shopper, the patron of the arts, and the political enthusiast all came together at the site of the newspaper,

which encouraged every reader in some fashion to undertake every role —
to be a shopper *and* a voter, for instance.

The modern newspaper imposed a voice on all these streams. Elsewhere we have pointed out that the newspaper became monovocal in the
modern formation. One aspect of this monovocality was a sense of identity
for each specific newspaper. Readers developed a familiarity with recurring
aspects of a newspaper: its editorial positions, its columnists, its ties to specific sports franchises, its promotions, even its reporters. Moreover, habitual
newspaper readers could pick up a copy of an unfamiliar newspaper and figure out its character, doping out its politics, its style, its readership. This is
one sense in which a newspaper creates and readers experience an environment.

The logic of corporate journalism has worked for a couple of decades to
diminish a newspaper's distinctiveness. The Gannett newspapers exemplify
this trend, with their cookie-cutter designs, weak local ties, bland conservative politics, and overall obeisance to the demands of the chain. When
strong-voiced papers like the *Louisville Courier Journal* and the *Des Moines
Register* joined the other scalps on the wall of Allan Neuharth's office, it only
confirmed what everyone already knew: the conditions of corporate newspapering mute a paper's voice.

The Web goes a step farther. What Gannett did by purging the Web
does by bingeing. The modern newspaper achieved monovocality by sup-
pressing the multiple voices of the various streams of content it drew from.
The Web ultimately disentangles those streams. Even a conservative site,
such as the editorial page of the *New York Times,* opens itself up to the multiple voices of its sources, allowing readers to take their pick of editorial cartoonists (none of whom appears in the print edition). This potentially
endless multiplication of options for the reader makes it impossible for the
Web newspaper to impose a voice on its matter.

In the same way, the Web also disperses a newspaper's readers. The
modern newspaper brought all readers together in the same common space,
but a Web edition directs them all to discrete rooms. A reader with an interest in sports need never glance at a public affairs story along the way. In fact,
such a reader need no longer rely on the daily newspaper at all as a source of
news. A sports fan may go directly to the ESPN site — still at this writing
the most frequently visited content provider — and from there directly to a
team site. For that reason, despite the fact that many newspapers, especially
the *New York Times,* load up their sites with more matter than they make
available in print, the readers of these sites are likely to read less of it than
they would in print and are also less likely to remember what they read.

These are empirical questions that require further investigation, but the form of on-line news points to a greater volatility or mobility in reading. If the metropolitan daily encouraged a common space of general knowledge, then the Web encourages narrower spaces of specialized knowledge. Anyone interested in the politics of Togo, a tiny nation and home to Africa's longest ruling dictator, can browse widely (and automatically) through the Web to cull news stories from many sources. Thus general readers can imitate reading practices formerly reserved for scholars and other specialists.

Popularizing specialist knowledge has democratic potential, of course. Web design by its nature weakens the editor's mediation of news flow. Instead of relying on the editor of the *Enquirer* sports page, a Cincinnati Reds fan may go directly to some of the sources that the newspaper used that day — the Associated Press wire or the Reds front office. The fans can be their own editors. In fact all sorts of people can build their own news media this way, taking a little from a wide range of sites.

Although they may feel like free agents in an anarchic landscape, readers are simultaneously targets for increasingly well-aimed advertising messages and marketing campaigns, the end result of which strengthens the economic position of the most successful of the new media, the ones that can claim the most hits. Those sites overwhelmingly are the Web versions of old media, print and broadcast alike. The independent reader, with apparently increasing freedom, also becomes an increasingly precise market segment. The trend did not originate with the Web. Newspapers experimented for years with ways to narrowcast their products, and most major newspapers produce zoned editions, targeted to particular locales. Much of the motivation grew out of advertising. Newspapers that can identify and deliver well-chosen market segments can expect geometric increases in advertising revenue. The same holds for magazines, although on a national rather than a local level (Abrahamson, 1996), as well as for other commercial media (Turow, 1997).

The Web nevertheless allows a new level of disarticulation, and the ultimate driving factor remains promotional, as we have already stated. The *New York Times,* for instance, began to request demographic information from subscribers early on and employs technology that allows advertisers to target particular readers. At the same time, Amazon, the largest advertiser on the Web, is willing to maintain links to *Times* book reviews and kick back a fee to the *Times* when a reader jumps from the *Times* Book Review section to Amazon and orders a book. The line between the medium and the advertiser has blurred radically, in both agenda and style.

But dire predictions of newsprint's demise add little to an understanding of the process of change. In its actual functioning, the World Wide Web intersects with print journalism in much the same way as the advertising industry complements the newspaper industry. On-line news does not compete directly with printed newspapers as newspapers once competed with radio or movies with television.

The rise of electronic forms instead most closely parallels the spread of photography in the nineteenth century and the triumph of modern design in the twentieth. Newspapers incorporated photography into their pages slowly (see Chapter 5), resisting as long as the forms failed to serve the prevailing visual regime. When that regime no longer made sense in the U.S. political and economic scene, newspapers embraced photography as part of a general move toward modernism, which later accelerated in what looked like a sudden revolution. Likewise the adoption of page designs controlled by ideals and routines of visual mapping began early and again moved slowly at first before speeding up (see Chapter 6). The conventional wisdom of journalistic circles described the accelerations as a result of new technologies spawning head-to-head competition between newspapers and picture magazines or radio (in the 1930s and 1940s) and later television news (in the late 1960s and early 1970s). The much earlier origin of the shifts resists a naïve narrative of technologically determined change and suggests a pattern of visual innovation.

When the recent process of digital transformation can be examined from a longer perspective, studies will likely show that the burst of activity near century's end followed a slow rise in the forms most associated with on-line networks. Certainly the move toward segmentation of the audience began earlier. Other aspects of design on the Web, including its abundance of material and its often self-consciously retrograde visual style, already made an appearance in Late Modern design as well.

The printed press can and probably will continue to coexist with on-line news sites, whence newspapers can expect a continual flow of innovation. We can offer two observations on the likely course of change. First, newspapers will adapt elements from computer networks to fit news culture, just as press photography, as it grew out from the tradition of engraving, increasingly took on the values of journalism. Photojournalism emerged from the dialectic of new form (photographs) and existing content (journalism), as all invaders have done. The outcome resulted from melding and compromise, not utter rout or defeat for print, as some journalists predicted at the time. The same will hold for digital news, especially as it generates revenue. Mainstream dailies at first embraced the Web as a defensive move. Newspapers rushed into cyberspace to stake claims to their traditional monopolies — classified advertising, financial information, and sports information especially — before upstarts like the Microsoft Street pages preempted them. Newspapers at first did not anticipate profits from their Internet sites. It came as something of a surprise when, in 1998, a majority began to break even or make money, but even then the profitability depended on the free content available from the print edition. At century's end, it is still very doubtful that the *New York Times* could survive separately as a Web edition, and in fact every profitable Web news site of any significance depends on a non-Web news organization, drawing on but not paying for its news-gathering resources.

We anticipate that the various forms of newspaper delivery will coexist in the same way that the various forms of film exhibition do. Hollywood panicked over the videocassette in the same way that newspapers panicked over the Internet, but after two decades of the VCR, theatrical exhibition remained highly profitable. Video distribution became crucial to a film's bottom line and unexpectedly reinforced rather than undermined the status of big-budget blockbusters and the studios that produced and distributed them (Wasser, 1996). Many films are now shot with viewing on the small screen in mind; a range of video products corresponds to the B movies of Hollywood's golden age and helps to glamorize the A movies, the major theatrical releases, by contrast. The old product remains sturdy, however, and for a very good reason, one that reinforces the notion of the media as environment. The theatrical film, marketed at a far higher price than home video, then could command more from filmgoers willing to purchase an *experience,* not just a text. At some point newspapers will likewise market their already high-priced print versions as a reading experience of a unique and increasingly upscale variety.

Our second observation on the process of encountering the on-line world is that newspapers will change to reflect the emerging moment of U.S. political and economic culture. As modernism arrived in the United States, the mode of pictorial narrative changed. Newspapers accomplished the change first by using collage and then by filling entire picture pages, shifting pictorial representations from static iconism (stock campaign engravings) in the nineteenth century republican ideal to picture-as-content (journalist-produced candid shots) in the twentieth-century professional ideal. Clearly, computer networks have already had a parallel influence. Content from on-line sources has achieved greater status in the hierarchy of news. Newspapers began to advertise their electronic scoops in much the same way they had plugged photojournalism — the last picture, the latest picture — early on. The earlier change accompanied the loss of image-as-handicraft. Not only did engraving and sketch art end, replaced by the supposedly mechanical photograph, but also the change led to the disappearance of artists' signatures, which at first had appeared within press photography as autographs. Artists, like authors, were eventually swallowed up in technical expertise. A computer-based parallel could result in a loss to the handicraft of reporting, continuing the pattern set as telephones placed mediation between journalists and sources. Another result, the growth of homemade news in the utopian vision of the Internet, seems less likely. The first few years of the World Wide Web pointed not to homemade but to corporate news, with institutional arbiters claiming to manufacture the facts and filter out the gossip (the realm of e-mail and perhaps chat rooms).

Eventually Web news will absorb many functions of print, just as illustrations eventually took over much of the visual work previously done by verbal reports. Twentieth-century journalists, leaving description to the camera, turned especially to prediction. The future tense, although not absent in early reportage, had usually conveyed details ("the color guard of the 82nd infantry will follow the casket"). As photographs took over the details, reporters began to speak confidently of a wider future. On-line archives can supplant the background summaries central to explanatory news stories, as well as the repetition of pictures that have formed collective identity in the modern memory. The form of the Web moves news even further from event-centered reporting and toward analysis, interpretation, and prediction (Barnhurst & Mutz, 1997).

The changes would leave the journalist as expert, but also would suggest a return to the journalist as advocate. The disappearance of partisan journalism was surprisingly recent, accomplished more by the professional newspaper than by the industrial newspaper. The industrial newspaper produced economies of scale that led to conditions of local monopoly for newspapers; cultural factors then encouraged building a sense of professionalism on that foundation. Web newspapers, although somewhat monopolistic, also break down the barriers necessary to sustain monopoly. The local market we examined in western Massachusetts had gained a wider reach and had also lost its insularity in the electronic frontier. The spatial and economic geography of North America, which retarded the appearance of national newspapers in the United States, becomes attenuated on the Web. In an electronic marketplace, we can imagine a series of truly national newspapers competing. Why shouldn't these come to occupy partisan positions (of the European sort)? Even without the advent of partisan national media on-line, journalists might become partisan on their own. The availability of a largely free and linkable universe of information can allow a journalist the kind of autonomy that previously required entrepreneurial genius (of someone like I. F. Stone) or immense prominence (of someone like Seymour Hersh).

Most discussions of computer-based news tend to hyperbole and over-simplification. It is as if the visual landscape had changed abruptly, with the appearance of effects such as the link and the moving image within news text. Our examination of picture regimes showed that it is too simple to as-sert such sudden transformations. The visual was not simply missing before the rise of news photography in the twentieth century. In the same vein, motion in newspapers was not absent before the rise of the World Wide Web. Not only did all sorts of visual ways exist to represent the news, but also newspapers had textual ways of presenting an active vision of events. Even in the nineteenth century, newspapers could use techniques such as walking description to incorporate imagery as well as motion into text well before either cameras or computers entered newsrooms.

The role of on-line news in 2000s is ambiguous, but no more so than the role of photojournalism in the 1930s, the full adoption of which was more equivocal than is often acknowledged. Photojournalism, like the Web, resulted from technological advance, of course, and also from artistic innovation. The shift came about when newsworkers learned how to make photographs as lucid as engravings, a step that required not only advances in the speed and handling of cameras but also in the visual conception of news-paper pages. Instead of containing a narrative within a single engraving from sketches, photography required integrating pictures into news, coopting many tasks of text, and publishing multiple images to tell a story. It is not surprising that editors resisted at first, just as many of them now look askance at the on-line environment. Web designs, like picture pages, move news even further from contained, linear narrative. Newsworkers are now reconceptualizing journalism as they learn to make electronic pages do the work of news, a step fostered by advances in technology but also by the larger visual environment.

NEWSPAPER FUTURES

What will follow the high modernist moment of U.S. journalism (Hallin, 1994)? High Modern and especially Late Modern designs made sense of the world by removing the newspaper itself from the world. No longer a partisan advocate or even a competitor in the marketplace, the newspaper and its per-sonnel proclaimed detachment and rationality, inviting the fetishization of the newspaper form. Like all ascendancies, this one immediately anticipated its decadence, raised the alarm, and appealed for support. The popularity of the Internet and commercial information networks supplies the latest of many pseudocrises, each of which has threatened to make newspapers little more than a memory.

The Internet and the World Wide Web have so captivated the fin de siècle imagination that other sources of change tend to fade into obscurity. The most important innovations for newspapers, however, have always traveled from the margins to the front pages of newspapers themselves. Electronic news forms, in fact, draw heavily from the visual shenanigans pioneered in the tabloid format. Another dimension of news design that seems to be carrying into the future is the presence of vernacular design. It exists on the Web especially in the local press. In our close examination of electronic news in the Pioneer Valley of Massachusetts, we found vernacular design in sites such as that of the *Springfield Union-News,* and we expect that homemade designs will continue through whatever other changes occur in the form of news.

The same cannot be said for modern style. We have seen how the constraints of the tabloid newspaper page limited the phases of modernism, but compared to tabloids, Web designs face an even greater constraint on format, limited to screen size. As a result most phases of modern style do not exist in the electronic newspapers we studied. We did not encounter the Protomodern phase at all in Web editions. The expansion of space in newspapers accompanied the Classicist and High Modern phases in print, but news on-line offers too little contiguous space to accommodate either phase. Modern order and neatness would allow for very few items on each screen, but the commercial urgency of the medium contradicts the quiet of empty space. Few electronic newspapers go that route. The national Spanish daily *El País,* for example, did not extend its reserved design to the Internet, but opted instead for Late Modern forms on-line. Most of the highly designed electronic newspapers have preferred that phase, converging with the predominant design for both broadsheets and tabloids throughout the world (with the mainstream U.S. press as something of a laggard).

In other aspects, however, newspaper sites on the Web align with the pushy salesmanship of the supermarket tabloid and the new, emphatic broadsheet. Like its tabloid counterpart, the emphatic broadsheet bears a striking similarity to Web-based newspapers. They all adopt a promotional vocabulary to push events at consumers, selling their moral charge rather than the considered discourse of civic culture. Perhaps they point to a new, postmodern formation. In place of the coffeehouse metaphor, they propose the discotheque. Bright colors, many small items, a disorderly and disordered abundance, and howling diction reign. Consumers distractedly dance along with the pirouetting crowd or watch in stunned amazement. Mainstream newspapers, as they reflect U.S. culture, have considerable resistance to the disco metaphor, at least for now, but we take the qualities of electronic newspapers as a further indication of the demise of the modern formation.

Newspapers have entered another period of visual change that may seem directionless. With its underpinnings in postmodern ennui, the new visual form of news has no sense of history and seems to require no justification. The end game of modernism, as it expands beyond U.S. borders and confronts a borderless world of interactive computer networks, suggests the unraveling of the newspaper map. The austerities of the High Modern yield to a new abundance, or perhaps rather an old abundance. The most visually striking newspaper of the 1980s, *USA Today*, belied its proclaimed affinity to TV news with a perhaps unconsciously retro design, and its millennial redesign only heightens that effect. The crowded anarchy of a newspaper Webpage, with its pulsing ads and colored hyperlinks, has a similar neo-Victorian look.

The end of modernism holds more than antiquarian interest. As we pointed out previously (Chapter 7), the shift to modern newspaper form came about in large part because of bottlenecks that emerged in the media. Recently the bottlenecks that fostered modernism have begun to shift and erode. An abundance of new televisual outlets on cable, the rise of talk radio, and the like have begun to challenge the authority of journalism professionals. On a less visible level, newspapers have lost long-standing monopolies in classified advertising, financial information, and sports news. The change is best understood within the long-term historical context of the rise of the modernist newspaper; it is poorly understood by hyperbolic denunciations of MTV and *USA Today*.

Perhaps MTV and *USA Today* are the most obvious contenders for the characteristic media of the end of the century. The eroding market position of newspapers and network news shows, the rise of new contenders for the title Keeper of the Social Map, and the decline of faith in any privileged position of mapping might spell the demise of the modern newspaper form, although the judgment of history must not be rushed. Our overview of current experiments with electronic newspapering are to the point. Such forays themselves do not threaten the professional autonomy of journalists as authors and experts — a story is a story, transmitted electronically or on hard copy — but they do threaten modernism. Whatever else it is — a dictionary, an encyclopedia, a library, a card catalog, a data network — an electronic newspaper is not a map.

CHAPTER 9

SPECTATORS
AND THEIR SPECTACLES

Forms of Knowledge, Forms of Power

In 1978, a small group of graphic designers met at an American Press Institute seminar in Washington, D.C., and from their initial discussions grew the Society of Newspaper Design (SND). The organization spread slowly through the United States and Canada, moving eventually into Europe and Latin America and then on to other countries, including Australia and New Zealand, South Africa, Israel and the United Arab Emirates, and, in Asia, India, Japan, Taiwan, Hong Kong, and Thailand. Twenty years later, with more than two thousand members in forty-seven countries, the group portentously had changed its name to the Society for News Design.

The story of that first meeting became legend in the trade, marking the beginnings of the so-called revolution in newspaper design that led the way into electronic forms. Through traveling workshops, the founders, who hold a revered place among the membership, spread the gospel of modern (or what we would call Late Modern) design. The organization's conferences and publications claimed an international reach, including a competition that named The World's Best Designed Newspapers. Although tiny in a global setting, the members represented experts in news typography, layout, information graphics, illustrations, and so forth — a highly specialized group with considerable influence at newspapers, where staffers jokingly called them design czars. The membership clustered in countries most receptive to U.S. visual culture, and the society's new name not only hinted at its proselytizing aims but also reflected a trajectory away from traditional news on paper.

During the modern newspaper formation in U.S. history, such revolutions have been endemic. One chronicler identifies four in the twentieth century, in the 1910s, 1930s, 1960s, and 1970s, all before the founding of SND or *USA Today* (Hutt, 1973). To make much of the uprisings would yield a story with too many climaxes, full of exclamation points but finally pointless. The term *modern* has flown over a long string of revolutions since the Renaissance, when scholars rediscovering the classics first lifted the banner to declare battle on all things medieval. Constant revolution is a defining trait of the modern. Each rebellion invariably takes aim at a worn-out and irrational authority, beginning with that of the church in the early modern era but later extending to the divine right of kings and many other widely and firmly held beliefs. The modern invariably asserts itself by relegating the immediate past (the distant past is another matter) to the zone of superstition.

The newspaper design revolution typifies all the others. It began by asserting the accessibility of genuine knowledge and attacking the accretions of accidents and confusions that stood between knowledge and the people. Modern journalism proposed to reveal the external world and array it with clarity. The proposal, which as always aligned itself with science, aimed not at contemplation for its own sake but at the exercise of power, following Bacon's claim that "Knowledge is power." But power for whom? Compared with the Age of Reason, when the new epistemology accompanied, justified, and took credit for the discovery of the New World and the Protestant Reformation, the stakes for the modernist newspaper worker might seem paltry indeed. The design revolution would amount to little more than office politics if the particular office involved did not direct the house that the Enlightenment built for citizens to consummate the social contract. Newspapers gave physical form to the public sphere, and designers did battle over that legacy, however dissipated.

By moving the center of power from established practices accreted through long collective experience, modern journalists (like Enlightenment philosophers) centered power in the individual. Extracting an objective knowledge of the social world required an operator, a privileged observer. Relying on human subjects to produce objective knowledge introduced a key contradiction into the modern project. Naturalizing and humanizing knowledge made the world more egalitarian but required proper (that is, expert) methods. In all fields of knowledge in the nineteenth century practitioners developed protocols of observation that increasingly separated them from a lay public. The twentieth-century rise of modern news design and news professionalism extended this revolution from specialized to general knowledge. Modernists at newspapers, following a well-beaten path, invariably called into service a variety of machinery and procedures — the Web, most recently — to safeguard the truth, to make it reliable and predictable. In the process, power flowed to journalists themselves.

Although we discount the revolutionary rhetoric employed in the rise of newspaper modernism, we take its claims to power seriously. Over the long course of the modern and of U.S. history, the recent rhetoric among newsworkers does contain a nugget of truth: something is afoot, and it has to do with power and its spectators.

A SEA OF CHANGE; OR, WHO NEEDS A WEATHERMAN?

When a tsunami, or tidal wave, originates at sea, it does not always manifest itself on the surface. Moving at high speed as a subsurface pulse or shock wave, it may altogether escape the notice of sailors up above. Or they may feel a brief shudder. Their first real awareness that a tsunami has passed under them will come moments later, when dead fish, crushed by the immense pressure, float to the surface. In U.S. political culture, a lot of dead fish have floated to the surface lately — say, O. J. Simpson or Monica Lewinsky. We suspect that a tidal wave passed underneath some time ago.

Although stories of revolution overstate the case, changes in news forms, which the public receives and then uses in governing itself, did contribute to the tsunami. The forms of the news hail readers into a particular relationship with the events and personages of the day. As we have suggested, news forms recast readers on two levels, which for want of better terms we characterize as material and represented. Materially, news forms set up relationships between readers and other social actors, such as the New York Stock Exchange, the U.S. Congress, and the National Basketball Association. The existing forms of the legislative report, for example, materially configure the reader as a spectator and politics as a sporting event. The stock tables and the daily sports standings each cast the reader into a material relationship with an institution, and, in the process, such forms foreclose or eliminate other relationships.

A similar although not often consonant process occurs on the represented level. In the example of legislative reporting, the forms cast the reader as a voter/citizen, a member of the chorus that performs a role called public opinion, which legislators and reporters refer to as the ultimate moving force of politics. The disjuncture between the material and the representational work of each news form comes embedded in its very structure. That is, when a reporter as expert/insider, adopting an attitude of objectivity, condenses a complex legislative process into a story or series of contained stories operating according to news values — prominence, conflict, timeliness, proximity, and so forth — and disseminates it in a mainstream daily newspaper or on a nightly network news program, the very form makes the reader/viewer into a spectator. Yet at the same time that form, in constructing in advance the narrative of the report as a prelude to an election, represents the reader/viewer as a member of the active, judgmental citizenry of public opinion.

The example suggests that not every form of news produces disjunctures of equal severity. Take an alternative form of legislative reporting, the transcript of debate. The form flourished in the early through the mid–nineteenth century, when quasi-official newspapers such as the *National Intelligencer* acted as news services, and the nation's press duly copied large chunks of digested and sometimes verbatim speeches. That form of news disappeared from the mainstream press when daily newspapers yielded the function of record keeping to official government printers; it now survives in the *Congressional Record* and on the cable channels C-Span and C-Span 2. The transcript form also incorporated a disjuncture between material and representational relationships. On a material level, it cast the reader as a spectator in the halls of legislation viewing a dramaturgically constructed spectacle of decision making. On a representational level, however, it cast the reader as jury member, making an actual judgment during a real-time contest of argument. The falsity of the representational level lies in the fact that the very form of publicness always drives decision making away from the readers' gaze; even a casual C-Span watcher knows that no legislator ever makes up one's mind during or even on the basis of the televised debate. The very form of the news embeds a disjuncture between the material and the represented citizen.

Nevertheless, we consider the disjuncture more benign in the transcript than in the legislative report. Legislative reports perform a double trick, purporting to unveil the hidden decision-making process, but at the same time pulling a veil over the spectatorship of the reader and the constructedness of the report. Ultimately, the form empties the stage, leaving no politics for anyone to pretend to participate in, even as audience. The transcript, on the other hand, stoically refuses to unveil the decision-making process and stubbornly insists that the debate is the point, which affirms politics, albeit naïvely. By leading readers to believe that argument matters, the transcript form encourages them to remain politically active, helping bring about a situation in which argument *does* matter. Not by mere coincidence did the period when the transcript flourished coincide with the period when U.S. citizens most often voted, organized, volunteered, and asserted themselves in politics. Americans went to war over slavery and used politics to address fundamental questions of economic organization and social fairness. U.S. histories recall much of the political silliness of the period, such as the campaign spectacles of the Jacksonian era (Schudson, 1998), but neglect to note just how seriously the represented debates were conducted and observed. That seriousness waged war against and eventually lost out to the veiled agendas of political operators, right to the brink where politics tumbled into war. Politics in that age was finally tragic, not triumphant, but it was serious. Can anyone make the same claim for the Age of Lewinsky?

One example of a shift in news forms can reveal only so much. Each element of form is just that, one among many, existing within an overall environment of forms in relation to everything else. The form of news by itself could not revolutionize the political landscape. The decline of popular politics required many other actors and processes, such as the mobilization of upper-class reformers and the privatization of government tasks into specialized and depoliticized agencies (McGerr, 1986). The forms of news do not constitute the Archimedean point from which to move the world. Forms do, however, have deep and far-reaching meanings and consequences. It is silly to believe that improving the content of the news could revolutionize public life in the absence of formal change, as many media critics, particularly journalists, seem to assume. Better reporting from the campaign trail, for instance, is still reporting from the campaign trail. If reporters did better in 1996 than in 1992 or 1988, they still did nothing to reform the architecture of public life. We doubt that meaningful change will come from improved performance in the standard occupational routines.

Change in news forms throughout U.S. history occurred dialectically, as we have argued. Each of the major news formations presented a synthesis. The printerly newspaper synthesized an idealized public sphere with a craft-based type of manufacture, for example, but that synthesis generated contradictions between its economic and its political aims. The partisan newspaper resolved that conflict by embracing the marketplace model, and a new synthesis emerged, employing the competitive ideal not only for the business of newspapers but also for their political arguments. The partisan newspaper in turn generated contradictions between its editorial posture and its various other news and business departments that led to a new synthesis in the Victorian newspaper. Similar dialectics constituted not only subsequent formations but also the phases of advertising design, which in turn supplied the impulse toward changes in the news.

Another way to understand the interaction of forms and publics is through the concept of *voice*. We have noted repeatedly how news is voiced in different formations. The printerly newspaper suppressed the printer's voice and at the same time gave voice to gentlemen-readers. The partisan newspaper spoke in the editor's voice. The publisher's newspaper produced a de facto multivocality, with the editor's voice chanting alongside the staccato melodies of the marketplace: advertisers occupying newly fenced off suburbs on paper, and various external actors, including wire services and stock markets, voicing national and everyday news. The industrial newspaper continued this multivocality, and the jumbled, intense vernacular of Victorian sensibility nurtured the urgent racket of the marketplace and the department store.

The professional newspaper challenged multivocality. The reporter's soothing monotone overrode every other voice in the news, reducing all other speakers to sound bites and focusing attention on the unvoiced landscape behind everything else. Where voices could not be reduced, they were dumped into ghettoes: the Sports page, for instance, or the Editorial page, where they supplied mere amusement or opinion. On the front page, the modern forms of news remained essentially monovocal, as the typographic unity of Classicist and High Modern designs attest.

The monovocality of modern news forms justifies itself as democratic. The modernist newspaper proclaimed that its mission was to give a complete and accurate account of the day's news in a context that gives it meaning. The newspaper would be the intelligence agent (Lippmann, 1922), providing information that ordinary people need to orient themselves as responsible citizens in a complicated and ever-changing world. That common sense packs in the raft of assumptions we began with, about knowledge, power, and the individual's relationship to the social real. The modernist newspaper, and much of the twentieth-century culture of the press, followed the Baconian understanding of knowledge and power, presuming that the function of democratic media is to present knowledge to a citizenry composed of rational individuals. Simple rationality itself, however, cannot guarantee readers' ability to decode the news properly. They must first share a pool of taken-for-granted knowledge, a consensus on the larger features of an overall mapping of society. A prime instance is the boundary that readily separated the personal from the political. If empowerment came from acquiring information, journalism aimed to supply the information, preferably mapped according to the gross features that, common sense said, corresponded to the essential structure of society. Such mythical background knowledge expressed itself in one voice — hence the monovocality of modernist news.

We have emphasized one aspect of modern news repeatedly, the byline, because the fact that stories acquired bylines returns to the fundamental contradiction of modernism, in which objectivity presumes subjectivity. The byline tells readers that, although a subjectivity (a specific person) wrote a story, a set of procedures followed precisely can still warrant the story's objectivity. The writer implicitly certifies that any other reporter could replicate the report. Naming the writer, ironically, underscores the monovocality of news. The byline stipulates the irrelevancy of voice or persona.

In the late modern or neo-Victorian moment, the weaknesses of the Baconian model have become manifest: a public of rational individuals is no longer a believable fiction. Instead the great public has bifurcated into passive (readers and viewers) and active (newsmakers and opinion leaders) parts. Reporters, more aligned with newsmakers than with audiences, often become celebrities who speak from a position of race, gender, or other difference, as the notion of a universal observer has crumbled. Knowledge can no longer be viewed as socially neutral. Instead, the news media and their forms exhibit power effects that are better explained by Foucault's inversion of the power–knowledge relationship. The forms of the newspaper encode power in ways that a literate reader can decode, but the knowledge they engender does not claim to empower the public by making it more intelligent. Having lost the fiction of the Baconian public, late modern news organizations, in an ironic echo of a conceit of colonial printers, satisfy themselves by believing that they themselves are the public. The collapse of the categories of journalist and citizen into one marks neither an end to monovocality nor a return to multivocality. As journalists become more fond of talking to each other, they cannot wholly abandon the repressed monotone of the neutral expert. Instead they produce a pseudovocality that uses personal-sounding effects to speak from nowhere and everywhere.

IDEAL NEWS FORM

Our excursus on voice offers a normative guideline for news forms. Multiple voices enhance democracy. Multivocal forms invite readers to act as citizens in ways that monovocal forms, no matter how much mastery of facts or truth they promise, never can.

The historical record does not reveal an ideally multivocal form. The Federal period fantasy of a public sphere presents an alluring ideal, in which newspapers operate like town meetings, but the actual formation of the printerly newspaper reproduced the monotone of propertied gentlemen. The partisan newspaper, by virtue of its position within a competitive news and political environment, reproduced a strong, demotic voice representing itself as one of many, but at the same time its forms cast readers as party faithful, listening to only one voice (i.e., fully attending to only one newspaper). Although the editor represented himself (usually) as a debater, the Partisan period in fact set up the relationship between editor and reader as teacher–student or drill sergeant–recruit — discipline masqueraded as persuasion.

The Victorian newspaper was truly multivocal, but its multivocality was profane. The many voices of the marketplace shouted down the lonely voice of the political arena. Consumer freedom seduced readers away from politics, now recast by the news as a dismal realm of tawdry spectacle, idiotic discipline, and inevitable misgovernment. Modernism did not invent the depoliticized public; it merely took it out of the profane neighborhoods of the Victorian paper and enshrined it in the temple, where reporters, the new high priests of civic discourse, could lead it in prayer. Some truths will not set you free.

Perhaps an ideally multivocal newspaper is a contradiction in terms. If so, then we await the deformation of the newspaper. The melange of styles in news would then point to the rejection of forms expressing not only the type of news production but also any larger public ideal. Without its civic justification, the newspaper would have even less claim on reader loyalty. We are reluctant to accept that grim possibility. Granted, all the newspaper formations we discuss cast readers into contradictory material and represented relationships. All of them are deeply implicated in legitimating existing concentrations of power by making them seem simply obvious, but not all are equally culpable. The modernist newspaper is the most implicated here, because it has combined the inescapable function of visual representation with a journalistic claim to fully and neutrally map the social and with the economic power to make that claim believable. Put tersely, the project of mapping the social has always entailed more power for the mapper than for the citizen.

A broad irony of modernism is the pessimism it produced. Enlightenment philosophers, by placing the individual at the center of their project, treated all citizens as inherently good and equal, beginning from the same blank slate. The resulting egalitarianism gave sense to the American Revolution and produced the printerly and then the partisan newspapers, the most optimistic of the formations we examined. Each succeeding formation has moved further away from the belief in the power and inherent goodness of the people. With the Late Modern phase, news arrived at its nadir, thoroughly pessimistic in regard to readers, whom it conceived as lacking knowledge, paying little attention to public affairs, and requiring constant visual cajoling (by marketing techniques) to show any response.

The ideal of the newspaper then moved on from map to index. As the High Modern phase of news passed, the possibility of mapping the social receded from the ambitions of news professionals, even as the autonomy of newsworkers receded before the advancing power of the news corporation. Instead of retreating to the multivocality of the industrial newspaper, the multiplicity of neo-Victorian design has produced a new kind of monovocality. The index as guiding ideal suggests that the newspaper might become a daily almanac. The best known U.S. almanac, *Poor Richard's,* supplied a reference tool for the immediate use of readers, laced with tidbits of moralistic prose. It contributed not only to the financial success of Benjamin Franklin but also to his celebrity. The almanac, a hybrid form combining tabular material and raw listed facts with a miscellany of more narrative content, makes its distributor a practical authority, and gives him or her a textured and recognized voice.

But neo-Victorian forms are surely transitional. As the newspaper moves into cyberspace, we anticipate a coming formation that we might call the *network newspaper.* The network newspaper would combine the corporate structure of the Late Modern news with the free forms and easy interconnectedness of the Internet. The endurance of the corporate structure has so far defied the predictions of Internet utopians, who expected the disappearance of scarcities in production (no need for paper and presses anymore) and of bottlenecks in distribution (no need for trucks and newsstands either) to open opportunities for more entrepreneurial news businesses to compete with and eventually uproot the dominant corporations. Utopians expected the free flow of information to kill the dinosaurs, but instead all the important Web-based news sites grew from existing news organizations. The Internet greased some of the relationships within the old forms of news, but in material terms has not yet produced new relationships. True, readers can talk back more easily to their newspapers on the Web, but the act still resembles talking back to the television set — something akin to therapy, perhaps, but not to political action. At least at this point the network newspaper encourages reader response primarily as a form of surveillance intended to strengthen the marketing and advertising functions of the corporation.

The Web also relates news forms to each other quite differently. Some formerly solid barriers, lines that separated the sacred from the profane and the news from advertising, have become more permeable. Previously well-defined divisions of labor in news production also show signs of strain. To the good, the vast network of relationships that produces the news has made itself more visible to readers. The fixed vantage point from which professional journalists surveyed the world in the High Modern period has dissolved. Network newspapers reveal instead a shifting nexus of different lines of force, representing the reader as a fleeting atom in the net.

We can choose to face the prospect of the next newspaper formation with more hope than history warrants. Multivocality in its ideal form may come at last. A limited deprofessionalization of journalists, coupled with the enhanced autonomy of readers, may produce a dialogue capable of overcoming the intense bifurcation of the public into active and passive parts that has become more characteristic during the modern era. A form of public deliberation through the news would then become at least possible, however unlikely.

Throughout U.S. history, stylistic decisions have assigned and channeled much of the work of the newspaper. Such decisions have paid little attention to less immediate implications, but instead recapitulated rather thoughtlessly the dominant distributions of power. We can say fairly that in the newspaper and in print culture and the media generally, the play of power is more simple, more tame, and better legitimated than in the culture or practices of everyday life. In every period of U.S. history, the voices of political debate in taverns and public squares have been more diverse than the spectrum represented in the press. Before the Civil War, women accomplished many things in the world but only a few in print. In the Progressive era, African Americans found myriad ways to resist white power in the workplace but remained simply subaltern in the mainstream press. The formal decision by which newspapers elected to add the adjective *colored* to the name of every black person, whether in an obituary or a story about a prizefight, did much to represent African Americans as less than full citizens (and their own newspapers emerged to redress that treatment). Style can accomplish a lot.

At the end of the modern era, much attention has been called to the rhetorical impact of formal decisions. No news photographer can innocently ignore the implications of depicting blacks rather than whites among chained arrestees or drug users. No reporter can innocently ignore the implications of quoting and naming male sources while paraphrasing unidentified women. No designer can innocently ignore the implications of choosing to group gay rights and AIDS stories together on the page. The journalist's lost innocence merits our congratulations. It should be carried further, as we have intended to do here. The greatest harm for the common good redounds when power operates at the margins. The modern commitment to openness thus must extend to the decisions newspaper conductors make about their visual form. Without the gauze curtain of ignorance that once obscured the manipulation of visual form, journalism may become more democratic — an aim we heartily endorse. We have yet to reach a point where we understand all the ways in which style creates and distributes power.

We do not, however, propose to isolate style from all the other ways that power is created and distributed. To do so would be to yield to the logic of the Late Modern newspaper, in which style is supposedly freed from corporate structure to do whatever work designers bid. Late Modern styles, whatever the designer's intent, inevitably reproduce corporate power by their mere inclusion in the relations ordered by the corporate newspaper. Styles cannot by themselves overcome the limitations of the corporate structure and the surrounding economic and political culture. In the final analysis, the newspaper remains a creature of its environment. Despite the powers of the press, which we have duly celebrated here, the work of overcoming an unfair distribution of social, economic, and political power must also be undertaken elsewhere.

News forms nevertheless do some work in the world. Although restricted by class, the forms of news opened participatory opportunities to gentlemen in the Federal period. The forms of early illustrated news reproduced the civic gaze that sustained a republican ideal. The Victorian forms of news gave the industrial newspaper near universal reach. Finally, the forms of news sustained a factual reliability in the modern newspaper, despite its other failings.

A FINAL NOTE

Our belief that the form of news makes a difference goes beyond any simple nostalgia for the idea of the newspaper, although we readily confess our personal histories and proclivities. We see our own citizenship playing out on the backdrop of news forms. We remember not only events but the look of those events in the press. As our aging memories become less crisp and vivid, what remains is the pattern of how things looked: the environment that newspapers created in which we experienced the affairs of the day.

In the ten years we have dedicated to our analysis, our engagement with daily newspapers has soured as that news environment has changed. We no longer read print versions with the same pleasure, a pleasure that always went beyond our evaluations of their journalistic and design virtues. Today's *Chicago Tribune* probably is a better paper in both regards than the one we read in the 1980s, but we value it less because we see through its visual and civic pretensions. At the same time, we use electronic versions more often but with increasing ruthlessness, getting our information on the run and taking no pleasure in it at all. Perhaps this is because we can't carry it around with us, and droop over it on the bus, and gesture at friends with it, and stick yellowing clippings from it to our refrigerators. We would never consider lingering over the online crossword puzzle as a guilty treat. The computer is our *work* station.

The fact that our newspaper reading has begun to move to computers attests to the many ways in which news has moved out of the domestic and the public worlds and instead into the corporate world. The news on-line and in print beckons us into an environment driven by tasks and by the bottom line, and like many other readers we resist by ignoring the visual gimmicks of Internet-based and Late Modern newsprint designs. The corporate setting plunders the visual form in search of short-term gains, and our own activities respond to that set of values. The example provides one final illustration of how the form of news narrows and limits our options. We extract what information will serve immediate purposes, and although we intend our perfunctory attention as a form of resistance, it in fact reflects the extractive models of corporate environments. Throughout its history, the form of news has played a similar game of gotcha.

That is not to say that we do not harbor optimism. We have dedicated time and energy to the project of documenting the changing form of news to alert readers and journalists to its power, with the expectation that awareness can motivate change. Design decisions are more than mere cake decorating that disguises the substance of news; they add to or limit its nutritional value. In any activist agenda, the first step is to raise consciousness. Although we do not prescribe what the environment should be, we want to show what it has been and to take part in the process that will reimagine what it will be.

We hope that the newspaper survives and evolves into a formation that will encourage civic culture in new ways. Although not a panacea, a reformation of the newspaper could help achieve greater justice. We hope that future forms of news will combine the participatory opportunities that the printerly newspaper gave to gentlemen with the civic gaze of early illustrated news and the universal reach of the industrial newspaper and the factual reliability of the modern newspaper. No other institution offers more promise for the regeneration of civic life. After all, history has not stopped, as anyone who reads newspapers knows.

REFERENCES

Abrahamson, David. *Magazine-Made America: The Colonial Transformation of the Postwar Periodical*. Cresskill, N.J.: Hampton Press, 1996.

Adams, Henry. *The Education of Henry Adams*. 1906. New York: Modern Library, 1931.

Alden, Albert. *Wood Engraver's Book* (scrapbook). Collection of the American Antiquarian Society, n.d.

Allen, John E. *Newspaper Designing*. New York: Harper, 1947.

Althusser, Louis. "Ideology and Ideological State Apparatuses." In *"Lenin and Philosophy and Other Essays,"* pp. 127–86. 1969. Trans. Ben Brewster. New York: Monthly Review Press, 1971.

Amaral, Roberto, and Elizabeth Rondelli. "Medios de comunicación de masas y poder en América Latina: Un pequeño ensayo sobre la modernidad arcaica" (Mass communication media and power in Latin America: A brief essay on archaic modernity). *Telos*. Madrid: Complutense University, 1996. (*ftp.fundesco.es/publica/telos-47/Central/3.html*).

Anderson, Patricia. *The Printed Image and the Transformation of Popular Culture, 1790–1860*. Oxford, U.K.: Oxford University Press, 1991.

Anthony, Jay, and Kate Newton Anthony. "Typefaces, White Spaces, Splashes of Color." *Washington Journalism Review*, May 1985, p. 31.

Arendt, Hannah. *The Human Condition*. Chicago: University of Chicago Press, 1958.

Arens, Egmont, and Ray Sheldon. *Consumer Engineering: A New Technique for Prosperity*. New York: Harper & Brothers, 1932.

Arnold, Edmund. *Functional Newspaper Design*. New York: Harper, 1956.

Bailey, David. *Eastward Ho! Leaves from the Diary of a Centennial Pilgrim*. Highland County, Ohio: Author, 1877.

Baldasty, Gerald. *The Commercialization of News in Nineteenth Century America*. Madison: University of Wisconsin Press, 1993.

Barnhurst, Kevin G. *News as Art*. Journalism Monographs 130. Columbia, S.C.: Association for Education in Journalism and Mass Communication, December 1991.

———. *Seeing the Newspaper*. New York: St. Martin's Press, 1994.

———. "Newspapers as Twentieth Century Texture." In *The News Aesthetic*, pp. 22–35. Ed. Lawrence Mirsky and Silvana Tropea. New York: Cooper Union/Princeton Architectural Press, 1995.

———. *Political Engagement and the Audience for News: Lessons from Spain*. Journalism and

Communication Monographs 2 (1). Columbia, S.C.: Association for Education in Journalism and Mass Communication, Spring 2000.

Barnhurst, Kevin G., and Diana Mutz. "American Journalism and the Decline of Event-Centered News." *Journal of Communication* 47 (4) (Autumn 1997): 27–53.

Barnhurst, Kevin G., et al. "Los periódicos españoles, en la textura del siglo XX" (Spanish newspapers in the texture of the twentieth century). *Revista Latina de Comunicación Social* (La Laguna, Tenerife) *18* (June 1999). (*www.ull.es/publicaciones/latina/a1999gjn/79ke/vin.htm*).

Baynes, Ken, ed. *Scoop, Scandal and Strife: A Study of Photography in Newspapers.* New York: Pantheon Books, 1971.

Beniger, James. *The Control Revolution: Technological and Economic Origins of the Information Society.* Cambridge, Mass.: Harvard University Press, 1986.

Benjamin, Walter. "The Work of Art in the Age of Mechanical Reproduction." In *Illuminations*, pp. 217–51. Ed., with intro., by Hannah Arendt. Trans. Harry Zohn. New York: Schocken Books, 1969.

Berger, John. *Ways of Seeing.* London: BBC/Penguin Books, 1972.

Berger, Meyer. *The Story of the* New York Times, *1851–1951.* New York: Simon & Schuster, 1951.

Berman, Marshall. *All That Is Solid Melts into Air: The Experience of Modernity.* New York: Simon & Schuster, 1982.

Birkhead, Douglas. "The Power in the Image: Professionalism and the Communications Revolution." *American Journalism 1* (Winter 1984): 1–17.

Boswell, Sharon A., and Lorraine McConaghy. *Raise Hell and Sell Newspapers: Alden J. Blethen and the* Seattle Times. Pullman: Washington State University Press, 1996.

Botein, Stephen. " 'Meer Mechanics' and an Open Press: The Business and Political Strategies of Colonial American Printers." *Perspectives in American History 9* (1975): 130–211.

———. "Printers and the American Revolution." In *The Press and the American Revolution*, pp. 11–58. Ed. Bernard Bailyn and John B. Hench. Boston: Northeastern University Press, 1981.

Bronfenbrenner, Urie. "The Ecology of Cognitive Development: Research Models and Fugitive Findings." In *Scientific Environments*, pp. 3–44. Ed. R. H. Wozinak and K. Fischer. Hillsdale, N.J.: Erlbaum, 1993.

Brown, Dee. *The Year of the Century: 1876.* New York: Scribner's, 1966.

Brown, Joshua Emmett. Frank Leslie's Illustrated Newspaper*: The Pictorial Press and the Representations of America, 1855–1889.* Ph.D. dissertation, Columbia University, 1993.

Brown, Richard D. *Knowledge Is Power: The Diffusion of Information in Early America, 1700–1865.* New York: Oxford University Press, 1989.

Brucker, Herbert. *The Changing American Newspaper.* New York: Columbia University Press, 1937.

Bryson, Norman, ed. *Visual Culture: Images & Interpretations.* Hanover, N.H.: University Press of New England for Wesleyan University Press, 1994.

Burnett, Ron. *Cultures of Vision: Images, Media and the Imaginary.* Bloomington: Indiana University Press, 1995.

Carey, James W. *Communication as Culture: Essays on Media and Society.* Boston: Unwin Hyman, 1988.

Carlebach, Michael G. *The Origins of Photojournalism.* Washington, D.C.: Smithsonian Institute, 1992.

Clark, Charles. *The Public Prints: The Newspaper in Anglo-American Culture, 1665–1740.* New York: Oxford University Press, 1994.

Conroy, David. *In Public Houses: Drink and the Revolution of Authority in Colonial Massachusetts.* Chapel Hill: University of North Carolina Press, 1995.

Cook, Timothy E. *Governing with the News: The News Media as a Political Institution*. Chicago: University of Chicago Press, 1998.

Craig, Robert L. "Advertising as Visual Communication." *Communication 13* (1992): 165–79.

Crary, Jonathan. *Techniques of the Observer: On Vision and Modernity in the Nineteenth Century*. Cambridge, Mass.: MIT Press, 1990.

Craven, Wayne. *American Art: History and Culture*. New York: Abrams, 1994.

Emery, Michael B., Edwin Emery, and Nancy L. Roberts. *The Press and America: An Interpretive History of the Mass Media*. 8th ed. Needham Heights, Mass.: Allyn & Bacon, 1996.

Epstein, Edward Jay. *News from Nowhere: Television and the News*. New York: Vintage Books, 1974.

Ericson, Richard V., Patricia M. Baranek, and Janet B. L. Chan. *Visualizing Deviance: A Study of News Organization*. Toronto: University of Toronto Press, 1987.

Ewen, Stuart. *All Consuming Images: The Politics of Style in Contemporary Culture*. New York: Basic Books, 1988.

Fallows, James. *Breaking the News: How the Media Undermine American Democracy*. New York: Pantheon Books, 1996.

Ferebee, Ann. *A History of Design from the Victorian Era to the Present*. New York: Van Nostrand Reinhold, 1970.

Fischer, David Hackett. *The Revolution of American Conservatism: The Federalist Party in the Era of Jeffersonian Democracy*. New York: Harper & Row, 1965.

Folkerts, Jean, and Dwight L. Teeter. *Voices of a Nation: A History of the Mass Media in the United States*. 3rd ed. Needham Heights, Mass.: Allyn & Bacon, 1998.

"Front Pages: How Much Have They Changed?" *Editor and Publisher*, November 2, 1985, p. 15.

Gans, Herbert J. *Deciding What's News: A Study of "CBS Evening News," "NBC Nightly News,"* Newsweek *and* Time. New York: Pantheon Books, 1979.

García, Mario R. *Contemporary Newspaper Design: A Structural Approach*. Englewood Cliffs, N.J.: Prentice-Hall, 1981.

———. "Too Often, Redesigns Produce 'Cookie-Cutter' Newspapers." *ASNE Bulletin*, no. 694 (1987): 34–35.

Goodrum, Charles, and Helen Dalrymple. *Advertising in America: The First 200 Years*. New York: Abrams, 1990.

Green, Jonathan. *American Photography: A Critical History, 1945 to the Present*. New York: Abrams, 1984.

Habermas, Jürgen. *The Structural Transformation of the Public Sphere: An Inquiry into a Category of Bourgeois Society*. 1963. Cambridge, Mass.: MIT Press, 1989.

Hall, Stuart, ed. *Representation: Cultural Representation and Signifying Practices*. London: Sage, 1997.

Hallin, Daniel C. *We Keep America on Top of the World: Television Journalism and the Public Sphere*. New York: Routledge, 1994.

Hartley, John. *The Politics of Pictures*. London: Routledge, 1993.

Haskell, F. *History and Its Images: Art and the Interpretation of the Past*. New Haven, Conn.: Yale University Press, 1993.

Hicks, Wilson. *Words and Pictures: An Introduction to Photojournalism*. New York: Harper, 1952.

Horkheimer, Max, and Theodor W. Adorno. 1944. *Dialectic of Enlightenment*. New York: Continuum, 1991.

Howard, Philip. *We Thundered Out: 200 Years of* The Times, *1785–1985*. Maplewood, N.J.: Hammond, 1985.

Huggins, John Richard Desborus. *Hugginiana*. New York: Southwick, 1808. (Shaw & Shoemaker 11941)

Hutchins Commission. *A Free and Responsible Press.* Chicago: University of Chicago Press, 1947.

Hutt, Allen. *The Changing Newspaper: Typographic Trends in Britain and America, 1622–1972.* London: Gordon Fraser, 1973.

Innis, Harold Adams. *The Bias of Communication.* Toronto: University of Toronto Press, 1951.

Irwin, Will. *The American Newspaper.* 1916. Ames: Iowa State University Press, 1969.

Iser, Wolfgang. *Prospecting: From Reader Response to Literary Anthropology.* Baltimore: Johns Hopkins University Press, 1989.

Iyengar, Shanto. *Is Anyone Responsible? How Television Frames Political Issues.* Chicago: University of Chicago Press, 1991.

Jackson, Kenneth. *Crabgrass Frontier: The Suburbanization of the United States.* New York: Oxford University Press, 1985.

James, William. *The Principles of Psychology.* 2 vols. New York: Holt & Co., 1890.

Jameson, Fredric. *Postmodernism, or, The Cultural Logic of Late Capitalism.* Durham, N.C.: Duke University Press, 1991.

Jay, Martin. *Downcast Eyes: The Denigration of Vision in Twentieth-Century French Thought.* Berkeley and Los Angeles: University of California Press, 1993.

Jenks, Chris, ed. *Visual Culture.* New York: Routledge, 1994.

John, Richard. *Spreading the News: The American Postal System from Franklin to Morse.* Cambridge, Mass.: Harvard University Press, 1995.

Katz, Jon. "On Line or Not, Newspapers Suck." *Wired,* September 1994, pp. 50–58.

Kern, Stephen. *The Culture of Time and Space, 1880–1918.* Cambridge, Mass.: Harvard University Press, 1983.

Kielbowicz, Richard. *News in the Mail: The Press, Post Office and Public Information, 1700–1860s.* New York: Greenwood Press, 1989.

La France les Etats-Unis et Leurs Presses. Paris: Centre George Pompidou, 1977.

Laird, Pamela Walker. *Advertising Progress: American Business and the Rise of Consumer Marketing.* Baltimore, Md.: Johns Hopkins University Press, 1998.

Lallana, Fernando. *Tipografía y diseño.* Madrid: Síntesis, 1999.

Lalvani, Suren. *Photography, Vision, and the Production of Modern Bodies.* Albany: State University of New York Press, 1996.

Leach, William. *Land of Desire: Merchants, Power, and the Rise of a New American Culture.* New York: Vintage Books, 1993.

Lears, T. J. Jackson. *Fables of Abundance: A Cultural History of Advertising in America.* New York: Basic Books, 1994.

LeMahieu, D. L. *A Culture for Democracy.* Oxford, U.K.: Oxford University Press, 1988.

Leonard, Thomas C. *The Power of the Press: The Birth of American Political Reporting.* New York: Oxford University Press, 1986.

———. "News at the Hearth: A Drama of Reading in Nineteenth-Century America." *Proceedings of the American Antiquarian Society 102* (2) (1993): 379–401.

———. *News for All: America's Coming of Age with the Press.* New York: Oxford University Press, 1995.

Leslie's Illustrated Newspaper. *Historical Register of the Centennial Exposition.* New York: Frank Leslie's, 1876.

Lippard, George. *The Quaker City; or, The Monks of Monk Hall.* Philadelphia, 1844.

Lippmann, Walter. *Public Opinion.* 1922. New York: Free Press, 1965.

Lockwood, Robert. *News by Design.* Denver: Quark Press, 1992.

Lury, Celia. *Prosthetic Culture: Photography, Memory and Identity.* New York: Routledge, 1998.

Marchand, Roland. *Advertising the American Dream: Making Way for Modernity, 1920–1940.* Berkeley and Los Angeles: University of California Press, 1985.

McChesney, Robert W. *Rich Media, Poor Democracy: Communication Politics in Dubious Times*. Urbana: University of Illinois Press, 1999.

McGerr, Michael. *The Decline of Popular Politics*. New York: Oxford University Press, 1986.

McLuhan, Marshall. *The Gutenberg Galaxy: The Making of Typographic Man*. Toronto: University of Toronto Press, 1962.

———. *Understanding Media: The Extensions of Man*. New York: McGraw-Hill, 1964.

Meggs, Philip B. *A History of Graphic Design*. 3rd ed. New York: Wiley, 1998.

Merritt, Richard. *Symbols of American Community, 1735–1775*. New Haven, Conn.: Yale University Press, 1966.

Messaris, Paul. *Visual Literacy: Image, Mind, Reality*. Boulder, Colo.: Westview Press, 1993.

Michaels, Walter Benn. *The Gold Standard*. Chapel Hill: University of North Carolina Press, 1988.

Mirsky, Lawrence. "Brand News." In *The News Aesthetic*, pp. 36–51. Ed. Lawrence Mirsky and Silvana Tropea. New York: Cooper Union/Princeton Architectural Press, 1995.

Moeller, Susan. *Compassion Fatigue: How the Media Sell Disease, Famine, War and Death*. New York: Routledge, 1999.

Moore, R. Laurence. *Selling God: American Religion in the Marketplace of Culture*. New York: Oxford University Press, 1994.

Morison, Stanley. *The English Newspaper*. Cambridge, U.K.: Cambridge University Press, 1932.

Nasaw, David. *Going Out: The Rise and Fall of Public Amusements*. New York: Basic Books, 1993.

Nerone, John. *The Culture of the Press in the Early Republic: Cincinnati, 1793–1848*. New York: Garland, 1989.

———. "The Problem of Teaching Journalism History." *Journalism Educator* 45 (3) (Autumn 1990): 16–23.

———. "A Local History of the Early U.S. Press: Cincinnati, 1793–1848." In *Ruthless Criticism: New Perspectives in U.S. Communication History*, pp. 38–65. Ed. William S. Solomon and Robert W. McChesney. Minneapolis: University of Minnesota Press, 1993a.

———. "Theory and History." *Communication Theory* 3 (2) (May 1993b): 148–56.

———. *Violence against the Press: Policing the Public Sphere in U.S. History*. New York: Oxford University Press, 1994.

Nesbitt, Phil. "Reaching More Readers with Redesigned Papers." *ASNE Bulletin*, no. 703 (1988): 3–7.

Newhall, Beaumont. *The History of Photography, 1839 to the Present Day*. 1938. New York: Museum of Modern Art, 1982.

"The News-boy's Verses, for New-Year's Day, 1763: Humbly Address'd to his Patrons, to whom he Carries the Thursday's *New-York Gazette*." New York: John Holt, 1762. (Evans no. 9217)

Nord, David. "Teleology and News: The Religious Roots of American Journalism, 1630–1730." *Journal of American History* 77 (June 1990): 9–38.

Ohmann, Richard. *Selling Culture: Magazines, Markets and Class at the Turn of the Century*. New York: Verso, 1996.

Ong, Walter J. *Orality and Literacy: The Technologizing of the Word*. New York: Methuen, 1982.

Orvell, Miles. *The Real Thing: Imitation and Authenticity in American Culture, 1880–1940*. Chapel Hill: University of North Carolina Press, 1990.

Pauly, John. "The Professional Communicator as a Symbolic Figure." *American Journalism* 1 (Winter 1984): 18–35.

Pompey the Little Who Was Tied to the Kettle [illustrated children's book]. Philadelphia, 1812. (Shaw & Shoemaker 26492)

Postman, Neil. *Amusing Ourselves to Death: Public Discourse in the Age of Show Business.* New York: Viking Books, 1985.

Prints of Original Wood Blocks from the Archives of McLaughlin Bros. Publishers, N.Y. ca. 1865. Los Angeles: Dawson's Book Shop, 1980.

Quadros, Claudia Irene de. *Periodistas y diarios electrónicos: Las exigencias profesionales en la red: Estudio de los casos El País Digital, El Mundo del Siglo XXI, NetEstado y O Globo On.* Ph.D. dissertation, University of La Laguna, Tenerife, Spain, 1999.

Rabinbach, Anson. *The Human Motor: Energy, Fatigue, and the Origins of Modernity.* New York: Basic Books, 1990.

Radway, Janice A. *Reading the Romance: Women, Patriarchy and Popular Literature.* Chapel Hill: University of North Carolina Press, 1984.

Rawson, David Andrew. *"Guardians of Their Own Liberty": A Contextual History of Print Culture in Virginia Society, 1750 to 1820.* Ph.D. dissertation, College of William and Mary, 1998.

Rehe, Rolf. "The Emerging Patterns of Look-Alike Typography." *ASNE Bulletin,* no. 640 (1981): 22–23.

Reynolds, David S. *Beneath the American Renaissance: The Subversive Imagination in the Age of Emerson and Melville.* New York: Knopf, 1988.

Rothstein, Arthur. "Steelworkers Reading the Newspaper, Aliquippa, Pennsylvania." Farm Security Adminstration, Office of War Information Photograph Collection (LC-USF33–002822-M2), July 1938.

Rowell, George P., & Co. *American Newspaper Directory, Edition for 1876.* New York: Author, 1876.

Sampedro, Víctor. "Grounding the Displaced: Local Media Consumption in a Transnational Environment." *Journal of Communication* 48 (Spring 1998): 125–43.

Schiller, Herbert I. *Culture, Inc.: The Corporate Takeover of Public Expression.* New York: Oxford University Press, 1989.

Schudson, Michael. *Discovering the News: A Social History of American Newspapers.* New York: Basic Books, 1978.

———. "The Politics of Narrative Form: The Emergence of News Conventions in Print and Television." *Daedalus* 3 (4) (Winter–Fall 1982): 97–112.

———. *The Good Citizen: A History of American Civic Life.* New York: Free Press, 1998.

Sellers, Charles G. *The Market Revolution: Jacksonian America, 1815–1846.* New York: Oxford University Press, 1991.

Sinclair, Upton. *The Brass Check: A Study of American Journalism.* Pasadena, Calif.: Author, 1919.

Sloan, William David, and James D. Startt. *The Media in America: A History.* 3rd ed. Northport, Ala.: Vision Press, 1996.

Smith, Culver H. *The Press, Politics and Patronage: The American Government's Use of Newspapers, 1789–1875.* Athens: University of Georgia Press, 1977.

Soja, Edward W. *Postmodern Geographies: The Reassertion of Space in Critical Social Theory.* London: Verso, 1989.

Solomon, William. "The Site of Newsroom Labor: The Division of Editorial Practices." In *Newsworkers: Toward a History of the Rank and File,* pp. 110–34. Ed. Hanno Hardt and Bonnie Brennan. Minneapolis: University of Minnesota Press, 1995.

Spigel, Lynn. *Make Room for TV: Television and the Family Ideal in Postwar America.* Chicago: University of Chicago Press, 1992.

Steele, Ian K. *The English Atlantic, 1675–1740: An Exploration of Communication and Community.* New York: Oxford University Press, 1986.

Stephens, Mitchell. *The Rise of the Image, the Fall of the Word.* New York: Oxford University Press, 1998.

Stewart, Donald H. *The Opposition Press of the Federalist Period*. Albany: State University of New York Press, 1969.

Stone, Gerald C., John C. Schweitzer, and David H. Weaver. "Adoption of Modern Newspaper Design." *Journalism Quarterly* 55 (1978): 761–66.

Sutton, Albert. *Design and Makeup of the Newspaper.* Englewood Cliffs, N.J.: Prentice-Hall, 1969.

Szarkowski, John, *The Photographer's Eye.* New York: Museum of Modern Art, 1966.

———. ed. *From the Picture Press.* New York: Museum of Modern Art, 1973.

Taylor, Lucien, ed. *Visualizing Theory: Selected Essays from V.A.R., 1990–1994.* New York: Routledge, 1994.

Tompkins, Jane P., ed. *Reader-Response Criticism: From Formalism to Post-structuralism.* Baltimore: Johns Hopkins University Press, 1980.

Trachtenberg, Alan. *Reading American Photographs: Images as History, Mathew Brady to Walker Evans.* New York: Hill, 1990.

Tucher, Andie. *Froth and Scum: Truth, Beauty, Goodness, and the Ax Murder in America's First Mass Medium.* Chapel Hill: University of North Carolina Press, 1994.

Tuchman, Gaye. *Making News: A Study in the Construction of Reality.* New York: Free Press, 1978.

Turow, Joseph. *Breaking Up America: Advertisers and the New Media World.* Chicago: University of Chicago Press, 1997.

Universal Picture Books. Washington, D.C.: Charles Magnus, 1863.

Warner, Michael. *The Letters of the Republic: Publication and the Public Sphere in Eighteenth-Century America.* Cambridge, Mass.: Harvard University Press, 1990.

Wasser, Federick Anthony. *Flexible Home Entertainment: Hollywood's Response to Home Video.* Ph.D. dissertation, University of Illinois at Urbana Champaign, 1996.

Weaver, David H., L. E. Mullins, and Maxwell E. McCombs. "Competing Daily Newspapers: A Comparison of Content and Format." *ANPA News Research Bulletin*, no. 7 (January 1973).

Wiebe, Robert. *The Opening of American Society: From the Adoption of the Constitution to the Eve of Disunion.* New York: Knopf, 1984.

Wilson, Christopher. *The Labor of Words: Literary Professionalism in the Progressive Era.* Athens: University of Georgia Press, 1985.

Wood, Gordon. *The Radicalism of the American Revolution.* New York: Knopf, 1992.

Zboray, Ronald J. *A Fictive People: Antebellum Economic Development and the American Reading Public.* New York: Oxford University Press, 1993.

Zboray, Ronald J., and Mary Saracino Zboray. "Books, Reading, and the World of Goods in Antebellum New England." *American Quarterly* 48(4) (December 1996a): 587–622.

———. "Political News and Female Readership in Antebellum Boston and Its Region." *Journalism History* 22(1) (1996b): 2–14.

Zelizer, Barbie. *Covering the Body: The Kennedy Assassination, the Media, and the Shaping of Collective Memory.* Chicago: University of Chicago Press, 1992.

INDEX

(page numbers in italics refer to figures or tables)

Index

Index

ABOUT THE AUTHORS

KEVIN G. BARNHURST grew up in Salt Lake City and completed a PhD (1997) at the University of Amsterdam. He was a Fulbright professor in Lima, Peru, was a research fellow at Columbia University in New York, and taught journalism in Urbana and graphic design in Syracuse before joining the communication faculty at the University of Illinois at Chicago. He has been a shoe salesman in Utah and a farm hand in Idaho, was in the U.S. Army Infantry, and has worked as an economist and as an editor and graphic designer. His first book, *Seeing the Newspaper*, was named a Best Book of 1994 by *In These Times* magazine, and he has written for the *Christian Science Monitor*, the *Chicago Tribune*, *Commentary*, and the *American Scholar*. He lives in Chicago and New Hampshire with his partner, Richard Doherty, and he has three sons, Joel, Andrew, and Matthew.

JOHN NERONE was born in Cincinnati and educated at Xavier University and the University of Notre Dame, where he received a PhD (1982). After brief stints as a paperboy, freelance journalist, and proofreader/copyeditor, he found academic employment in 1983 in the College of Communications, University of Illinois at Urbana–Champaign, where he continues to teach courses in the history of the media and normative press theory. He is the author of three previous books: *The Culture of the Press in the Early Republic*, *Violence against the Press*, and *Last Rights: Revisiting Four Theories of the Press*, which he edited and coauthored with seven of his colleagues in Urbana. He married Ivy Glennon in 1990, and their daughter, Miranda, will turn five as this book is published.